# Scientific and Technical Writing

## *From Problem to Proposal*

### Fifth Revised Edition

*William Magrino*

RUTGERS, THE STATE UNIVERSITY OF NEW JERSEY

**Kendall Hunt**
publishing company

**Kendall Hunt**
publishing company

www.kendallhunt.com
*Send all inquiries to:*
4050 Westmark Drive
Dubuque, IA  52004-1840

# Contents

# Preface to Instructors

This is the fifth revised edition of a text built around a single concept—students learn professional writing through ownership of their ideas. The composition of this book, and its evolution through subsequent editions, coincided with the development of the course it was intended to serve as the main instructional resource at the Business & Technical Writing division of the Writing Program at Rutgers, The State University of New Jersey. At this time, this text is the primary resource for one of our most popular upper-level writing courses, Scientific and Technical Writing.

The first chapter is an introduction to the text and the course that it serves. First and foremost, this is a proposal writing text. In line with our learner-centered philosophy, this book assists students in building a proposal, in a very real way, from the ground up. The development of their proposals is based on a heuristic we constructed, known as the *Six P's.* This is a concept that students put into practice very early in the proposal writing process, and carry with them throughout the rest of the course. For each sequential assignment, leading up to the project proposal, the development of the Six P's assists each student in understanding the information accumulated up to a given point and, more importantly, where he or she needs to go next in the research process. The evolution of the Six P's mirrors the development of the project proposal, from its inception at the White Paper and Annotated Bibliography, through the Letter of Inquiry and Oral Presentation, until reaching the point of the Project Proposal.

In chapter two, we offer a number of readings to help acclimate students to the idea of working within paradigms and how these paradigms help inform our ideas in the scientific and technical fields. As in the previous editions, we begin this series of readings with a selection from Thomas Kuhn's *The Structure of Scientific Revolutions.* Kuhn's concept of *paradigm* serves as the foundation for our text and the series of assignments that it supports. Throughout this chapter, we provide both essays and articles that illustrate the influence of Kuhn's ideas concerning paradigms, as well as a number of pieces that show how this use of paradigms informs the fields of scientific and technical writing and, specifically, the assignments our students will be developing as they use this text. Each reading is followed by a number of discussion questions to allow for vigorous class debate, as well as consideration of the significant links between the concepts in the readings to the students' project ideas.

Frequently, other authors of professional writing texts present the employment application chapter toward the end of their books. We feature ours much earlier, in preparation for subsequent, and less familiar, assignments. Chapter three discusses a foundational task in any scientific and technical writing course—The Job Search Assignment. However, in keeping with the real-world setting of this text, the entire assignment is a product of the student's independent research, in light of what he or she personally brings to the individual employment search. This is one of the most practical ways to get a student engaged in the process of professional writing. The Job Search Assignment functions on a number of related levels: Foremost, this is an assignment that every student at this point in his or her college career will find valuable either immediately or in the near future. Similarly, this is an opportunity for a student to write for a professional audience in a way that he or she will have at least some familiarity. In addition, since these job application documents are persuasive, in which the student is selling his or her unique skills and experiences to a potential employer, it relates directly to the rhetoric that guides the future assignments, in which ideas are addressed to a specific funding source. As with each edition, all of the student samples are new. In this fifth revised edition, we are following an actual student through every assignment. In keeping with the learner-centered theme of this text and course upon which it is based, you will find a series of peer review workshop exercises for a number of the key assignments. It is our belief that as students work through the assignments, routine and guided peer review will help them acquire an expertise in the assignment criteria and, in turn, become better proofreaders of their own work. We offer a number of duplicate peer review forms in each chapter, which can be removed from the text, for in-class group evaluation.

Chapter four discusses the types of research students will need to do in the process of developing the project proposal, as well as the assignments that precede it. There is a detailed discussion of the secondary, including scholarly, research that must be done throughout the proposal writing process. In addition, there is significant discussion of the primary fieldwork that normally needs to be completed to help document and quantify the first three P's. This chapter also introduces students to APA Style, which is the citation and bibliographic format that is used for the research-based assignments. As with the Job Search Assignment, you will find respective student samples and peer review workshop forms in this chapter. At this point, we introduce students to the White Paper, the first of a series of assignments designed to assist them in their work toward the project proposal, and the Annotated Bibliography, which will help them collate and describe the relevance of their sources as they identify their first three P's and begin to develop their paradigms.

In chapter five, we discuss the document that represents the first contact that is made with a potential funding source, which is referred to as the Letter of Inquiry. This is the first assignment that requires a significant amount of scholarly research, cited in-text, as well as a list of References. At this point in the proposal writing process, awareness of the role of the patron takes the forefront. Within the real-world milieu of the course, this assignment marks the first level of communication with the funding source. Assuming the patron's interest is piqued, this letter will be followed by their presence at the oral presentation, which will culminate, hopefully, in a review of the full project proposal. Although the Letter of Inquiry, in light of the point in which the students are engaged in the research process, will focus more heavily on the first three P's, all of the P's should be represented in some way. As a result, this is where scholarly research should be presented and analyzed in support of an emerging paradigm. In this chapter, we present a detailed description of the Letter of Inquiry, as well as a sample from the student who produced the previous assignments and the corresponding peer review forms.

Chapter six addresses the Oral Presentation. This chapter includes a number of resources to assist students in developing an oral presentation in support of their proposals. Chronologically speaking, within the context of this course, the funding source has received and read the Letter of Inquiry and this document has generated enough interest for the patron to attend a presentation in support of a potential project proposal. In accord with the precepts of the course for which this text has been developed, each student is responsible to deliver an oral presentation to his or her respective patron. The instructor and classmates normally play the part of the funding source, especially during the question and answer period. This chapter contains relevant peer review forms and concludes with an evaluation form to assist in measuring the level of success for each presentation.

The final chapter of the text, chapter seven, examines the complete project proposal and the many inter-dependent parts that compose it. Each of the thirteen parts of the proposal are delineated and described. Here, the paradigm, as a justification for a specific course of action, takes center stage. As in the real-word professional fields, this proposal will succeed or fail in large part upon the quality and level of analysis of current, peer-reviewed research. At this point, the higher-level proposals will showcase the theoretical framework that guides the thinking, as well as the models of success that inform the detailed plan. Again, the sample assignment included is from the student we have been following throughout the proposal writing process. The peer review workshop materials in this chapter are divided into three sections to allow for a thorough review of the entire proposal. In addition, a final evaluation form with a condensed view of the criteria is provided.

I hope your students will find this text as valuable as mine have. From its inception, our goal has been to equip students with the real-world skills that today's employers seek. It is incredibly gratifying when a student from a previous semester contacts me following graduation to tell me about how this text and course helped him or her transition into the workplace, in terms of writing and communication. It's even more exciting when a student returns to my office to tell me about a research proposal developed in our course that was ultimately funded and put into action.

William Magrino
September, 2022

# The Project Proposal From the Ground Up

*Chapter*

**1**

S omeone once said, "those who know *how* will always have a job, but those who know *why* will lead the way." When you write a project proposal, you need to answer two critical *why* questions: "why do this?" and "why *this way* as opposed to some *other* way?" A key premise of this text is that you can only answer those *why* questions through research. Without research, you will not have knowledge (or, at least, you will not be able to persuade other people that you have knowledge), and without knowledge you cannot answer "why" in a way that persuades people to follow you.

We live in a society where knowledge is at the heart of the decision-making process. In this *knowledge society,* as Peter Drucker (1994) has called it, *knowledge workers* need many complex skills and abilities to get things done. They need to be able to:

- guide their own learning to master new knowledge and skills,
- analyze new situations, assess information needs, and locate that information,
- understand and digest both factual and theoretical material,
- think creatively to combine or improve available ideas,
- harness knowledge to justify a plan,
- develop and explain complex plans of action to others, and
- manage people and resources by putting information into action.

Knowledge workers need to be prepared for the creative challenge of solving problems through research, and they need practice in communicating their research to others. Having the experience of writing a project proposal where they use research to rationalize a plan of action can be a great first step toward professional competence. This book is designed to help you through the process of writing such a proposal.

## The Six Parts of any Project Proposal

Though formats differ from organization to organization, there are always six basic parts to any strong project proposal:

- Patron (the person who will fund your proposal)
- Population (the people who will benefit from it)

- Problem (the need that your proposal addresses)
- Paradigm (the research rationale for your plan)
- Plan (the way you will address the problem)
- Price (the budget to implement your plan)

A good project proposal will always help a specific *population* to address a *problem* by developing a *paradigm*-based *plan* of action that stays within the *price* that your *patron* is willing to pay. Though formats will differ from place to place, all strong proposals will have these six basic elements. The difficult part of developing a strong proposal is having all of the parts fit together into a coherent whole.

The *Six P Formula* can be used to organize both your written product and your writing process. The ideal process will follow the Six P's in order, more or less, focusing first on identifying a population to assist, a problem to solve, and a patron who would be willing to fund; then developing a paradigm through research that will help you design a well-justified plan of action; and once you have your plan you can develop your budget. Until you have a firm grasp on the first three P's, you will not be able to deal adequately with the last three. The first three help direct you to the right research to justify your plan and the last three present that research and use it to advance a coherent plan of action.

## Patron

Who will fund your project? This is the person to whom you will literally address your proposal, and therefore the person whose name will be on your cover letter or memo. He or she will be your chief audience or reader. This is the person you most need to persuade. The patron could be your boss, the people at headquarters, a government group, or any public or private foundation. Like the *patrons* of the arts who paid for public and private projects during the Renaissance, your patron is the person whose hand controls the purse. The interests of your patron will ultimately influence the proposal. If you choose a funding source that is most compatible with your approach, you will have fewer problems justifying your plan to them.

## Population

Who will benefit from your project? These are the people who will directly or indirectly be affected by your proposal. This must be a significant, measurable number of people. In a business setting, they may be your customers or people in your organization. In the case of a scientific project, the population should be thought of as both the people in your field who want certain questions answered and the people in the world who might benefit from your research. In any case, a persuasive project proposal will have a well-thought-out human dimension. After all, why should a proposal be funded if no one but you will benefit from it?

Sometimes students choose a project proposal (such as any reform at their college) where they themselves are part of the population to be served. If you do that, it is especially important for you to remain objective. No one wants to fund a self-serving project, and until you can imagine other beneficiaries for your work (the larger population of students to be served, for example) you will not be able to make a persuasive case for funding.

## Problem

What instigates your project? As any leader in the profession will tell you, "If there is no problem, there is no reason to develop a proposal." All strong proposals begin with a problem. If you find yourself beginning with a plan of action, then you have really jumped to conclusions. Before anyone should consider acting, after all, they need to be convinced that the problem is objectively real and that it needs to be addressed. You must first define and quantify your problem so that your patron can understand its scale, scope, and significance. In the case of a theoretical question, you will need to show how this question arose in prior research. In a business proposal, you will typically need to quantify the problem so that your patron can weigh the costs and benefits of action and inaction. Why does the problem even need to be addressed? Ultimately, you need to provide evidence to answer that question. You are not advancing a course of action just *because it sounds like a good idea.* If there is no problem, then there is no need to write a proposal.

## *Paradigm*

Why is your plan of action the best one available for addressing the problem? To answer *why* you need a research-based rationale that answers these two questions: *How do you know* that your plan will solve the problem? And *why* try to solve the problem *this way* rather than any number of other ways? A good research-based rationale will show that you have a consensus within your field that justifies your approach. It might also show that the plan you want to implement has strong precedents to suggest that it will succeed. This is basically what we mean by a *paradigm.*

The way we use the term *paradigm* today has been greatly influenced by the work of Thomas Kuhn. In Kuhn's (1970) view, experiments form the basis of scientific knowledge by being what he called *exemplars,* or models of how problems can be solved. The larger theory that explains why the models work, which he called the *disciplinary matrix,* often comes much later. But the part and the whole are mutually dependent. When there is a consensus within a field of endeavor that this model and this matrix agree with each other, you have a paradigm. In terms of writing a persuasive project proposal, a paradigm can be either a model of success (or benchmark) that you think should be imitated or it can be a theoretical framework for understanding why your plan should succeed. The ideal paradigm will feature both an exemplar and a disciplinary matrix: it will have both a model of success and a theory of why that model succeeds. It will have both the part and the whole.

Paradigms describe the rhetorical and conceptual spaces that practitioners of any discipline generally follow. In the sciences and some areas of social research, paradigms are so commonly shared that a shorthand has developed for describing them, so that many paradigms can be summed up in a phrase that names a theory within a specific discipline: *integrated pest management* in agriculture, or *experiential learning* in education, or *ecological risk assessment* in environmental planning, or *the broken windows theory* in sociology or law enforcement. These terms grew out of exemplary practices that became common knowledge within a field of endeavor.

If you want to develop a paradigm for your project, you might ask these questions: How have other people solved this problem or addressed this question in the past? What models of successful practice are available to give me ideas and help justify a plan or experiment? What theories or ideas might help me to develop a logical approach to this problem or to develop experimental procedures? How might language from my discipline help describe and understand the problem?

Once you have a paradigm, you will be able to construct your plan based on research. Without a paradigm you will be inventing your plan out of whole cloth with nothing but your own ethos to justify it, and that is not likely to take you very far with your patron.

## *Plan*

Your plan might be a construction project, a training or education program, an experiment to test a hypothesis, a study to determine what course of action is best, or some other specific initiative. Since a good plan will have to grow organically out of the people, problem, and paradigm, it is generally not the first thing you will work on for the project. It has to be responsive to your research findings.

How you present your plan will depend upon your project, but you should strive to be as explicit as possible about all that will be involved. If you can find a way to visually organize this part of your proposal, it will help your reader to understand it better. If the project will take place in a series of steps, you might be able to set up a calendar showing the sequence of events. If the plan requires construction, you will probably want to draw a diagram of the thing you are going to build. But a good plan needs to look back at its problem and paradigm: it should detail the specific ways you are going to address the problem and suggest how it follows logically from your models and theoretical research.

## Price

Once you have your plan in place, you will need to calculate a budget. Often, your budget is restricted before you begin your project, and you should recognize the ways that price can have a strong influence over choices you make in dealing with the other five P's. If you are making a case for overall long-term savings from your project, you may want to include those in your calculations. If the materials for your project can be broken down and detailed, then do so. Find out the price of the materials you need, either by contacting suppliers or looking up prices online. Talk to people who have done this sort of work before if you can. Use your judgment if you are not certain of costs, but try to be as realistic as possible.

## Other Considerations

The Six P's are not an exhaustive list, but they should handle the critical issues you need to cover in any good proposal. We could add some other P's here, and I would like to mention two more, since they often come up: Partners and Politics.

By *partners* I mean the people who will help you achieve your goals yet who will not necessarily be benefiting from the project or providing funding for it. They might be other organizations or other people in your company. They can sometimes be very important to discuss in your proposal, since mentioning their support will show that you already have convinced other people that you have a good project idea.

By *politics* I mean the larger cultural, economic, legal, or political situation that may impact your proposal. As we know, projects that might gain support at one time or in one place will not gain support in another time or place. If your project runs counter to prevailing ideology, you may have a problem on your hands. For example, it would be politically difficult to get backing to promote the medical use of illegal drugs in a state with tough anti-drug laws; it would be difficult to organize a deer hunt to address a deer overpopulation issue in a community that is anti-hunting; it might be foolhardy to propose new accounting tricks in the wake of accounting scandals like Enron's; and costly projects will not be well received during times of fiscal difficulty. At the very least, you may need to give special attention to your rhetorical frame (that is, how you argue for your project) or you may need to adjust some of your assumptions to make your proposal more feasible given current realities (or *politics*).

# The Interdependence of the Six P's

You should imagine the Six P's spatially, as the parts of a coherent project that might come together in any temporal order. Making the Six P's fit together can sometimes feel like building a structure with six interlocking parts. As previously stated, the last three P's rely upon your command of the first three. The Six P's are completely interdependent entities, so choices in one area impact choices in other areas. You need to be open to revising the different parts of your project as it develops. How will decisions about the funding source (the addressee for your proposal) affect the way you approach the problem? How will the population to be served by the project impact the approach you might take?

For example, suppose your lab has expanded beyond its present capacity to give experimental space to all who need it. The people in charge of finding a solution to this problem will begin by asking themselves a number of questions:

- Patron: Where might we get money to solve this problem?

- Population: Who is most affected by the problem?

- Problem: What are some of the causes of the problem? What is its scope? What objective evidence do we have that there really is a problem?

- Paradigm: How have other labs succeeded in solving this problem? What innovative approaches (such as time sharing) have they used? What areas of knowledge can be brought to bear on the problem?

- Plan: What plans are feasible given current fiscal and political realities?

- Price: How much do you think you might be able to raise to fund your project? How much have similar projects cost?

If you find a patron willing to give you whatever money you need, then that will make it possible to build additional space. However, if your funds are limited and you need to make do with the space available, then that will clearly change your approach. In the case of limited funds, you may need to make decisions about which researchers should have priority over others, and that will create a narrower population that needs extra assistance. At each step of your project you should recognize how your choices can have cascading effects down the line.

## The Six P's in Action

Because you are likely to make changes in your proposal at each step of its development, you should be prepared to revise your project as you go in order to make it more coherent. While not every project develops in a coherent step-by-step process following the order of the Six P's, they all need to put the Six P's together in a way that meshes. The order in which they are discussed here, however, is the order in which they will appear in the project proposal. Some projects begin logically but then require extensive revision to resolve conflicts between various areas of the Six P's (such as when the patron doesn't like the price).

A computer science student taking a professional writing course—let's call her Sandy—wanted to build a web page for a restaurant where she worked, but she didn't see how that web page could be used to improve business. She had begun with the plan (*I want to build a website*), and her dilemma was that she didn't see the problem to be solved or the paradigm to solve it. As a result, she had to go back to the beginning and ask some of the questions that had been skipped over in leaping to the plan of action. This is why you should avoid *working backward* and find the best research before identifying a course of action. You do not want to advocate for a plan for which there is no justification.

Sandy already knew the funding source: the restaurant owners would pay to develop a good website. But she had not yet thought about the people to be served (Who are our customers? What are their needs?), or the problem (How could a website improve business? What opportunities are we missing out on by not having one?), or the paradigm to guide her (What principles or models of success might give us ideas?). Without answers to these questions, the website could very well become a waste of resources. She had to work on the Six P's from the beginning.

A good project always depends on good research. And what Sandy most needed was a paradigm to guide her research. Always remember that the success of a proposal is dependent upon the quality of the paradigm research—not the ambition of the plan.

In her initial writings about the project, Sandy had made the textbook distinction between *target marketing,* which seeks to attract new consumers from a specific group, and *relationship marketing,* which involves improving loyalty among the base of consumers who already use your product or service. She suggested that the internet was probably more useful for relationship marketing than for target marketing because of how expensive and difficult it is to reach consumers who haven't already heard of your business. In fact, she recognized it might be easier to attract people to the website by using the restaurant than to attract people to the restaurant by using the website.

What Sandy did not recognize right away was that the term *relationship marketing* describes a researchable concept, literally a marketing paradigm. Sandy had stumbled upon the term in her initial research, but because she was not a marketing major (she was a computer science major, after all) it had not occurred to her that she could explore that concept further through more focused research and reading. To do that, she needed to look at resources in the marketing field and examples of relationship marketing in action. A brief stop at the library index *Business Source Premier* (which indexes business sources and even offers full-text versions online) showed her that there was a wealth of source material within easy reach. A single search turned up almost 500 potential sources on *relationship marketing* alone. Though she found no examples of restaurants using the concept, she did discover quite a few service-sector models for using a website to build relationships with loyal customers. One of the best examples she found, described at length in one article, was of a dry cleaner that used a sophisticated website not only to communicate with customers but also to offer other services that helped to develop a sense of community around the establishment. The site even had a singles meeting page that allowed people going to this dry cleaner to connect with local singles, many of whom would post their pictures both online and in the lobby of the establishment.

You might say that Sandy's paradigm was supported by both the exemplar (or example) of the dry cleaner and the disciplinary matrix (or theory) of *relationship marketing,* two things she knew nothing about when she began her research. There were other approaches she could have explored (for example, there is a large body of research on building a *virtual community,* a term coined by Howard Rheingold). But the approach she found gave her what she needed to begin developing a paradigm for a workable plan. The idea Sandy ended up developing was quite creative and went beyond the things she had learned as a computer science major. In many ways, the project helped her to understand the human dimensions of her field.

After looking at how a number of other companies used their websites to develop relationships with customers, Sandy was able to synthesize an original yet proven plan for her workplace. She decided to work on developing a sense of community around the restaurant, so that even when customers were not there they could participate in the social life of the institution, developing a relationship with it like the patrons of the television bar *Cheers.* To entice current customers of the restaurant to visit the website, she would offer them online coupons, based upon the models offered by a number of other establishments. Customers visiting the site could find out more about the staff, e-mail suggestions directly to the chef, check out the calendar of upcoming events, join the restaurant mailing list to receive announcements and advertisements, or check out what was going on at one of the live chat rooms. In a business built on loyal customers, a website that helped build loyalty was a concept worth implementing.

It took research to lead the way.

# References

Drucker, P. F. (1994, November). The age of social transformation. *The Atlantic Monthly, 274*(5), 53–80.

Kuhn, T. S. (1970). *The structure of scientific revolutions* (2nd ed.). University of Chicago Press.

# The Newspaper Assignment

## Preparation

To complete this assignment, you should read several print or online news articles and choose **one** article that could be the basis for a project proposal. The best articles will suggest a viable, **specific problem** that could be addressed by a project proposal. The purpose of this exercise is *not* to get you to choose the topic that you will actually work on for this class (though it is possible that some of you might stumble upon your topic this way). Rather, this exercise is intended to get you to practice the process of project development. After reading Chapter 1, take notes on the Six P's that you could imagine developing from the article you have chosen. Be prepared to support your analysis.

## In Class

Get into small groups, and do the following:

1. Each of you, in turn, should present your article to the other group members. Describe the article and explain how this illustrates a problem that could lead to a good project idea. (About 10 minutes)

2. After the individual presentations, decide, as a group, which of them would make the most interesting basis for a project. (About 5 minutes)

3. Elect a group leader. This person does not have to be the one whose article was chosen, but he or she should present your ideas to the class. (About 5 minutes)

4. Once you have elected a group leader, begin developing a project idea based upon the article and on your own general knowledge. Obviously, to develop a strong project you would have to do a significant amount of research, but do the best you can with the information provided in the article. Use the following questions as a guide to discussion: (About 20 minutes)

   • Patron: Who might fund your idea? Why would they want to fund it?

   • Population: Who is affected by this problem? What specific population will your project serve?

   • Problem: What is the basic problem or need your project will address? Why is it a problem? How could you illustrate the extent of this problem? What are the tangible effects of this issue upon the population?

   • Paradigm: What disciplines (e.g., marketing, education, nutrition, medicine, etc.) might be useful in addressing this problem? What specific types of research would help?

   • Plan: How might you address the problem you have identified? What is your plan of action? Who will carry out this plan?

   • Price: What resources or assistance will you need? How much do you think your project might cost?

5. Present your ideas to the class and answer any questions. (About 5 minutes for each group)

# The Six P's Assignment

Use the following form in a class exercise as directed by your instructor to analyze your project idea or the idea of someone else in your class.

## Patron

Who would be willing to fund this project? Why would they want to fund it?

## Population

Who does the problem affect? That is, who has a stake in seeing that there is a solution to the problem? Does your population have the same interests as the patron?

## Problem

What are the main problems that need to be addressed? How could research shed light on these problems to emphasize their scale, scope, and significance? What sources of information about the problem would the patron find most persuasive?

## Paradigm

What disciplines (e.g., computer science, marketing, education, psychology, etc.) might be useful in developing a disciplinary matrix for providing a rationale for action? Where might models of success be found to help shape the plan? What specific *types* of research would help?

## Plan

What possible plans of action can you already imagine at this point? What plans are politically feasible? What would you need to know in order to develop a logical plan?

## Price

How might your budget be limited? How much do you think the project might cost? How can that spending be justified?

# Readings in Scientific and Technical Writing

## Chapter

## Introduction

Each of the following readings was chosen to facilitate class discussion of the *paradigm* concept, which is central to understanding the social situation of research writing in scientific and technical fields. Without an understanding of the concept of paradigm, you will have trouble conducting your research and successfully supporting your argument. You will also be missing a key concept of our times that has had a broad impact on thinking in many disciplines.

This chapter begins with a selection from a pivotal work by Thomas Kuhn (1979). Kuhn is a major figure in the history of science and his book *The Structure of Scientific Revolutions* remains one of the most cited academic works of the last century. His use of the term *paradigm* has had a lasting impact on the language, twisting a term that had previously meant *model* or *example* so that it signifies a consensus within a field of research (among other things), which can sometimes very quickly follow innovations (what Kuhn termed "paradigm shifts"). This selection is from a conference talk he presented at the University of Utah to academics interested in creativity and the development of scientific talent. It retains much of the flavor of a public presentation and, as such, makes many of Kuhn's concepts accessible to a general audience.

Unless you have a familiarity with the paradigm concept, you might not think of how important it is to review the tradition in your field to support innovative work, as Thomas Kuhn discusses in the first reading. Paradigms are central to the work that Kuhn calls *normal science*, but we must remember that paradigms both shape and are shaped by cultural and technological forces, as Atul Gawande (2013) suggests. In "Slow Ideas," Gawande discusses how paradigms develop and how they are sometimes stalled, due to public perception and conventional wisdom. While it is clear that paradigms support innovative research, as in Peter Andrey Smith's (2015) article, "Can the Bacteria in Your Gut Explain Your Mood?," adherence to paradigms can also lead to overly dogmatic applications. Current research links an array of human behaviors, and possibly some of our most chronic and baffling psychological conditions, to the presence, and absence, of certain bacteria in our bodies—that is the radical view of the prominent scientists and researchers Smith cites. The work described in this piece strongly suggests a reevaluation of our use of antibiotics and other modern medical practices, which are based upon adherence to a germ theory paradigm that originated more than a century ago. Concurrently, a more acute understanding of the human microbiome presents some significant implications for the treatment of a number of neurological conditions.

A path toward innovation that avoids dogmatism is to either adapt paradigms from other fields to your own, similar to what is being described in Smith's article, or consider a reframing of existing paradigms. The disparity, at times, between public perception and science on *hot* topics such as global climate change, the subject of "Framing and Re-framing in Environmental Science," is a case in point. Here, Justin King Rademaekers and Richard Johnson-Sheehan (2014) demonstrate that our understanding of climate change is a result of how the issue has been framed. As these authors argue, if any progress is to be made with climate change, it will need to be presented to the public in a clear and understandable way through a metaphoric reframing of the issue.

This chapter also includes a number of readings that will help you understand how the notion of *paradigm,* as well as the other key concepts featured in this text, relates to the subsequent assignments. Peek et al. (2014) talk about how changes in health care fields affects how research needs to be conducted. In preparation for developing the Oral Presentation and solidifying the Project Proposal, Andrea Hill et al.'s article discusses how the paradigms that shape a given subject area can affect pedagogical practices, such as the use of as PowerPoint, within that field of study. Jane E. Miller (2007) demonstrates how organization and order of numeric data must work in conjunction with a given author's intentions concerning how that data is to be used. In the final reading, Stephanie Huffman (2010) discusses how we need to change our views about citation in the digital age.

Paradigms, which are the product of consensus, are ultimately social products, and as such they are rarely without critics, because they can dramatically affect people's lives. Consequently, in the professional arenas, paradigms determine whose work is funded and whose work is not. Being able to situate your work within such traditions and use them to innovate is the key to being a strong research writer in the scientific and technical fields. I hope that you find these essays worthwhile both in this course and in your future careers.

# References

Gawande, A. (2013, July 29). Slow ideas. *New Yorker.*

Hill, A., Arford, T., Lubitow, A., & Smallin, L. M. (2012). "I am ambivalent about it": The dilemmas of PowerPoint. *Teaching Sociology, 40*(3), 242–256.

Huffman, S. (2010). The missing link: The lack of citations and copyright notices in multimedia presentations. *Springer Science+Business Media: Tech Trends, 54*(3), 38–44.

Kuhn, T. S. (1979). *The essential tension: Selected studies in scientific tradition and change* (pp. 225–239). University of Chicago Press.

Miller, J. E. (2007, August). Organizing data in tables and charts: Different criteria for different tasks. *Teaching Statistics, 29*(3), 98–101. John Wiley and Sons.

Peek, C. J., Glassgow, R. E., Stange, K. C., Klesges, L. M., Purcell, E. P., & Kessler, R. S. (2014, September/October). The 5 R's: An emerging bold standard for conducting relevant research in a changing world. *Annals of Family Medicine, 12*(5).

Rademaekers, J. K., & Johnson-Sheehan, R. (2014). Framing and re-framing in environmental science: Explaining climate change to the public. *Journal of Technical Writing and Communication. 44*(1), 3–21.

Smith, P. A. (2015, June 28) Can the bacteria in your gut explain your mood? *The New York Times.*

# The Essential Tension

## Tradition and Innovation in Scientific Research

## Thomas Kuhn

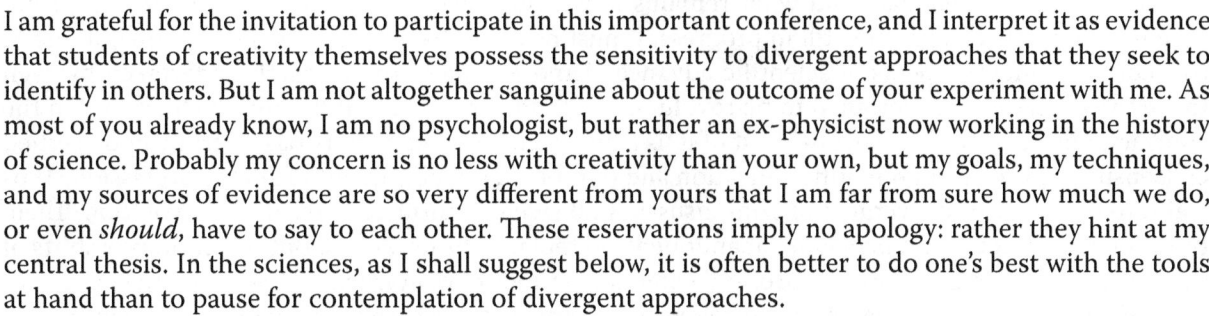

I am grateful for the invitation to participate in this important conference, and I interpret it as evidence that students of creativity themselves possess the sensitivity to divergent approaches that they seek to identify in others. But I am not altogether sanguine about the outcome of your experiment with me. As most of you already know, I am no psychologist, but rather an ex-physicist now working in the history of science. Probably my concern is no less with creativity than your own, but my goals, my techniques, and my sources of evidence are so very different from yours that I am far from sure how much we do, or even *should*, have to say to each other. These reservations imply no apology: rather they hint at my central thesis. In the sciences, as I shall suggest below, it is often better to do one's best with the tools at hand than to pause for contemplation of divergent approaches.

If a person of my background and interests has anything relevant to suggest to this conference, it will not be about your central concerns, the creative personality and its early identification. But implicit in the numerous working papers distributed to participants in this conference is an image of the scientific process and of the scientist; that image almost certainly conditions many of the experiments you try as well as the conclusions you draw; and about it the physicist-historian may well have something to say. I shall restrict my attention to one aspect of this image—an aspect epitomized as follows in one of the working papers: The basic scientist "must lack prejudice to a degree where he can look at the most 'self-evident' facts or concepts without necessarily accepting them, and, conversely, allow his imagination to play with the most unlikely possibilities" (Selye, 1959). In the more technical language supplied by other working papers (Getzels and Jackson), this aspect of the image recurs as an emphasis upon "divergent thinking, . . . the freedom to go off in different directions, . . . rejecting the old solutions and striking out in some new direction."

I do not at all doubt that this description of "divergent thinking" and the concomitant search for those able to do it are entirely proper. Some divergence characterizes all scientific work, and gigantic divergences lie at the core of the most significant episodes in scientific development. But both my own experiences in scientific research and my reading of the history of the sciences lead me to wonder whether flexibility and open-mindedness have not been too exclusively emphasized as the characteristics requisite for basic research. I shall therefore suggest below that something like "convergent thinking" is just as essential to scientific advances as is divergent. Since these two modes of thought are inevitably in conflict, it will follow that the ability to support a tension that can occasionally become almost unbearable is one of the prime requisites for the very best sort of scientific research.

I am elsewhere studying these points more historically, with emphasis on the importance to scientific development of "revolutions."[1] These are episodes—exemplified in their most extreme and readily recognized form by the advent of Copernicanism, Darwinism, or Einsteinianism—in which a scientific community abandons one time-honored way of regarding the world and of pursuing science in favor of some other, usually incompatible, approach to its discipline. I have argued in the draft that the historian constantly encounters many far smaller but structurally similar revolutionary episodes and that they are central to scientific advance. Contrary to a prevalent impression, most new discoveries and theories in the sciences are not merely additions to the existing stockpile of scientific knowledge. To assimilate them the scientist must usually rearrange the intellectual and manipulative equipment he has previously relied upon, discarding some elements of his prior belief and practice while finding new significances in and new relationships between many others. Because the old must be revalued and reordered when assimilating the new, discovery and invention in the sciences are usually intrinsically revolutionary. Therefore, they do demand just that flexibility and open-mindedness that characterize, or indeed define, the divergent thinker. Let us henceforth take for granted the need for these characteristics. Unless many scientists possessed them to a marked degree, there would be no scientific revolutions and very little scientific advance.

Yet flexibility is not enough, and what remains is not obviously compatible with it. Drawing from various fragments of a project still in progress, I must now emphasize that revolutions are but one of two complementary aspects of scientific advance. Almost none of the research undertaken by even the greatest scientists is designed to be revolutionary, and very little of it has any such effect. On the contrary, normal research, even the best of it, is a highly convergent activity based firmly upon settled consensus acquired from scientific education and reinforced by subsequent life in the profession. Typically, to be sure, this convergent or consensus-bound research ultimately results in revolution. Then, traditional techniques and beliefs are abandoned and replaced by new ones. But revolutionary shifts of a scientific tradition are relatively rare, and extended periods of convergent research are the necessary preliminary to them. As I shall indicate below, only investigations break that tradition and give rise to a new one. That is why I speak of an "essential tension" implicit in scientific research. To do his job the scientist must undertake a complex set of intellectual and manipulative commitments. Yet his claim to fame, if he has the talent and good luck to gain one, may finally rest upon his ability to abandon this net of commitments in favor of another of his own invention. Very often the successful scientist must simultaneously display the characteristics of the traditionalist and of the iconoclast.[2]

The multiple historical examples upon which any full documentation of these points must depend are prohibited by the time limitations of the conference. But another approach will introduce you to at least part of what I have in mind—an examination of the nature of education in the natural sciences. One of the working papers for this conference (Getzels and Jackson) quotes Guilford's very apt description of scientific education as follows: "[It] has emphasized abilities in the areas of convergent thinking and evaluation, often at the expense of development in the area of divergent thinking. We have attempted to teach students how to arrive at 'correct' answers that our civilization has taught us are correct. . . . Outside the arts [and I should include most of the social sciences] we have generally discouraged the development of divergent-thinking abilities, unintentionally." That characterization seems to me eminently just, but I wonder whether it is equally just to deplore the product that results. Without defending plain bad teaching, and granting that in this country the trend to convergent thinking in all education may have proceeded entirely too far, we may nevertheless recognize that a rigorous training in convergent thought has been intrinsic to the sciences almost from their origin. I suggest that they could not have achieved their present state or status without it.

Let me try briefly to epitomize the nature of education in the natural sciences, ignoring the many significant yet minor differences between the various sciences and between the approaches of different educational institutions. The single most striking feature of this education is that, to an extent totally unknown in other creative fields, it is conducted entirely through textbooks. Typically, undergraduate and graduate students of chemistry, physics, astronomy, geology, or biology acquire the substance of their fields from books written especially for students. Until they are ready, or even nearly ready, to commence work on their own dissertations, they are neither asked to attempt trial research projects nor exposed to the immediate products of research done by others, that is, to the professional communications that scientists write for each other. There are no collections of "readings" in the natural sciences. Nor are science students encouraged to read the historical classics of their fields—works in which they might discover other ways of regarding the problems discussed in their textbooks, but in which they would also meet problems, concepts, and standards of solution that their future professions have long since discarded and replaced.

In contrast, the various textbooks that the student does encounter display different subject matters, rather than, as in many of the social sciences, exemplifying different approaches to a single problem field. Even books that compete for adoption in a single course differ mainly in level and in pedagogic detail, not in substance or conceptual structure. Last, but most important of all, is the characteristic technique of textbook presentation. Except in their occasional introductions, science textbooks do not describe the sorts of problems that the professional may be asked to solve and the variety of techniques available for their solution. Rather, these books exhibit concrete problem solutions that the profession has come to accept as paradigms, and they then ask the student, either with a pencil and paper or in the laboratory, to solve for himself problems very closely related in both method and substance to those through which the textbook or the accompanying lecture has led him. Nothing could be better calculated to produce "mental sets" or *Einstelleungen*. Only in their most elementary courses do other academic fields offer as much as a partial parallel.

Even the most faintly liberal educational theory must view this pedagogic technique as anathema. Students, we would all agree, must begin by learning a good deal of what is already known, but we also insist that education give them vastly more. They must, we say, learn to recognize and evaluate problems to which no unequivocal solution has yet been given; they must be supplied with an arsenal of techniques for approaching these future problems; and they must learn to judge the relevance of these techniques and to evaluate the possibly partial solutions that they can provide. In many respects these attitudes toward education seem to me entirely right, and yet we must recognize two things about them. First, education in the natural sciences seems to have been totally unaffected by their existence. It remains a dogmatic initiation in a pre-established tradition that the student is not equipped to evaluate. Second, at least in the period when it was followed by a term in an apprenticeship relation, this technique of exclusive exposure to a rigid tradition has been immensely productive of the most consequential sorts of innovations.

I shall shortly inquire about the pattern of scientific practice that grows out of this educational initiation and will then attempt to say why that pattern proves quite so successful. But first, an historical excursion will reinforce what has just been said and prepare the way for what is to follow. I should like to suggest that the various fields of natural science have not always been characterized by rigid education in exclusive paradigms, but that each of them acquired something like that technique at precisely the point when the field began to make rapid and systematic progress. If one asks about the origin of our contemporary knowledge of chemical composition, of earthquakes, of biological reproduction, of motion through space, or of any other subject matter known to the natural sciences one immediately encounters a characteristic pattern that I shall here illustrate with a single example.

Today, physics textbooks tell us that light exhibits some properties of a wave and some of a particle: both textbook problems and research problems are designed accordingly. But both this view and these textbooks are products of an early twentieth-century revolution. (One characteristic of scientific revolutions is that they call for the rewriting of science textbooks.) For more than half a century before 1900, the books employed in scientific education had been equally unequivocal in stating that light was wave motion. Under those circumstances scientists worked on somewhat different problems and sometimes embraced rather different sorts of solutions to them. The nineteenth-century textbook tradition does not, however, mark the beginning of our subject matter. Throughout the eighteenth century and into the early nineteenth, Newton's *Opticks* and the other books from which men learned science taught almost all students that light was particles, and research guided by this tradition was again different from that which succeeded it. Ignoring a variety of subsidiary changes within these three successive traditions, we may therefore say that our views derive historically from Newton's views by way of two revolutions in optical thought, each of which replaced one tradition of convergent research with another. If we make appropriate allowances for changes in the locus and materials of scientific education, we may say that each of these three traditions was embodied in the sort of education by exposure to unequivocal paradigms that I briefly epitomized above. Since Newton, education and research in physical optics have normally been highly convergent.

The history of theories of light does not, however, begin with Newton. If we ask about knowledge in the field before his time, we encounter a significantly different pattern—a pattern still familiar in the arts and in some social sciences, but one that has largely disappeared in the natural sciences. From remote antiquity until the end of the seventeenth century there was no single set of paradigms for the study of physical optics. Instead, many men advanced a large number of different views about the nature of light. Some of these views found few adherents, but a number of them gave rise to continuing schools of optical thought. Although the historian can note the emergence of new points of view as well as changes in the relative popularity of older ones, there was never anything resembling consensus. As a result, a new man entering the field was inevitably exposed to a variety of conflicting viewpoints; he was forced to examine the evidence for each, and there always was good evidence. The fact that he made a choice and conducted himself accordingly could not entirely prevent his awareness of other possibilities. This earlier mode of education was obviously more suited to produce a scientist without prejudice, alert to novel phenomena, and flexible in his approach to his field. On the other hand, one can scarcely escape the impression that, during the period characterized by this more liberal educational practice, physical optics made very little progress.[3]

The pre-consensus (we might here call it the divergent) phase in the development of physical optics is, I believe, duplicated in the history of all other scientific specialties, excepting only those that were born by the subdivision and recombination of pre-existing disciplines. In some fields, like mathematics and astronomy, the first firm consensus is prehistoric. In others, like dynamics, geometric optics, and parts of physiology, the paradigms that produced a first consensus date from classical antiquity. Most other natural sciences, though their problems were often discussed in antiquity, did not achieve a first consensus until after the Renaissance. In physical optics, as we have seen, the first firm consensus dates only from the end of the seventeenth century; in electricity, chemistry, and the study of heat, it dates from the eighteenth; while in geology and the non-taxonomic parts of biology no very real consensus developed until after the first third of the nineteenth century. This century appears to be characterized by the emergence of a first consensus in parts of a few of the social sciences.

In all the fields named above, important work was done before the achievement of the maturity produced by consensus. Neither the nature nor the timing of the first consensus in these fields can be understood without a careful examination of both the intellectual and the manipulative techniques developed before the existence of unique paradigms. But the transition to maturity is not less significant because individuals practiced science before it occurred. On the contrary, history strongly suggests that, though one can practice science—as one does philosophy or art or political science—without a firm consensus, this more flexible practice will not produce the pattern of rapid consequential scientific advance to which recent centuries have accustomed us. In that pattern, development occurs from one consensus to another, and alternate approaches are not ordinarily in competition. Except under quite special conditions, the practitioner of a mature science does not pause to examine divergent modes of explanation or experimentation.

I shall shortly ask how this can be so—how a firm orientation toward an apparently unique tradition can be compatible with the practice of the disciplines most noted for the persistent production of novel ideas and techniques. But it will help first to ask what the education that so successfully transmits such a tradition leaves to be done. What can a scientist working within a deeply rooted tradition and little trained in the perception of significant alternatives hope to do in his professional career? Once again limits of time force me to drastic simplification, but the following remarks will at least suggest a position that I am sure can be documented in detail.

In pure or basic science—that somewhat ephemeral category of research undertaken by men whose most immediate goal is to increase understanding rather than control of nature—the characteristic problems are almost always repetitions, with minor modifications, of problems that have been undertaken and partially resolved before. For example, much of the research undertaken within a scientific tradition is an attempt to adjust existing theory or existing observation in order to bring the two into closer and closer agreement. The constant examination of atomic and molecular spectra during the years since the birth of wave mechanics, together with the design of theoretical approximations for the prediction of complex spectra, provides one important instance of this typical sort of work. Another was provided by the remarks about the eighteenth-century development of Newtonian dynamics in the paper on measurement supplied to you in advance of the conference.][4] The attempt to make existing theory and observation conform more closely is not, of course, the only standard sort of research problem in the basic sciences. The development of chemical thermodynamics or the continuing attempts to unravel organic structure illustrate another type—the extension of existing theory to areas that it is expected to cover but in which it has never before been tried. In addition, to mention a third common sort of research problem, many scientists constantly collect the concrete data (e.g.; atomic wrights, nuclear moments) required for the application and extension of existing theory.

These are normal research projects in the basic sciences, and they illustrate the sorts of work on which all scientists, even the greatest, spend most of their professional lives and on which many spend all. Clearly their pursuit is neither intended nor likely to produce fundamental discoveries or revolutionary changes in scientific theory. Only if the validity of the contemporary scientific tradition is assumed do these problems make much theoretical or any practical sense. The man who suspected the existence of a totally new type of phenomenon or who had basic doubts about the validity of existing theory would not think problems so closely modeled on textbook paradigms worth undertaking. It follows that the man who does undertake a problems of this sort—and that means all scientists at most times—aims to elucidate the scientific tradition in which he was raised rather than to change it. Furthermore, the fascination of his work lies in the difficulties of elucidation rather than in any surprises that the work is likely to produce. Under normal conditions the research scientist is not an innovator. Under normal conditions the research scientist is not an innovator but a solver of puzzles, and the puzzles upon which he concentrates are just those that he believes can be both stated and solved within the existing scientific tradition.

Yet—and this is the point—the ultimate effect of this tradition-bound work has invariably been to change the tradition. Again and again the continuing attempt to elucidate a currently received tradition has at least produced one of those shifts in fundamental theory, in problem field, and in scientific standards to which I previously referred as scientific revolutions. At least for the scientific community as a whole, work within a well-defined and deeply ingrained tradition seems more productive of tradition-shattering novelties than work in which no similarly convergent standards are involved. How can this be so? I think it is because no other sort of work is nearly so well suited to isolate for continuing and concentrated attention those loci of trouble or causes of crisis upon whose recognition the most fundamental advances in basic science depend.

As I have indicated in the first of my working papers, new theories and, to an increasing extent, novel discoveries in the mature sciences are not born de novo. On the contrary, they emerge from old theories and within a matrix of old beliefs about the phenomena that the world does *and does not* contain. Ordinarily such novelties are far too esoteric and recondite to be noted by the man without a great deal of scientific training. And even the man with considerable training can seldom afford simply to go out and look for them, let us say by exploring those areas in which existing data and theory have failed to produce understanding. Even in a mature science there are always far too many such areas, areas in which no existing paradigms seem obviously to apply and for whose exploration few tools and standards are available. More likely than not the scientist who ventured into them, relying merely upon his receptivity to new phenomena and his flexibility to new patterns of organization, would get nowhere at all. He would rather return his science to its pre-consensus or natural history phase.

Instead, the practitioner of a mature science, from the beginning of his doctoral research, continues to work in the regions for which the paradigms derived from his education and from the research of his contemporaries seem adequate. He tries, that is, to elucidate topographical detail on a map whose main outlines are available in advance, and he hopes—if he is wise enough to recognizes the nature of his field—that he will some day undertake a problem in which the anticipated does *not* occur, a problem that goes wrong in ways suggestive of a fundamental weakness in the paradigm itself. In the mature sciences the prelude to much discovery and to all novel theory is not ignorance, but the recognition that something has gone wrong with existing knowledge and beliefs.

What I have said so far may indicate that it is sufficient for the productive scientist to adopt existing theory as a lightly held tentative hypothesis, employ it *faut de mieux* in order to get a start in his research, and then abandon it as soon as it leads him to a trouble spot, a point at which something has gone wrong. But though the ability to recognize trouble when confronted by it is surely a requisite for scientific advance, trouble must not be too easily recognized. The scientist requires a thoroughgoing commitment to the tradition with which, if he is fully successful, he will break. In part this commitment is demanded by the nature of the problems the scientist normally undertakes. These, as we have seen, are usually esoteric puzzles whose challenge lies less in the information disclosed by their solutions (all but its details are often known in advance) than in the difficulties of technique to be surmounted in providing any solution at all. Problems of this sort are undertaken only by men assured that there is a solution that ingenuity can disclose, and only current theory could possibly provide assurance of that sort. That theory alone gives meaning to most of the problems of normal research. To doubt it is often to doubt that the complex technical puzzles which constitute normal research have any solutions at all. Who, for example, would have developed the elaborate mathematical techniques required for the study of the effects of interplanetary attractions upon basic Keplerian orbits if he had not assumed that Newtonian dynamics, applied to the planets then known, would explain the last details of astronomical observation? But without that assurance, how would Neptune have been discovered and the list of planets changed?

In addition, there are pressing practical reasons for commitment. Every research problem confronts the scientist with anomalies whose sources he cannot quite identify. His theories and observations never quite agree; successive observations never yield quite the same results; his experiments have both theoretical and phenomenological by-products that it would take another research project to unravel. Each of these anomalies or incompletely understood phenomena could conceivably be the clue to a fundamental innovation in scientific theory or technique, but the man who pauses to examine them one by one never completes his first project. Reports of effective research repeatedly imply that all but the most striking and central discrepancies could be taken care of by current theory if only there were time to take them on. The men who make these reports find most discrepancies trivial or uninteresting, an evaluation that they can ordinarily base only upon their faith in current theory. Without that faith their work would be wasteful of time and talent.

Besides, lack of commitment too often results in the scientist's undertaking problems that he has little chance of solving. Pursuit of an anomaly is fruitful only if the anomaly is more than non-trivial. Having discovered it, the scientist's first efforts and those of his profession are to do what nuclear physicists are now doing. They strive to generalize the anomaly, to discover other and more revealing manifestations of the same effect, to give it structure by examining its complex interrelationships with phenomena they still feel they understand. Very few anomalies are susceptible to this sort of treatment. To be so they must be in explicit and unequivocal conflict with some structurally central tenet of current scientific belief. Therefore, their recognition and evaluation once again depend upon a firm commitment to the contemporary scientific tradition.

This central role of an elaborate and often esoteric tradition is what I have principally had in mind when speaking of the essential tension in scientific research. I do not doubt that the scientist must be, at least potentially, an innovator, that he must possess mental flexibility, and that he must be prepared to recognize troubles where they exist. That much of the popular stereotype is surely correct, and it is important accordingly to search for indices of the corresponding personality characteristics. But what is no part of our stereotype and what appears to need careful integration with it is the other face of this same coin. We are, I think, more likely fully to exploit our potential scientific talent if we recognize the extent to which the basic scientist must also be a firm traditionalist, or, if I am using your vocabulary at all correctly, a convergent thinker. Most important of all, we must seek to understand how these two superficially discordant modes of problem solving can be reconciled both within the individual and within the group.

Everything said above needs both elaboration and documentation. Very likely some of it will change in the process. This paper is a report on work in progress. But, though I insist that much of it is tentative and all of it incomplete, I still hope that the paper has indicated why an educational system best described as an initiation into an unequivocal tradition should be thoroughly compatible with successful scientific work. And I hope, in addition, to have made plausible the historical thesis that no part of science has progressed very far or very rapidly before this convergent education and correspondingly convergent normal practice became possible. Finally, though it is beyond my competence to derive personality correlates from this view of scientific development, I hope to have made meaningful the view that the productive scientist must be a traditionalist who enjoys playing intricate games by pre-established rules in order to be a successful innovator who discovers new rules and new pieces with which to play them.

As first planned, my paper was to have ended at this point. But work on it, against the background supplied by the working papers distributed to conference participants, has suggested the need for a postscript. Let me therefore briefly try to eliminate a likely ground of misunderstanding and simultaneously suggest a problem that urgently needs a great deal of investigation.

Everything said above was intended to apply strictly only to basic science, an enterprise whose practitioners have ordinarily been relatively free to choose their own problems. Characteristically, as I have indicated, these problems have been selected in areas where paradigms were clearly applicable but where exciting puzzles remained about how to apply them and how to make nature conform to the results of the application. Clearly the inventor and applied scientist are not generally free to choose puzzles of this sort. The problems among which they may choose are likely to be largely determined by social, economic, or military circumstances external to the sciences. Often the decision to seek a cure for a virulent disease, a new source of household illumination, or an alloy able to withstand the intense heat of rocket engines must be made with little reference to the state of the relevant science. It is, I think, by no means clear that the personality characteristics requisite for pre-eminence in this more immediately practical sort of work are altogether the same as those required for a great achievement in basic science. History indicates that only a few individuals, most of whom worked in readily demarcated areas, have achieved eminence in both.

I am by no means clear where this suggestion leads us. The troublesome distinctions between basic research, applied research, and invention need far more investigation. Nevertheless, it seems likely, for example, that the applied scientist, to whose problems no scientific paradigm need be fully relevant, may profit by a far broader and less rigid education than that to which the pure scientist has characteristically been exposed. Certainly there are many episodes in the history of technology in which lack of more than the most rudimentary scientific education has proved to be an immense help. This group scarcely needs to be reminded that Edison's electric light was produced in the face of unanimous scientific opinion that the arc light could not be "subdivided," and there are many other episodes of this sort.

This must not suggest, however, that mere differences in education will transform the applied scientist into a basic scientist or vice versa. One could at least argue that Edison's personality, ideal for the inventor and perhaps also for the "oddball" in applied science, barred him from fundamental achievements in the basic sciences. He himself expressed great scorn for scientists and thought of them as wooly-headed people to be hired when needed. But this did not prevent his occasionally arriving at the most sweeping and irresponsible scientific theories of his own. (The pattern recurs in the early history of electrical technology: both Tesla and Gramme advanced absurd cosmic schemes that they thought deserved to replace the current scientific knowledge of their day.) Episodes like this reinforce an impression that the personality requisites of the pure scientist and of the inventor may be quite different, perhaps with those of the applied scientist lying somewhere between.[5]

Is there a further conclusion to be drawn from all this? One speculative thought forces itself upon me. If I read the working papers correctly, they suggest that most of you are really in search of the *inventive* personality, a sort of person who does emphasize divergent thinking but whom the United States has already produced in abundance. In the process you may be ignoring certain of the essential requisites of the basic scientist, a rather different sort of person, to whose ranks America's contributions have as yet been notoriously sparse. Since most of you are, in fact, Americans, this correlation may not be entirely coincidental.

# Notes

1. *The Structure of Scientific Revolutions* (Chicago, 1962).

2. Strictly speaking, it is the professional group rather than the individual scientist that must display both these characteristics simultaneously. In a fuller account of the ground covered in this paper that distinction between individual and group characteristics would be basic. Here I can only note that, though recognition of the distinction weakens the conflict or tension referred to above it does not eliminate it. Within the group some individuals may be more traditionalistic, others more iconoclastic, and their contributions may differ accordingly. Yet education, institutional norms, and the nature of the job to be done will inevitably combine to insure that all group members will, to a greater or lesser extent, be pulled in both directions.

3. The history of physical optics before Newton has recently been well described by Vasco Ronchi in *Histoire de la lumière*, trans. J. Taton (Paris, 1956). His account does justice to the element I elaborate too little above. Many fundamental contributions to physical optics were made in the two millennia before Newton's work. Consensus is not prerequisite to a sort of progress in the natural sciences, any more than it is to progress in the social sciences or the arts. It is, however, prerequisite to the sort of progress that we now generally refer to when distinguishing the natural sciences from the arts and from most social sciences.

4. A revised version appeared in *Isis* 52 (1961): 161–93.

5. For the attitude of scientists toward the technical possibility of the incandescent light see Francis A. Jones, *Thomas Alva Edison* (New York, 1908), pp. 99–100, and Harold C. Passer, *The Electrical Manufacturers, 1875–1900* (Cambridge, Mass., 1953). pp. 82–83. For Edison's attitude toward scientists see Passer, ibid., pp. 180–181. For a sample of Edison's theorizing in realms otherwise subject to scientific treatments see Dagobert D. Runes, ed., *The Diary and Sundry Observations of Thomas Alva Edison* (New York, 1948), pp. 205–44, passim.

# Chapter 2 ■ The Essential Tension

## Questions for Discussion

1. Kuhn uses the term *paradigm* many times in his talk without pausing to define it. Based on your reading of how he uses the term, how would you define a *paradigm*?

2. As part of the process of developing a definition, get into small groups and try to draw a picture of a paradigm. Of course, the word describes an abstract concept and so there can be no actual picture of a paradigm. But in drawing a picture you will be able to objectify it and thus make it easier to describe in your own words. What would a paradigm look like? How might you describe it metaphorically?

3. Students often say that they are prevented from being original by the requirement that they use research to provide a rationale for their plan. After all, they ask, where is the room for pure invention if everything needs to be supported by research into what other people have done? How can new ideas come out of old ones? How might Kuhn respond to these questions? According to Kuhn, how does tradition actually *support* original research? What evidence does Kuhn use to back up this claim? By what logic does consensus support rapid progress within a research field?

4. Kuhn was speaking at a conference whose main objective was to help foster scientific talent and creativity. How might colleges do more to encourage their students to pursue original ideas? What are some of the problems that Kuhn identifies in our typical science education system, and how might they be remedied?

5. Kuhn points out several times that the arts and social sciences have multiple paradigms while the sciences tend toward a single unifying paradigm in each field. What reasons does he suggest for this disparity? What does this suggest about the potential difficulties of people working in the arts and social sciences? Should scientists necessarily adopt more of a liberal arts model? What would be gained and lost by doing so?

6. Within what specific field of study is your own project situated? What paradigm governs that field? How does that paradigm inform your own work? Would you say that there is a *mini-paradigm* within your specific subfield of research? How would you describe that paradigm? Does it derive more from a theory or from a specific experiment or model?

# Slow Ideas

## Atul Gawande

Why do some innovations spread so swiftly and others so slowly? Consider the very different trajectories of surgical anesthesia and antiseptics, both of which were discovered in the nineteenth century. The first public demonstration of anesthesia was in 1846. The Boston surgeon Henry Jacob Bigelow was approached by a local dentist named William Morton, who insisted that he had found a gas that could render patients insensible to the pain of surgery. That was a dramatic claim. In those days, even a minor tooth extraction was excruciating. Without effective pain control, surgeons learned to work with slashing speed. Attendants pinned patients down as they screamed and thrashed, until they fainted from the agony. Nothing ever tried had made much difference. Nonetheless, Bigelow agreed to let Morton demonstrate his claim.

On October 16, 1846, at Massachusetts General Hospital, Morton administered his gas through an inhaler in the mouth of a young man undergoing the excision of a tumor in his jaw. The patient only muttered to himself in a semi-conscious state during the procedure. The following day, the gas left a woman, undergoing surgery to cut a large tumor from her upper arm, completely silent and motionless. When she woke, she said she had experienced nothing at all.

Four weeks later, on November 18th, Bigelow published his report on the discovery of "insensibility produced by inhalation" in the *Boston Medical and Surgical Journal*. Morton would not divulge the composition of the gas, which he called Letheon, because he had applied for a patent. But Bigelow reported that he smelled ether in it (ether was used as an ingredient in certain medical preparations), and that seems to have been enough. The idea spread like a contagion, travelling through letters, meetings, and periodicals. By mid-December, surgeons were administering ether to patients in Paris and London. By February, anesthesia had been used in almost all the capitals of Europe, and by June in most regions of the world.

There were forces of resistance, to be sure. Some people criticized anesthesia as a "needless luxury"; clergymen deplored its use to reduce pain during childbirth as a frustration of the Almighty's designs. James Miller, a nineteenth-century Scottish surgeon who chronicled the advent of anesthesia, observed the opposition of elderly surgeons: "They closed their ears, shut their eyes, and folded their hands. . . . They had quite made up their minds that pain was a necessary evil, and must be endured." Yet soon even the obstructors, "with a run, mounted behind—hurrahing and shouting with the best." Within seven years, virtually every hospital in America and Britain had adopted the new discovery.

Sepsis—infection—was the other great scourge of surgery. It was the single biggest killer of surgical patients, claiming as many as half of those who underwent major operations, such as a repair of an open fracture or the amputation of a limb. Infection was so prevalent that suppuration—the discharge of pus from a surgical wound—was thought to be a necessary part of healing.

In the eighteen-sixties, the Edinburgh surgeon Joseph Lister read a paper by Louis Pasteur laying out his evidence that spoiling and fermentation were the consequence of microorganisms. Lister became convinced that the same process accounted for wound sepsis. Pasteur had observed that, besides filtration and the application of heat, exposure to certain chemicals could eliminate germs. Lister had read about the city of Carlisle's success in using a small amount of carbolic acid to eliminate the odor of sewage, and reasoned that it was destroying germs. Maybe it could do the same in surgery.

During the next few years, he perfected ways to use carbolic acid for cleansing hands and wounds and destroying any germs that might enter the operating field. The result was strikingly lower rates of sepsis and death. You would have thought that, when he published his observations in a ground-breaking series of reports in *The Lancet*, in 1867, his antiseptic method would have spread as rapidly as anesthesia.

Far from it. The surgeon J. M. T. Finney recalled that, when he was a trainee at Massachusetts General Hospital two decades later, hand washing was still perfunctory. Surgeons soaked their instruments in carbolic acid, but they continued to operate in black frock coats stiffened with the blood and viscera of previous operations—the badge of a busy practice. Instead of using fresh gauze as sponges, they reused sea sponges without sterilizing them. It was a generation before Lister's recommendations became routine and the next steps were taken toward the modern standard of asepsis—that is, entirely excluding germs from the surgical field, using heat-sterilized instruments and surgical teams clad in sterile gowns and gloves.

In our era of electronic communications, we've come to expect that important innovations will spread quickly. Plenty do: think of in-vitro fertilization, genomics, and communications technologies themselves. But there's an equally long list of vital innovations that have failed to catch on. The puzzle is why.

Did the spread of anesthesia and antisepsis differ for economic reasons? Actually, the incentives for both ran in the right direction. If painless surgery attracted paying patients, so would a noticeably lower death rate. Besides, live patients were more likely to make good on their surgery bill. Maybe ideas that violate prior beliefs are harder to embrace. To nineteenth-century surgeons, germ theory seemed as illogical as, say, Darwin's theory that human beings evolved from primates. Then again, so did the idea that you could inhale a gas and enter a pain-free state of suspended animation. Proponents of anesthesia overcame belief by encouraging surgeons to try ether on a patient and witness the results for themselves—to take a test drive. When Lister tried this strategy, however, he made little progress.

The technical complexity might have been part of the difficulty. Giving Lister's methods "a try" required painstaking attention to detail. Surgeons had to be scrupulous about soaking their hands, their instruments, and even their catgut sutures in antiseptic solution. Lister also set up a device that continuously sprayed a mist of antiseptic over the surgical field.

But anesthesia was no easier. Obtaining ether and constructing the inhaler could be difficult. You had to make sure that the device delivered an adequate dosage, and the mechanism required constant tinkering. Yet most surgeons stuck with it—or else they switched to chloroform, which was found to be an even more powerful anesthetic, but posed its own problems. (An imprecise dosage killed people.) Faced with the complexities, they didn't give up; instead, they formed an entire new medical specialty—anesthesiology.

So what were the key differences? First, one combatted a visible and immediate problem (pain); the other combatted an invisible problem (germs) whose effects wouldn't be manifest until well after the operation. Second, although both made life better for patients, only one made life better for doctors. Anesthesia changed surgery from a brutal, time-pressured assault on a shrieking patient to a quiet, considered procedure. Listerism, by contrast, required the operator to work in a shower of carbolic acid. Even low dilutions burned the surgeons' hands. You can imagine why Lister's crusade might have been a tough sell.

This has been the pattern of many important but stalled ideas. They attack problems that are big but, to most people, invisible; and making them work can be tedious, if not outright painful. The global destruction wrought by a warming climate, the health damage from our over-sugared modern diet, the economic and social disaster of our trillion dollars in unpaid student debt—these things worsen imperceptibly every day. Meanwhile, the carbolic-acid remedies to them, all requiring individual sacrifice of one kind or another, struggle to get anywhere.

The global problem of death in childbirth is a pressing example. Every year, three hundred thousand mothers and more than six million children die around the time of birth, largely in poorer countries. Most of these deaths are due to events that occur during or shortly after delivery. A mother may hemorrhage. She or her baby may suffer an infection. Many babies can't take their first breath without assistance, and newborns, especially those born small, have trouble regulating their body temperature after birth. Simple, lifesaving solutions have been known for decades. They just haven't spread.

Many solutions aren't ones you can try at home, and that's part of the problem. Increasingly, however, women around the world are giving birth in hospitals. In India, a government program offers mothers up to fourteen hundred rupees—more than what most Indians live on for a month—when they deliver in a hospital, and now, in many areas, the majority of births are in facilities. Death rates in India have fallen, but they're still ten times greater than in high-income countries like our own.

Not long ago, I visited a few community hospitals in north India, where just one-third of mothers received the medication recommended to prevent hemorrhage; less than ten per cent of the newborns were given adequate warming; and only four per cent of birth attendants washed their hands for vaginal examination and delivery. In an average childbirth, clinicians followed only about ten of twenty-nine basic recommended practices.

Here we are in the first part of the twenty-first century, and we're still trying to figure out how to get ideas from the first part of the twentieth century to take root. In the hopes of spreading safer childbirth practices, several colleagues and I have teamed up with the Indian government, the World Health Organization, the Gates Foundation, and Population Services International to create something called the BetterBirth Project. We're working in Uttar Pradesh, which is among India's poorest states. One afternoon in January, our team travelled a couple of hours from the state's capital, Lucknow, with its bleating cars and ramshackle shops, to a rural hospital surrounded by lush farmland and thatched-hut villages. Although the sun was high and the sky was clear, the temperature was near freezing. The hospital was a one-story concrete building painted goldenrod yellow. (Our research agreement required that I keep it unnamed.) The entrance is on a dirt road lined with rows of motorbikes, the primary means of long-distance transportation. If an ambulance or an auto-rickshaw can't be found, women in labor sit sidesaddle on the back of a bike.

The hospital delivers three thousand newborns a year, a typical volume in India but one that would put it in the top fifth of American hospitals. Yet it had little of the amenities that you'd associate with a modern hospital. I met the physician in charge, a smart and capable internist in his early thirties who had trained in the capital. He was clean-shaven and buzz-cut, with an Argyle sweater, track shoes, and a habitual half smile. He told me, apologetically, that the hospital staff had no ability to do blood tests, to give blood transfusions, or to perform emergency obstetrics procedures such as Cesarean sections. There was no electricity during the day. There was certainly no heating, even though the temperature was barely forty degrees that day, and no air-conditioning, even though summer temperatures routinely reach a hundred degrees. There were two blood-pressure cuffs for the entire facility. The nurse's office in my neighborhood elementary school was better equipped.

The hospital was severely understaffed, too. The doctor said that half of the staff positions were vacant. To help with child deliveries for a local population of a quarter of a million people, the hospital had two nurses and one obstetrician, who happened to be his wife. The nurses, who had six months of childbirth training, did most of the deliveries, swapping shifts year-round. The obstetrician covered the outpatient clinic, and helped with complicated births whenever she was required, day or night. During holidays or sickness, the two nurses covered for each other, but, if no one was available, laboring women were either sent to another hospital, miles away, or an untrained assistant might be forced to step in.

It may be surprising that mothers are better off delivering in such places than at home in a village, but studies show a consistently higher survival rate when they do. The staff members I met in India had impressive experience. Even the youngest nurses had done more than a thousand child deliveries. They've seen and learned to deal with countless problems—a torn placenta, an umbilical cord wrapped around a baby's neck, a stuck shoulder. Seeing the daily heroism required to keep such places going, you feel foolish and ill-mannered asking how they could do things better.

But then we hung out in the wards for a while. In the delivery room, a boy had just been born. He and his mother were lying on a cot, bundled under woollen blankets, resting. The room was coffin-cold; I was having trouble feeling my toes. I tried to imagine what that baby must have felt like. Newborns have a high body-surface area and lose heat rapidly. Even in warm weather, hypothermia is common, and it makes newborns weak and less responsive, less able to breast-feed adequately and more prone to infection. I noticed that the boy was swaddled separately from his mother. Voluminous evidence shows that it is far better to place the child on the mother's chest or belly, skin to skin, so that the mother's body can regulate the baby's until it is ready to take over. Among small or premature babies, kangaroo care (as it is known) cuts mortality rates by a third.

So why hadn't the nurse swaddled the two together? She was a skilled and self-assured woman in her mid-thirties with twinkly eyes, a brown knit hat, and a wool sweater over her shalwar kameez. Resources clearly weren't the issue—kangaroo care costs nothing. Had she heard of it? Oh, yes, she said. She'd taken a skilled-birth-attendant class that taught it. Had she forgotten about it? No. She had actually offered to put the baby skin to skin with the mother, and showed me where she'd noted this in the record.

"The mother didn't want it," she explained. "She said she was too cold."

The nurse seemed to think it was strange that I was making such an issue of this. The baby was fine, wasn't he? And he was. He was sleeping sweetly, a tightly wrapped peanut with a scrunched brown face and his mouth in a lowercase "o."

But had his temperature been taken? It had not. The nurse said that she had been planning to do so. Our visit had disrupted her routine. Suppose she had, though, and his temperature was low. Would she have done anything differently? Would she have made the mom unswaddle the child and put him to her chest?

Everything about the life the nurse leads—the hours she puts in, the circumstances she endures, the satisfaction she takes in her abilities—shows that she cares. But hypothermia, like the germs that Lister wanted surgeons to battle, is invisible to her. We picture a blue child, suffering right before our eyes. That is not what hypothermia looks like. It is a child who is just a few degrees too cold, too sluggish, too slow to feed. It will be some time before the baby begins to lose weight, stops making urine, develops pneumonia or a bloodstream infection. Long before that happens—usually the morning after the delivery, perhaps the same night—the mother will have hobbled to an auto-rickshaw, propped herself beside her husband, held her new baby tight, and ridden the rutted roads home.

From the nurse's point of view, she'd helped bring another life into the world. If four per cent of the newborns later died at home, what could that possibly have to do with how she wrapped the mother and child? Or whether she washed her hands before putting on gloves? Or whether the blade with which she cut the umbilical cord was sterilized?

We're infatuated with the prospect of technological solutions to these problems—baby warmers, say. You can still find high-tech incubators in rural hospitals that sit mothballed because a replacement part wasn't available, or because there was no electricity for them. In recent years, though, engineers have produced designs specifically for the developing world. Dr. Steven Ringer, a neonatologist and BetterBirth leader, was an adviser for a team that made a cheap, ingenious, award-winning incubator from old car parts that are commonly available and easily replaced in low-income environments. Yet it hasn't taken off, either. "It's in more museums than delivery rooms," he laments.

As with most difficulties in global health care, lack of adequate technology is not the biggest problem. We already have a great warming technology: a mother's skin. But even in high-income countries we do not consistently use it. In the United States, according to Ringer, more than half of newborns needing intensive care arrive hypothermic. Preventing hypothermia is a perfect example of an unsexy task: it demands painstaking effort without immediate reward. Getting hospitals and birth attendants to carry out even a few of the tasks required for safer childbirth would save hundreds of thousands of lives. But how do we do that?

The most common approach to changing behavior is to say to people, "Please do X." Please warm the newborn. Please wash your hands. Please follow through on the twenty-seven other childbirth practices that you're not doing. This is what we say in the classroom, in instructional videos, and in public-service campaigns, and it works, but only up to a point.

Then, there's the law-and-order approach: "You must do X." We establish standards and regulations, and threaten to punish failures with fines, suspensions, the revocation of licenses. Punishment can work. Behavioral economists have even quantified how averse people are to penalties. In experimental games, they will often quit playing rather than risk facing negative consequences. And that is the problem with threatening to discipline birth attendants who are taking difficult-to-fill jobs under intensely trying conditions. They'll quit.

The kinder version of "You must do X" is to offer incentives rather than penalties. Maybe we could pay birth attendants a bonus for every healthy child who makes it past a week of life. But then you think about how hard it would be to make a scheme like that work, especially in poor settings. You'd need a sophisticated tracking procedure, to make sure that people aren't gaming the system, and complex statistical calculations, to take prior risks into account. There's also the impossible question of how you split the reward among all the people involved. How much should the community health worker who provided the prenatal care get? The birth attendant who handled the first twelve hours of labor? The one who came on duty and handled the delivery? The doctor who was called in when things got complicated? The pharmacist who stocked the antibiotic that the child required?

Besides, neither penalties nor incentives achieve what we're really after: a system and a culture where X is what people do, day in and day out, even when no one is watching. "You must" rewards mere compliance. Getting to "X is what we do" means establishing X as the norm. And that's what we want: for skin-to-skin warming, hand washing, and all the other lifesaving practices of childbirth to be, quite simply, the norm.

To create new norms, you have to understand people's existing norms and barriers to change. You have to understand what's getting in their way. So what about just working with health-care workers, one by one, to do just that? With the BetterBirth Project, we wondered, in particular, what would happen if we hired a cadre of childbirth-improvement workers to visit birth attendants and hospital leaders, show them why and how to follow a checklist of essential practices, understand their difficulties and objections, and help them practice doing things differently. In essence, we'd give them mentors.

The experiment is just getting under way. The project has recruited only the first few of a hundred or so workers whom we are sending out to hospitals across six regions of Uttar Pradesh in a trial that will involve almost two hundred thousand births over two years. There's no certainty that our approach will succeed. But it seemed worth trying.

Reactions that I've heard both abroad and at home have been interestingly divided. The most common objection is that, even if it works, this kind of one-on-one, on-site mentoring "isn't scalable." But that's one thing it surely is. If the intervention saves as many mothers and newborns as we're hoping—about a thousand lives in the course of a year at the target hospitals—then all that need be done is to hire and develop similar cadres of childbirth-improvement workers for other places around the country and potentially the world. To many people, that doesn't sound like much of a solution. It would require broad mobilization, substantial expense, and perhaps even the development of a new profession. But, to combat the many antisepsis-like problems in the world, that's exactly what has worked. Think about the creation of anesthesiology: it meant doubling the number of doctors in every operation, and we went ahead and did so. To reduce illiteracy, countries, starting with our own, built schools, trained professional teachers, and made education free and compulsory for all children. To improve farming, governments have sent hundreds of thousands of agriculture extension agents to visit farmers across America and every corner of the world and teach them up-to-date methods for increasing their crop yields. Such programs have been extraordinarily effective. They have cut the global illiteracy rate from one in three adults in 1970 to one in six today, and helped give us a Green Revolution that saved more than a billion people from starvation.

In the era of the iPhone, Facebook, and Twitter, we've become enamored of ideas that spread as effortlessly as ether. We want frictionless, "turnkey" solutions to the major difficulties of the world—hunger, disease, poverty. We prefer instructional videos to teachers, drones to troops, incentives to institutions. People and institutions can feel messy and anachronistic. They introduce, as the engineers put it, uncontrolled variability.

But technology and incentive programs are not enough. "Diffusion is essentially a social process through which people talking to people spread an innovation," wrote Everett Rogers, the great scholar of how new ideas are communicated and spread. Mass media can introduce a new idea to people. But, Rogers showed, people follow the lead of other people they know and trust when they decide whether to take it up. Every change requires effort, and the decision to make that effort is a social process.

This is something that salespeople understand well. I once asked a pharmaceutical rep how he persuaded doctors—who are notoriously stubborn—to adopt a new medicine. Evidence is not remotely enough, he said, however strong a case you may have. You must also apply "the rule of seven touches." Personally "touch" the doctors seven times, and they will come to know you; if they know you, they might trust you; and, if they trust you, they will change. That's why he stocked doctors' closets with free drug samples in person. Then he could poke his head around the corner and ask, "So how did your daughter Debbie's soccer game go?" Eventually, this can become "Have you seen this study on our new drug? How about giving it a try?" As the rep had recognized, human interaction is the key force in overcoming resistance and speeding change.

In 1968, *The Lancet* published the results of a modest trial of what is now regarded as among the most important medical advances of the twentieth century. It wasn't a new drug or vaccine or operation. It was basically a solution of sugar, salt, and water that you could make in your kitchen. The researchers gave the solution to victims of a cholera outbreak in Dhaka, the capital of what is now Bangladesh, and the results were striking.

Cholera is a violent and deadly diarrheal illness, caused by the bacterium *Vibrio cholera*, which the victim usually ingests from contaminated water. The bacteria secrete a toxin that triggers a rapid outpouring of fluid into the intestine. The body, which is sixty per cent water, becomes like a sponge being wrung out. The fluid pouring out is a cloudy white, likened to the runoff of washed rice. It produces projectile vomiting and explosive diarrhea. Children can lose a third of their body's water in less than twenty-four hours, a fatal volume. Drinking water to replace the fluid loss is ineffective, because the intestine won't absorb it. As a result, mortality commonly reached seventy per cent or higher. During the nineteenth century, cholera pandemics killed millions across Asia, Europe, Africa, and North America. The disease was dubbed the Blue Death because of the cyanotic blue-gray color of the skin from extreme dehydration.

In 1906, a partially effective treatment was found: intravenous fluid solutions reduced mortality to thirty per cent. Prevention was the most effective approach. Modern sewage and water treatment eliminated the disease in affluent countries. Globally, though, millions of children continued to die from diarrheal illness each year. Even if victims made it to a medical facility, the needles, plastic tubing, and litres of intravenous fluid required for treatment were expensive, in short supply, and dependent on medical workers who were themselves in short supply, especially in outbreaks that often produced thousands of victims.

Then, in the nineteen-sixties, scientists discovered that sugar helps the gut absorb fluid. Two American researchers, David Nalin and Richard Cash, were in Dhaka during a cholera outbreak. They decided to test the scientific findings, giving victims an oral rehydration solution containing sugar as well as salt. Many people doubted that victims could drink enough of it to restore their fluid losses, typically ten to twenty litres a day. So the researchers confined the Dhaka trial to twenty-nine patients. The subjects proved to have no trouble drinking enough to reduce or even eliminate the need for intravenous fluids, and none of them died.

Three years later, in 1971, an Indian physician named Dilip Mahalanabis was directing medical assistance at a West Bengal camp of three hundred and fifty thousand refugees from Bangladesh's war of independence when cholera struck. Intravenous-fluid supplies ran out. Mahalanabis instructed his team to try the Dhaka solution. Just 3.6 per cent died, an unprecedented reduction from the usual thirty per cent. The solution was actually better than intravenous fluids. If cholera victims were alert, able to drink, and supplied with enough of it, they could almost always save their own lives.

One might have expected people to clamor for the recipe after these results were publicized. Oral rehydration solution seems like ether: a miraculous fix for a vivid, immediate, and terrifying problem. But it wasn't like ether at all.

To understand why, you have to imagine having a child throwing up and pouring out diarrhea like you've never seen before. Making her drink seems only to provoke more vomiting. Chasing the emesis and the diarrhea seems both torturous and futile. Many people's natural inclination is to not feed the child anything.

Furthermore, why believe that this particular mixture of sugar and salt would be any different from water or anything else you might have tried? And it *is* particular. Throw the salt concentration off by a couple of teaspoons and the electrolyte imbalance could be dangerous. The child must also keep drinking the stuff even after she feels better, for as long as the diarrhea lasts, which is up to five days. Nurses routinely got these steps wrong. Why would villagers do any better?

A decade after the landmark findings, the idea remained stalled. Nothing much had changed. Diarrheal disease remained the world's biggest killer of children under the age of five.

In 1980, however, a Bangladeshi nonprofit organization called BRAC decided to try to get oral rehydration therapy adopted nationwide. The campaign required reaching a mostly illiterate population. The most recent public-health campaign—to teach family planning—had been deeply unpopular. The messages the campaign needed to spread were complicated.

Nonetheless, the campaign proved remarkably successful. A gem of a book published in Bangladesh, "A Simple Solution," tells the story. The organization didn't launch a mass-media campaign—only twenty per cent of the population had a radio, after all. It attacked the problem in a way that is routinely dismissed as impractical and inefficient: by going door to door, person by person, and just talking.

It started with a pilot project that set out to reach some sixty thousand women in six hundred villages. The logistics were daunting. Who, for instance, would do the teaching? How were those workers going to travel? How was their security to be assured? The BRAC leaders planned the best they could and then made adjustments on the fly.

They recruited teams of fourteen young women, a cook, and a male supervisor, figuring that the supervisor would protect them from others as they travelled, and the women's numbers would protect them from the supervisor. They travelled on foot, pitched camp near each village, fanned out door to door, and stayed until they had talked to women in every hut. They worked long days, six days a week. Each night after dinner, they held a meeting to discuss what went well and what didn't and to share ideas on how to do better. Leaders periodically debriefed them, as well.

The workers were only semi-literate, but they helped distill their sales script into seven easy-to-remember messages: for instance, severe diarrhea leads to death from dehydration; the signs of dehydration include dry tongue, sunken eyes, thirst, severe weakness, and reduced urination; the way to treat dehydration is to replace salt and water lost from the body, starting with the very first loose stool; a rehydration solution provides the most effective way to do this. BRAC's scientists had to figure out how the workers could teach the recipe for the solution. Villagers had no precise measuring implements—spoons were locally made in nonstandard sizes. The leaders considered issuing special measuring spoons with the recipe on the handle. But these would be costly; most people couldn't read the recipe; and how were the spoons to be replaced when lost? Eventually, the team hit upon using finger measures: a fistful of raw sugar plus a three-finger pinch of salt mixed in half a "seer" of water—a pint measure commonly used by villagers when buying milk and oil. Tests showed that mothers could make this with sufficient accuracy.

Initially, the workers taught up to twenty mothers per day. But monitors visiting the villages a few weeks later found that the quality of teaching suffered on this larger scale, so the workers were restricted to ten households a day. Then a new salary system was devised to pay each worker according to how many of the messages the mothers retained when the monitor followed up. The quality of teaching improved substantially. The field workers soon realized that having the mothers make the solution themselves was more effective than just showing them. The workers began looking for diarrhea cases when they arrived in a village, and treating them to show how effective and safe the remedy was. The scientists also investigated various questions that came up, such as whether clean water was required. (They found that, although boiled water was preferable, contaminated water was better than nothing.)

Early signs were promising. Mothers seemed to retain the key messages. Analysis of their sugar solutions showed that three-quarters made them properly, and just four in a thousand had potentially unsafe salt levels. So BRAC and the Bangladeshi government took the program nationwide. They hired, trained, and deployed thousands of workers region by region. The effort was, inevitably, imperfect. But, by going door to door through more than seventy-five thousand villages, they showed twelve million families how to save their children.

The program was stunningly successful. Use of oral rehydration therapy skyrocketed. The knowledge became self-propagating. The program had changed the norms.

Coaxing villagers to make the solution with their own hands and explain the messages in their own words, while a trainer observed and guided them, achieved far more than any public-service ad or instructional video could have done. Over time, the changes could be sustained with television and radio, and the growth of demand led to the development of a robust market for manufactured oral rehydration salt packets. Three decades later, national surveys have found that almost ninety per cent of children with severe diarrhea were given the solution. Child deaths from diarrhea plummeted more than eighty per cent between 1980 and 2005.

As other countries adopted Bangladesh's approach, global diarrheal deaths dropped from five million a year to two million, despite a fifty-per-cent increase in the world's population during the past three decades. Nonetheless, only a third of children in the developing world receive oral rehydration therapy. Many countries tried to implement at arm's length, going "low touch," without sandals on the ground. As a recent study by the Gates Foundation and the University of Washington has documented, those countries have failed almost entirely. People talking to people is still how the world's standards change.

Surgeons finally did upgrade their antiseptic standards at the end of the nineteenth century. But, as is often the case with new ideas, the effort required deeper changes than anyone had anticipated. In their blood-slick, viscera-encrusted black coats, surgeons had seen themselves as warriors doing hemorrhagic battle with little more than their bare hands. A few pioneering Germans, however, seized on the idea of the surgeon as scientist. They traded in their black coats for pristine laboratory whites, refashioned their operating rooms to achieve the exacting sterility of a bacteriological lab, and embraced anatomic precision over speed.

The key message to teach surgeons, it turned out, was not how to stop germs but how to think like a laboratory scientist. Young physicians from America and elsewhere who went to Germany to study with its surgical luminaries became fervent converts to their thinking and their standards. They returned as apostles not only for the use of antiseptic practice (to kill germs) but also for the much more exacting demands of aseptic practice (to prevent germs), such as wearing sterile gloves, gowns, hats, and masks. Proselytizing through their own students and colleagues, they finally spread the ideas worldwide.

In childbirth, we have only begun to accept that the critical practices aren't going to spread themselves. Simple "awareness" isn't going to solve anything. We need our sales force and our seven easy-to-remember messages. And in many places around the world the concerted, person-by-person effort of changing norms is under way.

I recently asked BetterBirth workers in India whether they'd yet seen a birth attendant change what she does. Yes, they said, but they've found that it takes a while. They begin by providing a day of classroom training for birth attendants and hospital leaders in the checklist of practices to be followed. Then they visit them on site to observe as they try to apply the lessons.

Sister Seema Yadav, a twenty-four-year-old, round-faced nurse three years out of school, was one of the trainers. (Nurses are called "sisters" in India, a carryover from the British usage.) Her first assignment was to follow a thirty-year-old nurse with vastly more experience than she had. Watching the nurse take a woman through labor and delivery, she saw how little of the training had been absorbed. The room had not been disinfected; blood from a previous birth remained in a bucket. When the woman came in—moaning, contractions speeding up—the nurse didn't check her vital signs. She didn't wash her hands. She prepared no emergency supplies. After delivery, she checked the newborn's temperature with her hand, not a thermometer. Instead of warming the baby against the mother's skin, she handed the newborn to the relatives.

When Sister Seema pointed out the discrepancy between the teaching and the practice, the nurse was put out. She gave many reasons that steps were missed—there was no time, they were swamped with deliveries, there was seldom a thermometer at hand, the cleaners never did their job. Sister Seema—a cheerful, bubbly, fast talker—took her to the cleaner on duty and together they explained why cleaning the rooms between deliveries was so important. They went to the medical officer in charge and asked for a thermometer to be supplied. At her second and third visits, disinfection seemed more consistent. A thermometer had been found in a storage closet. But the nurse still hadn't changed much of her own routine.

By the fourth or fifth visit, their conversations had shifted. They shared cups of chai and began talking about why you must wash hands even if you wear gloves (because of holes in the gloves and the tendency to touch equipment without them on), and why checking blood pressure matters (because hypertension is a sign of eclampsia, which, when untreated, is a common cause of death among pregnant women). They learned a bit about each other, too. Both turned out to have one child—Sister Seema a four-year-old boy, the nurse an eight-year-old girl. The nurse lived in the capital, a two-hour bus ride away. She was divorced, living with her mother, and struggled with the commute. She'd been frustrated not to find a hospital posting in the city. She worked for days at a stretch, sleeping on a cot when she got a break. Sister Seema commiserated, and shared her own hopes for her family and her future. With time, it became clearer to the nurse that Sister Seema was there only to help and to learn from the experience herself. They even exchanged mobile-phone numbers and spoke between visits. When Sister Seema didn't have the answer to a question, she made sure she got one.

Soon, she said, the nurse began to change. After several visits, she was taking temperatures and blood pressures properly, washing her hands, giving the necessary medications—almost everything. Sister Seema saw it with her own eyes.

She'd had to move on to another pilot site after that, however. And although the project is tracking the outcomes of mothers and newborns, it will be a while before we have enough numbers to know if a difference has been made. So I got the nurse's phone number and, with a translator to help with the Hindi, I gave her a call.

It had been four months since Sister Seema's visit ended. I asked her whether she'd made any changes. Lots, she said.

"What was the most difficult one?" I asked.

"Washing hands," she said. "I have to do it so many times!"

"What was the easiest?"

"Taking the vital signs properly." Before, she said, "we did it haphazardly." Afterward, "everything became much more systematic."

She said that she had eventually begun to see the effects. Bleeding after delivery was reduced. She recognized problems earlier. She rescued a baby who wasn't breathing. She diagnosed eclampsia in a mother and treated it. You could hear her pride as she told her stories.

Many of the changes took practice for her, she said. She had to learn, for instance, how to have all the critical supplies—blood-pressure cuff, thermometer, soap, clean gloves, baby respiratory mask, medications—lined up and ready for when she needed them; how to fit the use of them into her routine; how to convince mothers and their relatives that the best thing for a child was to be bundled against the mother's skin. But, step by step, Sister Seema had helped her to do it. "She showed me how to get things done practically," the nurse said.

"Why did you listen to her?" I asked. "She had only a fraction of your experience."

In the beginning, she didn't, the nurse admitted. "The first day she came, I felt the workload on my head was increasing." From the second time, however, the nurse began feeling better about the visits. She even began looking forward to them.

"Why?" I asked.

All the nurse could think to say was "She was nice."

"She was nice?"

"She smiled a lot."

"That was it?"

"It wasn't like talking to someone who was trying to find mistakes," she said. "It was like talking to a friend."

That, I think, was the answer. Since then, the nurse had developed her own way of explaining why newborns needed to be warmed skin to skin. She said that she now tells families, "Inside the uterus, the baby is very warm. So when the baby comes out it should be kept very warm. The mother's skin does this."

I hadn't been sure if she was just telling me what I wanted to hear. But when I heard her explain how she'd put her own words to what she'd learned, I knew that the ideas had spread. "Do the families listen?" I asked.

"Sometimes they don't," she said. "Usually, they do."

# Chapter 2 ■ Slow Ideas

## Questions for Discussion

1. In "Slow Ideas," Gawande presents the following:

    In the 1860s, the Edinburgh surgeon Joseph Lister read a paper by Louis Pasteur laying out his evidence that spoiling and fermentation were the consequence of microorganisms. Lister became convinced that the same process accounted for wound sepsis. Pasteur had observed that, besides filtration and the application of heat, exposure to certain chemicals could eliminate germs. Lister had read about the city of Carlisle's success in using a small amount of carbolic acid to eliminate the odor of sewage, and reasoned that it was destroying germs. Maybe it could do the same in surgery.

    a.  As researchers, how might you be limited by the paradigms you employ within your specific research field?

    b.  How can reading interdisciplinary research help expand your own research and help you discover new models of success?

2. The process of discovering successful paradigms can, at times, be painstakingly long. As Gawande outlines, "This has been the pattern of many important but stalled ideas. They attack problems that are big but, to most people, invisible; and making them work can be tedious, if not outright painful." How will your research process benefit from the fact that, at this point in time, much of this tedious work has already been done for you? On the other hand, could this potentially stifle you from uncovering groundbreaking information?

3. Gawande discusses the "unsexy tasks" that go into making permanent and meaningful changes. You will undoubtedly discover some of these "unsexy," yet successful, tasks in your research. How might you illustrate the benefits of such tasks to your patron so that they are willing to back the implementation of your proposal?

4. As researchers, we don't always have the luxury of visiting sites to experience the problem firsthand, conducting long-standing fieldwork, or overseeing the implementation of positive changes in person. How can we, as researchers, get a better feel for these processes even though we may not be able to be there in person?

5. Gawande cites Everett Rogers in the following: "Diffusion is essentially a social process through which people talking to people spread an innovation." How can you incorporate diffusion into your proposal in order to ensure that you can spread the word on the work you will be doing?

6. Do you anticipate any resistance to your proposal? If so, how will you utilize human interaction to try to counteract that resistance? Explain the specific steps you will take and outline whose help you will need with this task.

# Can the Bacteria in Your Gut Explain Your Mood?

The rich array of microbiota in our intestines can tell us more than you might think.

Peter Andrey Smith

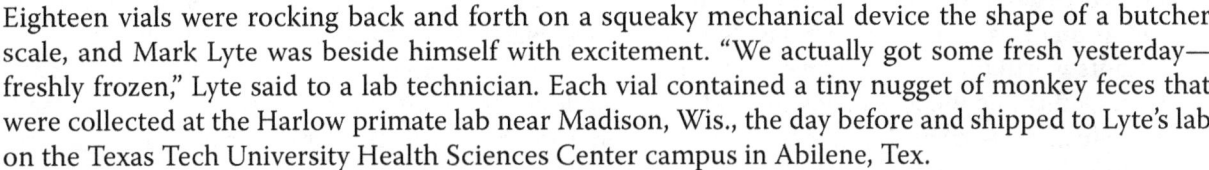

Eighteen vials were rocking back and forth on a squeaky mechanical device the shape of a butcher scale, and Mark Lyte was beside himself with excitement. "We actually got some fresh yesterday— freshly frozen," Lyte said to a lab technician. Each vial contained a tiny nugget of monkey feces that were collected at the Harlow primate lab near Madison, Wis., the day before and shipped to Lyte's lab on the Texas Tech University Health Sciences Center campus in Abilene, Tex.

Lyte's interest was not in the feces per se but in the hidden form of life they harbor. The digestive tube of a monkey, like that of all vertebrates, contains vast quantities of what biologists call gut microbiota. The genetic material of these trillions of microbes, as well as others living elsewhere in and on the body, is collectively known as the microbiome. Taken together, these bacteria can weigh as much as six pounds, and they make up a sort of organ whose functions have only begun to reveal themselves to science. Lyte has spent his career trying to prove that gut microbes communicate with the nervous system using some of the same neurochemicals that relay messages in the brain.

Inside a closet-size room at his lab that afternoon, Lyte hunched over to inspect the vials, whose samples had been spun down in a centrifuge to a radiant, golden broth. Lyte, 60, spoke fast and emphatically. "You wouldn't believe what we're extracting out of poop," he told me. "We found that the guys here in the gut make neurochemicals. We didn't know that. Now, if they make this stuff here, does it have an influence there? Guess what? We make the same stuff. Maybe all this communication has an influence on our behavior."

Since 2007, when scientists announced plans for a Human Microbiome Project to catalog the microorganisms living in our body, the profound appreciation for the influence of such organisms has grown rapidly with each passing year. Bacteria in the gut produce vitamins and break down our food; their presence or absence has been linked to obesity, inflammatory bowel disease and the toxic side effects of prescription drugs. Biologists now believe that much of what makes us human depends on microbial activity. The two million unique bacterial genes found in each human microbiome can make the 23,000 genes in our cells seem paltry, almost negligible, by comparison. "It has enormous implications for the sense of self," Tom Insel, the director of the National Institute of Mental Health, told me. "We are, at least from the standpoint of DNA, more microbial than human. That's a phenomenal insight and one that we have to take seriously when we think about human development."

Given the extent to which bacteria are now understood to influence human physiology, it is hardly surprising that scientists have turned their attention to how bacteria might affect the brain. Microorganisms in our gut secrete a profound number of chemicals, and researchers like Lyte have found that among those chemicals are the same substances used by our neurons to communicate and regulate mood, like dopamine, serotonin and gamma-aminobutyric acid (GABA). These, in turn, appear to play a function in intestinal disorders, which coincide with high levels of major depression and anxiety. Last year, for example, a group in Norway examined feces from 55 people and found certain bacteria were more likely to be associated with depressive patients.

At the time of my visit to Lyte's lab, he was nearly six months into an experiment that he hoped would better establish how certain gut microbes influenced the brain, functioning, in effect, as psychiatric drugs. He was currently compiling a list of the psychoactive compounds found in the feces of infant monkeys. Once that was established, he planned to transfer the microbes found in one newborn monkey's feces into another's intestine, so that the recipient would end up with a completely new set of microbes—and, if all went as predicted, change their neurodevelopment. The experiment reflected an intriguing hypothesis. Anxiety, depression and several pediatric disorders, including autism and hyperactivity, have been linked with gastrointestinal abnormalities. Microbial transplants were not invasive brain surgery, and that was the point: Changing a patient's bacteria might be difficult but it still seemed more straightforward than altering his genes.

When Lyte began his work on the link between microbes and the brain three decades ago, it was dismissed as a curiosity. By contrast, last September, the National Institute of Mental Health awarded four grants worth up to $1 million each to spur new research on the gut microbiome's role in mental disorders, affirming the legitimacy of a field that had long struggled to attract serious scientific credibility. Lyte and one of his longtime colleagues, Christopher Coe, at the Harlow primate lab, received one of the four. "What Mark proposed going back almost 25 years now has come to fruition," Coe told me. "Now what we're struggling to do is to figure out the logic of it." It seems plausible, if not yet proved, that we might one day use microbes to diagnose neurodevelopmental disorders, treat mental illnesses and perhaps even fix them in the brain.

**In 2011, a team** of researchers at University College Cork, in Ireland, and McMaster University, in Ontario, published a study in Proceedings of the National Academy of Science that has become one of the best-known experiments linking bacteria in the gut to the brain. Laboratory mice were dropped into tall, cylindrical columns of water in what is known as a forced-swim test, which measures over six minutes how long the mice swim before they realize that they can neither touch the bottom nor climb out, and instead collapse into a forlorn float. Researchers use the amount of time a mouse floats as a way to measure what they call "behavioral despair." (Antidepressant drugs, like Zoloft and Prozac, were initially tested using this forced-swim test.)

For several weeks, the team, led by John Cryan, the neuroscientist who designed the study, fed a small group of healthy rodents a broth infused with Lactobacillus rhamnosus, a common bacterium that is found in humans and also used to ferment milk into probiotic yogurt. Lactobacilli are one of the dominant organisms babies ingest as they pass through the birth canal. Recent studies have shown that mice stressed during pregnancy pass on lowered levels of the bacterium to their pups. This type of bacteria is known to release immense quantities of GABA; as an inhibitory neurotransmitter, GABA calms nervous activity, which explains why the most common anti-anxiety drugs, like Valium and Xanax, work by targeting GABA receptors.

Cryan found that the mice that had been fed the bacteria-laden broth kept swimming longer and spent less time in a state of immobilized woe. "They behaved as if they were on Prozac," he said. "They were more chilled out and more relaxed." The results suggested that the bacteria were somehow altering the neural chemistry of mice.

Until he joined his colleagues at Cork 10 years ago, Cryan thought about microbiology in terms of pathology: the neurological damage created by diseases like syphilis or H.I.V. "There are certain fields that just don't seem to interact well," he said. "Microbiology and neuroscience, as whole disciplines, don't tend to have had much interaction, largely because the brain is somewhat protected." He was referring to the fact that the brain is anatomically isolated, guarded by a blood-brain barrier that allows nutrients in but keeps out pathogens and inflammation, the immune system's typical response to germs. Cryan's study added to the growing evidence that signals from beneficial bacteria nonetheless find a way through the barrier. Somehow—though his 2011 paper could not pinpoint exactly how—micro-organisms in the gut tickle a sensory nerve ending in the fingerlike protrusion lining the intestine and carry that electrical impulse up the vagus nerve and into the deep-brain structures thought to be responsible for elemental emotions like anxiety. Soon after that, Cryan and a co-author, Ted Dinan, published a theory paper in Biological Psychiatry calling these potentially mind-altering microbes "psychobiotics."

It has long been known that much of our supply of neurochemicals—an estimated 50 percent of the dopamine, for example, and a vast majority of the serotonin—originate in the intestine, where these chemical signals regulate appetite, feelings of fullness and digestion. But only in recent years has mainstream psychiatric research given serious consideration to the role microbes might play in creating those chemicals. Lyte's own interest in the question dates back to his time as a postdoctoral fellow at the University of Pittsburgh in 1985, when he found himself immersed in an emerging field with an unwieldy name: psychoneuroimmunology, or PNI, for short. The central theory, quite controversial at the time, suggested that stress worsened disease by suppressing our immune system.

By 1990, at a lab in Mankato, Minn., Lyte distilled the theory into three words, which he wrote on a chalkboard in his office: Stress->Immune->Disease. In the course of several experiments, he homed in on a paradox. When he dropped an intruder mouse in the cage of an animal that lived alone, the intruder ramped up its immune system—a boost, he suspected, intended to fight off germ-ridden bites or scratches. Surprisingly, though, this did not stop infections. It instead had the opposite effect: Stressed animals got sick. Lyte walked up to the board and scratched a line through the word "Immune." Stress, he suspected, directly affected the bacterial bugs that caused infections.

To test how micro-organisms reacted to stress, he filled petri plates with a bovine-serum-based medium and laced the dishes with a strain of bacterium. In some, he dropped norepinephrine, a neurochemical that mammals produce when stressed. The next day, he snapped a Polaroid. The results were visible and obvious: The control plates were nearly barren, but those with the norepinephrine bloomed with bacteria that filigreed in frostlike patterns. Bacteria clearly responded to stress.

Then, to see if bacteria could induce stress, Lyte fed white mice a liquid solution of Campylobacter jejuni, a bacterium that can cause food poisoning in humans but generally doesn't prompt an immune response in mice. To the trained eye, his treated mice were as healthy as the controls. But when he ran them through a plexiglass maze raised several feet above the lab floor, the bacteria-fed mice were less likely to venture out on the high, unprotected ledges of the maze. In human terms, they seemed anxious. Without the bacteria, they walked the narrow, elevated planks.

Each of these results was fascinating, but Lyte had a difficult time finding microbiology journals that would publish either. "It was so anathema to them," he told me. When the mouse study finally appeared in the journal Physiology & Behavior in 1998, it garnered little attention. And yet as Stephen Collins, a gastroenterologist at McMaster University, told me, those first papers contained the seeds of an entire new field of research. "Mark showed, quite clearly, in elegant studies that are not often cited, that introducing a pathological bacterium into the gut will cause a change in behavior."

Lyte went on to show how stressful conditions for newborn cattle worsened deadly E. coli infections. In another experiment, he fed mice lean ground hamburger that appeared to improve memory and learning—a conceptual proof that by changing diet, he could change gut microbes and change behavior. After accumulating nearly a decade's worth of evidence, in July 2008, he flew to Washington to present his research. He was a finalist for the National Institutes of Health's Pioneer Award, a $2.5 million grant for so-called blue-sky biomedical research. Finally, it seemed, his time had come. When he got up to speak, Lyte described a dialogue between the bacterial organ and our central nervous system. At the two-minute mark, a prominent scientist in the audience did a spit take.

"Dr. Lyte," he later asked at a question-and-answer session, "if what you're saying is right, then why is it when we give antibiotics to patients to kill bacteria, they are not running around crazy on the wards?"

Lyte knew it was a dismissive question. And when he lost out on the grant, it confirmed to him that the scientific community was still unwilling to imagine that any part of our neural circuitry could be influenced by single-celled organisms. Lyte published his theory in Medical Hypotheses, a low-ranking journal that served as a forum for unconventional ideas. The response, predictably, was underwhelming. "I had people call me crazy," he said.

But by 2011—when he published a second theory paper in Bioessays, proposing that probiotic bacteria could be tailored to treat specific psychological diseases—the scientific community had become much more receptive to the idea. A Canadian team, led by Stephen Collins, had demonstrated that antibiotics could be linked to less cautious behavior in mice, and only a few months before Lyte, Sven Pettersson, a microbiologist at the Karolinska Institute in Stockholm, published a landmark paper in Proceedings of the National Academy of Science that showed that mice raised without microbes spent far more time running around outside than healthy mice in a control group; without the microbes, the mice showed less apparent anxiety and were more daring. In Ireland, Cryan published his forced-swim-test study on psychobiotics. There was now a groundswell of new research. In short order, an implausible idea had become a hypothesis in need of serious validation.

**Late last year,** Sarkis Mazmanian, a microbiologist at the California Institute of Technology, gave a presentation at the Society for Neuroscience, "Gut Microbes and the Brain: Paradigm Shift in Neuroscience." Someone had inadvertently dropped a question mark from the end, so the speculation appeared to be a definitive statement of fact. But if anyone has a chance of delivering on that promise, it's Mazmanian, whose research has moved beyond the basic neurochemicals to focus on a broader class of molecules called metabolites: small, equally druglike chemicals that are produced by microorganisms. Using high-powered computational tools, he also hopes to move beyond the suggestive correlations that have typified psychobiotic research to date, and instead make decisive discoveries about the mechanisms by which microbes affect brain function.

Two years ago, Mazmanian published a study in the journal Cell with Elaine Hsiao, then a graduate student and now a neuroscientist at Caltech, and others, that made a provocative link between a single molecule and behavior. Their research found that mice exhibiting abnormal communication and repetitive behaviors, like obsessively burying marbles, were mollified when they were given one of two strains of the bacterium Bacteroides fragilis.

The study added to a working hypothesis in the field that microbes don't just affect the permeability of the barrier around the brain but also influence the intestinal lining, which normally prevents certain bacteria from leaking out and others from getting in. When the intestinal barrier was compromised in his model, normally "beneficial" bacteria and the toxins they produce seeped into the bloodstream and raised the possibility they could slip past the blood-brain barrier. As one of his colleagues, Michael Fischbach, a microbiologist at the University of California, San Francisco, said: "The scientific community has a way of remaining skeptical until every last arrow has been drawn, until the entire picture is colored in. Other scientists drew the pencil outlines, and Sarkis is filling in a lot of the color".

Mazmanian knew the results offered only a provisional explanation for why restrictive diets and antibacterial treatments seemed to help some children with autism: Altering the microbial composition might be changing the permeability of the intestine. "The larger concept is, and this is pure speculation: Is a disease like autism really a disease of the brain or maybe a disease of the gut or some other aspect of physiology?" Mazmanian said. For any disease in which such a link could be proved, he saw a future in drugs derived from these small molecules found inside microbes. (A company he co-founded, Symbiotix Biotherapies, is developing a complex sugar called PSA, which is associated with Bacteroides fragilis, into treatments for intestinal disease and multiple sclerosis.) In his view, the prescriptive solutions probably involve more than increasing our exposure to environmental microbes in soil, dogs or even fermented foods; he believed there were wholesale failures in the way we shared our microbes and inoculated children with these bacteria. So far, though, the only conclusion he could draw was that disorders once thought to be conditions of the brain might be symptoms of microbial disruptions, and it was the careful defining of these disruptions that promised to be helpful in the coming decades.

The list of potential treatments incubating in labs around the world is startling. Several international groups have found that psychobiotics had subtle yet perceptible effects in healthy volunteers in a battery of brain-scanning and psychological tests. Another team in Arizona recently finished an open trial on fecal transplants in children with autism. (Simultaneously, at least two offshore clinics, in Australia and England, began offering fecal microbiota treatments to treat neurological disorders, like multiple sclerosis.) Mazmanian, however, cautions that this research is still in its infancy. "We've reached the stage where there's a lot of, you know, 'The microbiome is the cure for everything,'" he said. "I have a vested interest if it does. But I'd be shocked if it did."

Lyte issues the same caveat. "People are obviously desperate for solutions," Lyte said when I visited him in Abilene. (He has since moved to Iowa State's College of Veterinary Medicine.) "My main fear is the hype is running ahead of the science." He knew that parents emailing him for answers meant they had exhausted every option offered by modern medicine. "It's the Wild West out there," he said. "You can go online and buy any amount of probiotics for any number of conditions now, and my paper is one of those cited. I never said go out and take probiotics." He added, "We really need a lot more research done before we actually have people trying therapies out."

If the idea of psychobiotics had now, in some ways, eclipsed him, it was nevertheless a curious kind of affirmation, even redemption: an old-school microbiologist thrust into the midst of one of the most promising aspects of neuroscience. At the moment, he had a rough map in his head and a freezer full of monkey fecals that might translate, somehow, into telling differences between gregarious or shy monkeys later in life. I asked him if what amounted to a personality transplant still sounded a bit far-fetched. He seemed no closer to unlocking exactly what brain functions could be traced to the same organ that produced feces. "If you transfer the microbiota from one animal to another, you can transfer the behavior," Lyte said. "What we're trying to understand are the mechanisms by which the microbiota can influence the brain and development. If you believe that, are you now out on the precipice? The answer is yes. Do I think it's the future? I think it's a long way away."

# Chapter 2 ■ Can the Bacteria in Your Gut Explain Your Mood?

## Questions for Discussion

1. At the end of the article, Peter Andrey Smith discusses the possible dangers associated with stretching a discovery too far. Smith cites Mark Lyte, the researcher studying the connection between microbes and brain physiology in the following: "You can go online and buy any amount of probiotics for any number of conditions now, and my paper is one of those cited. I never said go out and take probiotics . . . We really need a lot more research done before we actually have people trying therapies out." Clearly, the application of any paradigm has its limits. How might a larger context affect our work in this class? At any point in your research, have you stopped to think about subsidiary or unintended consequences of conducting your research or implementing your plan? Are there any glaring, or underlying, outcomes from your plan that you could envision having negative effects down the line?

2. Smith talks about the difficulty researchers face when they are trying to share new research and have it be taken seriously. Tom Insel, the director of the National Institute of Mental Health explains: "We are, at least from the standpoint of DNA, more microbial than human. That's a phenomenal insight and one that we have to take seriously when we think about human development." Since this is a relatively new idea, not every scientist is thinking about the brain in terms of microbial studies. After reading this article, list what you think would be included in a general set of guidelines for analyzing new paradigms and determining their scientific promise. Create a list of at least three rules that would help determine whether or not a study is worth investing time and money in.

3. In this article, Smith focuses a great deal on Mark Lyte's work. As Smith explains, "When Lyte began his work on the link between microbes and the brain three decades ago, it was dismissed as a curiosity." Why, consequently, has Lyte's work been successful? How can you make sure that you are pitching your ideas to your patron in a way that ensures that they won't write it off as a "curiosity"? What cues can you take from Lyte's research and apply to your own?

4. As we know from Thomas Kuhn's discussion of the "disciplinary matrix," the research you do for your proposal will fall into more than one field of study. In this article, scientist John Cryan highlights the fact in the following: "There are certain fields that just don't seem to interact well." As he goes on to explain, "Microbiology and neuroscience, as whole disciplines, don't tend to have had much interaction, largely because the brain is somewhat protected." List all of the disciplines you will need to consider while conducting your research. Discuss with a partner some of the originality and promise associated with crossing over multiple disciplines in developing your proposals. Then, discuss the potential pitfalls when trying to use research from more than one discipline in a given research project.

5. Smith cites Michael Fischbach, a microbiologist at the University of California, San Francisco in the following: "The scientific community has a way of remaining skeptical until every last arrow has been drawn, until the entire picture is colored in." Now that you've amassed a significant amount of research for your own proposal, can you find a trend that proves this to be true? Take note of how long it took for the paradigms you'll use to be considered meaningful models of success. How many scientists/researchers had to provide evidence to back the paradigm before it was taken seriously by the science world?

6. Sarkis Mazmanian, a microbiologist, sees great promise in his research of gut microbes and their relation to the brain. Still, as he admits, "We've reached the stage where there's a lot of, you know, 'The microbiome is the cure for everything.'" He goes on to say, "I have a vested interest if it does. But I'd be shocked if it did." What can you learn from his candid realism when it comes to discussing research that is important to him? How can you incorporate this honesty into your own proposal while still enticing your patron to have a vested interest in your plan?

# Framing and Re-Framing in Environmental Science: Explaining Climate Change to the Public

Justin King Rademaekers and Richard Johnson-Sheehan

## Abstract

Environmental scientists and science communicators working to educate the public on the science of global climate change often work to present information through an environmentalist perspective. This article uses theories of metaphoric framing to present six guidelines that climate change communicators can use to reframe climate change science in public communication. In particular, the authors argue for environmental scientists to adopt frames that the broader public will find familiar and persuasive. This reframing of environmental science is necessary to counter the framing of skepticism that special interest groups have used to dominate attempts to communicate climate change science to the public.

# Introduction

In January 2007, the Union of Concerned Scientists (UCS) issued a report titled, "Smoke, Mirrors, and Hot Air: How ExxonMobil Uses Big Tobacco's Tactics to Manufacture Uncertainty on Climate Change." The tone of the article is confrontational, which is not characteristic of the UCS. The UCS typically advocates for the environment in non-partisan ways, producing science-based reports that rely on substantiated data. This UCS report, however, takes on ExxonMobil's marketing tactics with a frontal attack, charging the company with underwriting "the most sophisticated and most successful disinformation campaign since the tobacco industry misled the public about the scientific evidence linking smoking to lung cancer and heart disease" [1, p. 1]. This charge is a serious one. After all, the tobacco companies were successfully sued by states for billions of dollars, primarily for misleading the public about the risks of tobacco usage. If it can be shown that ExxonMobil is similarly misleading people about the risks and effects of climate change, then it too could be a target for expensive litigation.

The UCS report received some interest in the press, but it mostly went unnoticed. ExxonMobil's official response, released to the press, was interesting. The press release referred to an in-house document "Tomorrow's Energy" on its website:

> As stated in Tomorrow's Energy, a publication that may be found on our website and addresses important issues associated with energy supply and demand, including our position on climate change: "We recognize that the accumulation of greenhouse gases in the Earth's atmosphere poses risks that may prove significant for society and ecosystems. . . . Human activities have contributed to these increased concentrations [of greenhouse gases], mainly through the combustion of fossil fuels for energy use; land use changes [especially deforestation]; and agricultural, animal husbandry and waste-disposal practices. . . . Even with many scientific uncertainties, the risk that greenhouse gas emissions may have serious impacts justifies taking action." What is clear today is that greenhouse gas emissions are one of the factors that contribute to climate change, and that the use of fossil fuels is a major source of these emissions [1, para. 2].

From *Journal of Technical Writing and Communication*, Volume 44 (1), 2014, pp. 3–21. Copyright © 2014 Baywood Publishing Company, Inc. Reprinted by permission of SAGE Publications.

The "Tomorrow's Energy" document has since been taken down from the website, and this area of the ExxonMobil site, titled "Energy and the Environment," is now relabeled "Managing Climate Change Risks." It is interesting, however, that in this statement ExxonMobil openly concedes that its products are at least partly responsible for climate change and that the risks of climate change are significant. By making this concession, the company deflected the major premise of the UCS's report, which is that ExxonMobil denies that oil is partly responsible for climate change [1].

ExxonMobil's strategy is subtle, and it helps demonstrate how science-based advocacy groups often overplay their hand with the climate change issue. ExxonMobil's public relations strategy is more sophisticated than simple denial or a red herring claim that climate change is a "hoax." Instead, their strategy demonstrates that fossil fuel energy companies have actually learned from the experiences of the tobacco industry. The tobacco industry, we will point out, is still profitably manufacturing its product and people are still buying it—even though nearly everyone knows it causes lung cancer and heart disease among other ailments. ExxonMobil and other fossil fuel companies know that they will be allowed to continue manufacturing and selling their product as long as they can redirect and reframe the problem of climate change rather than deny its existence.

In this article, we will explore the use of metaphorical framing to explain how environmental scientists and science communicators can better discuss climate change with the public. Our premise is that environmental scientists habitually adopt the frames of the environmental movement, which often puts them at odds with the social frames familiar to the general public. As a result, even though environmental scientists form arguments that are persuasive to environmentalists, these arguments are often not persuasive to the broader public. Sometimes these arguments even cause resistance or denial of climate change. The lack of proper framing by environmental scientists creates a space in which public relations agents working for the fossil fuel industry sow doubt in the public and activate resistance by politicians and pundits. This resulting polarization can be exploited by the fossil fuel industry to preserve the status quo.

## Climate Change History

The science of climate change has existed longer than most people realize. The idea of climate change first emerged in the 1800s in the scientific works of Joseph Fourier (1827) John Tyndall (1861), Svante Arrhenius (1896), and Thomas Chamberlin (1897). Recognizing the effects of the industrial revolution, these scientists argued that the emissions of carbon, especially from the burning of coal and wood, would lead to a warming of the planet.

During the 1800s, much of climate change science stemmed from attempts to understand how heat energy, such as ultraviolet rays from the sun, interact with gas molecules. Fourier was a French physicist who suggested in an 1827 publication "Mémoire Sur Les Températures Du Globe Terrestre Et Des Espaces Planétaires," that mathematical equations based on the Earth's size could not explain the planet's hospitable climate. While far from the climate change science that would develop through the rest of the 19th century, Fourier's treatise sounded the call for scientists to study heat energy to help explain the phenomenon of the Earth's seemingly insulated climate [2].

In 1861, Tyndall, an Irish physicist, published a work in *Philosophical Magazine* that explained what Fourier's math had discovered—that atoms and molecules absorb heat in very specific ways. Tyndall's article "On the absorption and radiation of heat by gases and vapours, and on the physical connection of radiation, adsorption, and conduction" corroborates Fourier's findings and sets out to explore the role of gases in absorbing radiant heat from the sun—a phenomenon that might help explain why the Earth stays warmer than Fourier's calculation reveals it should [3].

While Tyndall was impressed with carbon dioxide's absorption power, he was even more impressed with the absorptive power of water vapor. Water vapor's role in climate change would become a point of dispute until the 1950s. As early as 1961, however, Tyndall doubted the role of water vapor in climate change, noting that if water vapor was the primary greenhouse molecule, the constant fluctuations of water vapor in the atmosphere (in both quantity and altitude) would cause frequent and drastic temperature swings [3, p. 277]. As a result, carbon dioxide, which is evenly and steadily spread throughout the atmosphere (about 3%) was soon understood to be a primary absorber and contributor to the greenhouse effect.

It was the Swedish scientist, Arrhenius, who would be one of the first scientists to put together the works of Fourier, Tyndall, and others in the 19th century, to form a theory of global climate change in which humans are crucial actors. Arrhenius published "On the Influence of Carbonic Acid in the Air upon the Temperature of the Ground" in *Philosophical Magazine* and *Journal of Science* in April of 1896. Arrhenius, like many scientists in the late 1800s, was intensely interested in the ice ages of the past. The theory that Arrhenius puts forth in his publication does not reveal a "gotcha moment" for the role of carbon dioxide in global climate change. Instead, Arrhenius posits that carbon dioxide should be added to the list of other factors effecting global climate such as the sun's output of radiation, the distance of the earth from the sun, and the abundance of carbon sinks (such as the earth's oceans and plant vegetation) [4].

To support his theory, Arrhenius extensively paraphrased his colleague, Professor Högbom, who was better established at the time, and from which one of the most important elements of Arrhenius' 1896 publication arises—that displacements of the carbon dioxide equilibrium in the atmosphere can occur, and that coal, specifically, contributes to one one-thousandth of the carbon content in the atmosphere. Arrhenius was perhaps the first scientist to recognize that burning coal could lead to human-induced global climate change [4].

Works citing Arrhenius continued through the early twentieth century with scientists like G. S. Callendar pursuing the connection between rises in carbon dioxide levels and rises in global temperature. The theory continued to be contested by critics who emphasized the role of carbon sinks, but by the mid-twentieth century scientists were increasingly confident that global climate change through fossil fuel releases of carbon dioxide was human-induced [5, p. 314].

This history explains in part why the science of climate change has been slow to reach the public's attention. Until the 1960s, climate change was primarily a thought experiment and an untestable geological phenomenon. If anything, climate change science was used as a geological theory to explain prehistoric ice ages, the Medieval Warm Period from 950–1250 AD, or perhaps the "Little Ice Age," the period of European cooling from 1550–1850 AD.

In the 1960s, however, climate change science began to enter the public sphere, including politics, as part of the environmental movement. Oceanographer Charles Keeling measured the amount of carbon dioxide in the atmosphere and determined that it was rising quickly. Keeling determined that the rise in carbon in the atmosphere was approximately the expected difference between the amount captured by oceans as "sinks" and the amount released by humans into the atmosphere [6–8]. A 1961 article in the *Science News Letter* titled "Warm Earth Man's Doing" [9] discusses the findings of a University of Utah geologist, William Lee Stokes. Stokes indicates that climate change may have been caused by ancient man's massive burnings 11,000 years prior. Other scientists began to confirm and extend these findings, and they began to sound the alarm about the potential effects of rising carbon dioxide levels. Environmentalists saw climate change as yet another reason why the public needed to begin addressing issues like pollution and waste.

Herein lies the problem. Climate change arguments since the 1960s, including those that are solidly based in scientific data, are typically framed in the language of environmentalism. Of course, this approach seems only natural because climate change is on its surface an environmental issue, and most environmental scientists probably identify themselves as environmentalists. As a result, they tend to frame climate change issues in terms that seem most familiar or commonsensical to them— i.e., the language of environmentalism. The problem, though, is that these frames are not familiar or commonsensical to much of the general public. Moreover, these environmentalist frames can be actively resisted or indirectly undermined by public relations and marketing campaigns, such as those from the fossil fuel industry and conservative think tanks.

# Fundamentals of Metaphoric Framing

To explain this problem, a closer look at framing theory is needed. Gamson and Modigliani [10] define a frame as "a central organizing idea or story line that provides meaning to an unfolding strip of events, weaving a connection among them. Similarly, Callahan and Schnell [11] define framing in the following way: "This process by which all political players, including the media, use linguistic cues to define and give meaning to issues and connect them to the larger political environment. . . . Essentially, frames set the boundaries of public policy debates" (p. 2). Entman [12] describes how frames work:

> To frame is to select some aspects of a perceived reality and make them more salient in a communicating text, in such a way as to promote a particular problem definition, causal interpretation, moral evaluation, and/or treatment recommendation for the item described [12, p. 52].

When repeated over time, a frame can be used to construct a hegemonic perspective in which a set of beliefs becomes accepted as common sense or what "everyone" believes [13]. Savvy politicians, political scientists, and corporate marketing specialists use frames to give specific ideas more authority or influence. A frame can become a conventional truth, especially if the mass media adopts it, working its way into how newsmakers and reporters express their view [13]. As the frame continues to be used and reinforced, it becomes a way of exerting and maintaining power in a culture because the frame itself becomes unseen and uncontested [14]. It shapes how people interpret and discourse about specific issues.

Frames are especially powerful when they are used to shape opinions about large-scale phenomena, like climate change, that are beyond an individual's direct experience. Complex issues, such as terrorism, economics, crime, and climate change are beyond an individual's ability to experience them directly. As a result, most people will use existing social and cultural frames to help them understand and make sense of these kinds of complex issues. According to Kinder and Nelson, these frames become cognitive structures that "provide order and meaning, making the world beyond direct experience seem natural" [15, p. 103]. In other words, what people take to be "normal" or "natural" are often deep-seated frames that have become mostly invisible to them. The frames themselves structure and constrain how they interpret issues.

In 2004, George Lakoff, a linguist from California—Berkeley, published a bestselling political treatise titled, *Don't Think of an Elephant: Know Your Values and Frame the Debate* [16]. In this book, Lakoff introduced the general public to the concept of framing as a political device. According to Lakoff, framing is the use of a structure of words that reflects a specific value set [16, p. xv]. Frames govern how people interpret what is happening around them and how they express their ideas in words. For the most part people don't even notice their own frames, as Lakoff points out, because their own frames express their cultural values. As a result, people accept their frame as true or common sense, while rejecting new frames or the frames of others as false.

To explain framing, Lakoff uses the example of "tax relief" [16, p. 3]. He demonstrates that arguments for "relief" establish a specific frame from which debates over taxes are often argued. In this case, the idea that taxpayers need "relief" can be a persuasive position, even when taxes are historically low and cutting taxes further would be bad for society and the economy. After all, as Lakoff points out, almost everyone would like to pay less taxes. All of us, in some way, feel burdened with taxes, no matter how low those taxes might be. As a result, framing the debate in terms of "relief" suggests that our burden could be lightened or even removed. As Lakoff suggests, people who provide relief are champions of common people, and people who argue against so-called tax relief are therefore villains [16, p. 3]. Spinning out that frame leads to further conclusions about who are the heroes and villains, what values are important, how we should talk about this issue, and the types of actions that should be taken. The frame itself leads people to arrive at—what they perceive to be—logical conclusions.

The frame casts opponents in the shadow of the issue. As soon as someone steps forward to question whether "tax relief" would be a prudent or an economically-sound policy, he or she adopts an inherently negative and vulnerable position. After all, arguing against relief means that you are really arguing for keeping a burden on suffering taxpayers. As Lakoff points out, opponents often mistakenly adopt the language of the frame itself. In this case, they argue against tax relief instead of arguing for something else. Consequently, it doesn't matter whether the opponents of tax relief are using facts and good reasoning to support their case. As long as they adopt their opponents' frame of tax relief, they find themselves on the weaker side of the argument.

Lakoff's solution is simple, but it makes sense: "This gives us a basic principle of framing, for when you are arguing against the other side: Do not use their language" [16, p. 3]. In other words, recognize that the other side of the argument is working from a particular frame that should be avoided. In this case, the better argument might be for "economic fairness" or perhaps "tax reform."

Interestingly, Lakoff, a leading scholar of metaphor theory, does not directly draw the obvious parallels between metaphors and frames; nevertheless metaphors and frames are basically the same things. This has been noted by authors like Davies and Mabin also [17]. Tax relief, pro-life, death penalty, right-to-work, equal opportunity, and global warming for example, are really just metaphors that are used to frame issues. Like any metaphor, they establish perspectives from which people interpret and discourse about reality. In his discussion of metaphor in *Grammar of Motives*, Kenneth Burke writes, "For *metaphor* we could substitute *perspective*" and follows with the definition "*Metaphor* is a device for seeing something in terms of something else" [18, 503; italics in original]. These perspectives become frames that pervade how we talk about specific issues. These frames' metaphorical origins tend to be forgotten as the perspective they create becomes the way people tend to view and talk about specific issues [19].

For this reason, we call frames "metaphoric frames" to highlight their basis in metaphors. Metaphoric frames can be used to create and maintain specific perspectives. For example, if you believe in the "war on cancer," then the frame encourages you to speak of cancer in terms of battle, attack, weapons, winning vs. losing, fronts, strategies, and tactics. The war frame encourages us to view cancer in belligerent terms, as a matter of life and death. Interestingly, as patients go into remission and increasingly live with cancer, alternative frames are being introduced such as "managing cancer." Instead of treating cancer as warfare, this alternative frame treats cancer as something to be managed much like a business. Doctors and cancer patients can now talk about assembling a team, setting goals, reviewing results, understanding risk, and assessing outcomes. The metaphoric frame not only changes the way we talk about cancer, it also shapes the actions patients take in response to a cancer diagnosis. The change in metaphor changes our perspective.

## Metaphoric Frames and Environmental Issues

When the general public and the mass media accept a metaphoric frame as true, it is difficult to argue against it. They tend to hear and absorb the facts and reasoning that fit their pre-existing frame. Facts that don't fit the frame are often not understood, not heard, or ignored. For example, if people believe that environmental progress only happens at the cost of jobs, then using facts, data, and reasoning alone to demonstrate the opposite probably won't be successful. For this reason, many environmental scientists often misread the rhetorical situation. They assume that data, scientifically-proven facts, and logical reasoning will eventually win over a skeptical public. They believe they simply need to tell the truth and people will understand what is going on. There are three problems with this assumption.

First, people rarely accept facts and reasoning that go against their pre-existing frames and the frames they hear in the media. They may listen. They may engage. But, if climate change facts just don't fit their worldview, they will assume the facts are flawed in some way or at least "open to debate." Environmental scientists often mistakenly assume that people who don't agree with the pro-environment argument are somehow being scoundrels or they are ignorant or unintelligent. That's not true. Most members of the public who are not persuaded by climate change arguments are simply working from metaphoric frames that are out of sync with the environmentalist message. Indeed, there are marketing specialists who are paid to reinforce those anti-environment frames. But, these efforts wouldn't be successful if large parts of the public and the media didn't already buy into metaphoric frames that are favorable to the fossil fuel industry's message.

Second, environmental scientists work from their own scientific frames, even when they firmly believe they are getting beyond "rhetoric" or "spin" and revealing the scientific truth. Because the frames they work from seem like common sense or truth to them, they often do not recognize our own frames. As a result, environmental scientists keep repeating the same "truths" over and over and often wonder why the public doesn't respond. Here's why. Many conservatives and libertarians do not trust scientific theories because they do not identify with the people who use scientific frames. Science is the domain of government and universities, entities many conservatives have already been conditioned to distrust. Scientific frames are also unfamiliar and difficult to understand. The terminologies that are common in the scientific frames (e.g., hypothesis, theory, method, results) do not fit the frames of people who are outside the scientific community.

Finally, the public tends to think within a consumerist frame, and the fossil fuel industry has become very good at sowing doubt about climate change by activating this consumerist frame. Even when people are ready to accept climate change arguments, they hesitate because they are concerned that taking action against climate change might mean hurting the economy or taking away jobs. It might mean changing the way people live their lives, including driving their car, using electricity, or traveling. Americans, especially, have been conditioned to believe in a consumerist frame, which assumes that economic progress (and job creation) happens at the expense of natural resources and even the environment itself. The concept of "sustainability," a common metaphoric frame among environmentalists and environmental scientists, is not in line with the American consumerist frame.

Information that *does* fit the public's consumerist frames includes facts and ideas that address their own concerns, such as jobs, health, and security. These are frames that people hold in common. People on both sides of the political spectrum may disagree about how we get to those goals, but they all agree that striving for good jobs, their own health, and their own security is a good thing.

## What's in a Name?

At this point, we will transition to discussing strategies for re-framing climate change in a way that the public will find acceptable. The re-framing starts with the name of climate change itself.

The term "global warming" began to be used in the popular media in the late 1960s and early 1970s. Newspaper articles of this time acknowledged the science behind greenhouse gases such as carbon dioxide and the link to fossil fuel burning [16, 20]. The tendency in these articles is to refer to global warming as the relationship between pollution and changes in global sea-levels. The majority of articles that used the phrase "global warming" over "climate change" were more interested in actions and effects than a discussion of a complex scientific process. For example, "global warming" articles of this time tend to cite sources of human pollution, the melting of ice caps, and statistics of sea level rises. One article discusses the inundation of New York and Washington, DC in which residents may one day "launch boats from the steps of the Capitol" [21]. The phrase "global warming" seems to have developed organically in the media as a way of describing the specific element of melting ice and its effect on American cities. Plus, the idea of "global warming" probably sounded more threatening, and therefore more attractive to journalists, than the title "climate change," which doesn't sound so ominous.

A 2009 study, "What's in a Name? Commonalities and Differences in Public Understanding of 'Climate Change' and 'Global Warming'" by Lorainne Whitmarsh [22], sheds interesting light on the public's different responses to the terms "global warming" and "climate change." The study was conducted using a mailed questionnaire to citizens of southern England. One interesting finding of the study dealt with familiarity of the terms. The study reported that "2.9 percent of the total sample said they had not heard of climate change/global warming." While this seems low, the familiarity between terms is less expected: "6.2 percent of respondents said they had not heard of 'climate change,'" and "no respondents claimed not to have heard of 'global warming'" [22, p. 405]. The study also pointed to causal relationships between the two terms. For example, respondents were more likely to associate heat-related effects (temperature increase), human causes of the phenomenon (humans are to blame), and ozone depletion to "global warming," whereas, "climate change" was more closely associated with a range of impacts (hot summers and cold winters), natural causes (natural atmospheric cycles—not human), and previously observed impacts. The study attributes possible causes to these differences-in-understanding:

> Firstly, source of information is significant. The variation in awareness by terminology may be a result of the media's tendency to refer to "global warming" instead of "climate change" [11], the latter being the term preferred by scientists and policy-makers. Given the public's reliance on media sources of information noted in this survey and elsewhere, this would explain the greater public familiarity with the term "global warming." Also "global warming" may be a more emotive term, in part because it suggests a clear direction of change towards increasing temperatures; while the implications of "climate change" are more ambiguous. Furthermore, "global warming" may be seen as a more concerning and salient issue because of its currency in the mass media, which tends to dramatize and politicize science news (Hargreaves et al., 2003). . . . It may also be the case that the lower levels of public concern associated with the term "climate change" are due to its scientific connotations [22, p. 416].

Of particular interest here is the acknowledgment of the media's role in deciding which term better activates the public's pre-existing frames. The media picked up the term "global warming" because it implicitly threatens people. People pay attention to issues that might threaten them physically or economically.

A more recent article that confirms the potential for selective use of the terms was conducted by Schuldt et al. [23]. "'Global Warming' OR 'Climate Change'? Whether the Planet is Warming Depends on Question Wording" reviews the results of an American Life Panel survey, which was directed toward Internet users over 18. The survey records information about opinions on "global warming," opinions on "climate change," and the politics associated with each respondent. According to the authors, "Republican respondents were more skeptical that global climate change is a real phenomenon when an otherwise identical question was worded in terms of "global warming" rather than "climate change"; no other political group (Democrats, Independents, and Others) was significantly affected by question wording" [23, p. 122]. The authors refer to Whitmarsh's 2009 study [22] to suggest that this difference has a lot to do with the human causation factor (anthropogenic), which is more closely associated to "global warming" than "climate change."

A good first step toward re-framing this issue is to exclusively use the term "climate change" and not use the term "global warming." Indeed, the term "global warming" should be challenged whenever it is used by the marketing, media, pundits, and politicians. The term itself activates a frame that is counterproductive to climate change science.

# Re-Framing Climate Change

Climate change itself is a frame, and a number of commentators have discussed how it has been used to frame and re-frame the debate about environmental practices and regulations [24]. However, it is not a dominant frame in the public, even though a slight majority of Americans believe humans are causing climate change to happen [25–27]. Almost all Americans have heard of climate change; however, a significant and vocal minority of Americans are skeptical about climate change science despite its conclusive evidence. The fossil fuel industry and its surrogates rely on that skeptical minority to maintain the status quo.

If so, how can environmental scientists re-frame climate change? Baumgartner, Berry, Hojnacki, Kimball, and Leech [28] argue that successful reframing is rare and often difficult to achieve. These scholars found that in a randomly selected set of policy debates occurring in Washington, DC between 1999 and 2002, only 4% of the issues underwent some degree of re-framing [28, p. 176]. Baumgartner et al. argue that re-framing is difficult for a number of reasons, including:

- opponents will likely try to counter or prevent the re-framing;

- frames are often institutionally embedded and therefore difficult to dislodge; and

- advocates confront a skeptical media who try to resist "spin" by lobbying groups.

In the case of climate change, though, re-framing is still possible for a couple reasons. First, the climate change frame already exists in the public consciousness. So, re-framing this issue is more a matter of consistently using elements of the "climate change" frame and not falling into defensive postures by using the fossil fuel industry's "global warming" or consumerist frames. Second, climate scientists don't need to undermine or defeat the frames of the fossil fuel industry. In fact, directly engaging with these frames only puts environmental scientists on the defensive and ultimately reinforces the frames used by the fossil fuel industry and their surrogates.

Instead, environmental scientists should work from the climate change frame exclusively and actively avoid frames that are used by the fossil fuel industry and their surrogates. Here are some guidelines toward reframing this issue.

## Guideline 1: Use the "Progress" Frame, and Avoid the "Trade-Off" Frame

A common frame used by the fossil fuel industry is the "trade-off" frame. A trade-off frame implies that in order for gains to be made in one area, something needs to be sacrificed in another area [29]. Trade-off frames also imply a process of prioritization whereby decision makers (implicitly or explicitly) rank some values, outcomes, and goals as more important than others. In climate change arguments, public relations agents and lobbyists for the fossil fuel industry will argue that economic growth (especially jobs) must be sacrificed if the government takes action against the rise of industrial greenhouse gas emissions. Therefore, prioritizing climate change means ranking other issues, like the economy, lower as a priority.

To re-frame this aspect of the debate, climate change scientists and technical communicators should work from the "progress" frame, which implies that a growing and dynamic economy needs to grow and change to meet new demands. Instead of responding to the trade-off frame by agreeing that jobs in the coal mining or petroleum industries will be sacrificed, they should instead point out that many more jobs (and better jobs) will be created in the growing energy sector. The progress frame suggests that economies naturally evolve, generally for the better, which creates a win-win situation for everyone. Prioritizing climate change issues is co-existent with prioritizing the economy.

## Guideline 2: Use the "Scientific Debate" Frame, and Avoid the "Balancing Norm" Frame

A common frame in the media is the "balancing norm" frame. Essentially, this frame implies that journalistic objectivity and fairness requires telling "both sides of the story" [26, 30]. For years, lobbyists and so-called policy experts from think tanks have been used by the fossil fuel industry to provide a counterweight to environmental scientists. If an environmental scientist is invited on television to present the case for climate change or explain the results of a study, a lobbyist or someone from a conservative think tank is often asked to "balance" that coverage. Predictably, the lobbyist or think tank expert is skeptical of the findings, claiming that more research on climate change needs to be done before any action can be taken. Consequently, the story turns into a quarrel between a scientist, who has scientific evidence to share, and a non-scientist, who is essentially a hired-gun lobbyist with no evidence to back up his or her skepticism. To the public, though, the debate looks like a simple difference in opinion, not a discussion of factual scientific evidence.

Environmental scientists should insist that any "balancing" of the coverage be done by debating credentialed scientists, not lobbyists from the fossil fuel industry or think tank policy experts. If a journalist claims that a scientist cannot be found to provide an oppositional view, environmental scientists should steer clear of these appearances. After all, these debates only reinforce the public's skepticism about climate change, even if the scientist is presenting solid scientific evidence. Why? The balancing norm frame is designed to imply that there are two mostly equal opinions available on the issue being discussed. That is true on social issues such as abortion, gay rights, or gun rights because these debates *are* reliant on opinion, not scientific evidence. In contrast, discussions about climate science should be about the validity of scientific methods and findings, not about opposing opinions.

A scientist should welcome a debate on scientific grounds, but he or she should avoid debates that appear to be balanced but really just give the fossil fuel industry an opportunity to imply that climate change science boils down to a difference of opinion.

## Guideline 3: Use the "Land Ethic" Frame, and Avoid the "Dominion" Frame

In his book on framing, Lakoff suggests that when making a public argument "you need to speak from your moral perspective at all times" [16, p. 33]. What he means is that any frame is embedded with a specific set of values. How an issue is framed will determine the set of values that are activated in the minds of the audience.

For example, many debates about environmental policies default to the "dominion" frame. The dominion frame is firmly established in the Judeo-Christian cultures. The 2012 Republican presidential candidate Rick Santorum echoed this frame at a Colorado energy summit during a speech that emphasized the need to continue harvesting fossil fuels. Santorum said, "We were put on this Earth as creatures of God to have dominion over the Earth, to use it wisely and steward it wisely, but for our benefit not for the Earth's benefit." At its worst, the dominion frame implies that humans have the right to use any natural resources however they see fit ("If you can afford it, you can use it."). At its best, it suggests that humans are gardeners or caretakers who should practice good stewardship of those resources ("Use as much as you want, but just don't waste it"). The dominion frame, as used by people like Santorum, expresses a set of values in which humans are seen as the reason why the environment is here. The Earth was created for humans, and therefore humans have the right to use its resources as they see fit. When environmental scientists respond within this frame, they accept its embedded value set, which puts humans in the center of the ecosystem.

Instead, environmental scientists should speak from Aldo Leopold's "Land Ethic" frame, a perspective that does not presume human dominion. In *A Sand County Almanac*, Leopold argued that the treatment of animals, plants, and landforms is an ethical issue:

> All ethics so far evolved rest upon a single premise: that the individual is a member of a community of interdependent parts. . . . The land ethic simply enlarges the boundaries of the community to include soils, waters, plants, and animals, or collectively: the land [31, p. 239].

When environmental scientists are communicating their findings with the public, they need to frame the debate in ethical terms. One of the most effective arguments through the land ethic frame has been preservation of the polar bear. The polar bear has stood, and stands still, as the symbol of the effects of climate change [32]. In this case, the argument isn't about whether preserving the habitat of polar bears is important to serve humans. The debate is whether polar bears have an ethical right to exist. Almost anyone would agree that they do. Therefore, when arguing climate change issues, environmental scientists should practice framing issues in terms of a greater land ethic. By using the land ethic frame, the environmental scientist will activate the set of values embedded in it, and compel critics to respond from within the land ethic frame.

## Guideline 4: Use the "Truth" Frame, and Avoid the "Theory" Frame

The word "theory" has a different meaning in general public than it does in the scientific community, and fossil fuel industry has exploited that ambiguity. To a scientist, the word theory means something very close to the truth. A theory, as the National Academy of Sciences defines the term, "a well-substantiated explanation of some aspect of the natural world, based on a body of facts that have been repeatedly confirmed through observation and experiment" [33, p. 2]. The only hesitation to call a theory "the truth" is due to the fundamental belief that even the strongest theories should be open to challenge and revision, but for all intents and purposes, a theory is held to be true. In the public, quite differently, the word "theory" means a guess or a speculation. So, many members of the public assume that even well-substantiated theories, such as evolution, relativity, or genetics, are still being actively challenged in the scientific community.

The problem with the theory frame is most evident when a weather-related catastrophe happens, such as a Category 5 hurricane, severe drought, massive forest fire, historic flood, or a series of tornadoes. A journalist will often ask an environmental scientist, "Do you think this catastrophe is due to climate change?" Environmental scientists have been conditioned to answer, "No, any single event cannot be proven to be caused climate change." This response, though technically correct, inevitably leads to questioning the larger theory of climate change itself. After all, in the minds of the public, if an extreme weather event cannot be linked to climate change, perhaps nothing can prove this theory. Interestingly, as deBoer concluded, people often only have the "vaguest ideas" about issues like energy [34]. However, they are very responsive to weather-related anomalies like flooding and persistent rainfall. In other words, facts and reasoning rarely invite people to question their existing frames. A severe weather event or weather-related tragedy, however, does offer an opening for inviting them to examine their existing frames.

When speaking with the public, environmental scientists should feel comfortable explaining theory as "the truth" without the usual qualifications and equivocations. A catastrophic event can urge members of the public to doubt their pre-existing frames. At that point, when people are willing to challenge their frames in a personal way, scientists have an opportunity to break through the usual frames that keep people from accepting climate change evidence. So, they should tell the "truth," which is that the severities of weather events are almost surely attributable to climate change and that the Earth will be experiencing more of these severe weather events in the future. When speaking with the public, environmental scientists can adopt a truth frame instead of qualifying all factual statements. Talking about the truth and what is really happening counters the ambiguity in the word "theory." If a journalist or a fossil fuel industry surrogate says something like, "But that's just a theory, and we don't have enough proof," then the scientist can respond with "it's the truth, and it's time we started doing something about it."

## Guideline 5: Use the "Problem-Solving" Frame, and Avoid the "Catastrophe" Frame

When scientists argue that climate change is a critical problem that must be dealt with, they tend to discuss the issue in catastrophic and even apocalyptic terms. For example, Al Gore and David Guggenheim's famous documentary *An Inconvenient Truth* [35] brings climate change science to the public by interweaving climate scientists' graphs and statistics with catastrophic depictions of global sea-level rises and rampant natural disasters.

Certainly, catastrophism is not exclusive to environmentalists or even left-wing activists. Right-wing politicians and their advocates regularly engage in catastrophism about economic, terrorism, and religious issues. However, the catastrophic frames that are embedded in these issues activate frames that actually lead to more conservative reactions. For example, let's say the New York Stock Exchange experiences a drop of 10% in one month. Even people who do not have money invested in the stock market will become more conservative with their finances. The vast majority of people still have money to spend, but they become more worried about what might happen than what was actually happening. So, they began to save more and borrow less, which causes the economy to further decline [36]. The same is true of crime. If the media suddenly plays up recent crime in an area, people will become more conservative about crime-related issues. They restrict their movements. They believe in harsher punishments. They will tend to vote for politicians who promise them security, even at the price of their own liberty [37].

Our point is that catastrophism is a metaphor that immediately plays into the hands of conservatives by activating one of their most common frames. Even if the arguments for the existence of climate change find their mark and succeed in scaring people, the tendency of most people is to become more conservative and withdraw—to ignore the argument or hide from it. That's exactly the opposite of what environmental scientists want people to do about climate change. To minimize the affects of climate change, scientists need to talk about solving the climate change problem in a positive way that leads to progress, even when the media wants to focus on its catastrophic consequences.

## Guideline 6: Use the "Adaptation" Frame, and Avoid the "Costs vs. Benefits" Frame

As Howarth and Monahan point out, people generally frame issues through a "criterion of economic efficiency," using a rudimentary cost-benefit analysis to help them make decisions about what to believe and how to behave [38]. Because climate change is such a complex problem in which the costs and benefits seem impossible to assess, especially on a personal level, people tend not to base decisions about their actions on climate change. The authors argue the following:

> (1) cost-benefit techniques are difficult to operationalize given the gross uncertainties surrounding climate change and its potential effects on future society; (2) the approach is insensitive to the distribution of impacts between present and future generations, yet climate change may have pronounced implications for future economic conditions and environmental quality [38, p. 188].

Even arguments that climate change will eventually cost billions and trillions of dollars make almost no impact on the public because these kinds of figures go far beyond an individual's ability to measure the costs and benefits to them personally.

For this reason, the best approach is to re-frame climate change in terms of "adaptation." This is adaptation in a totalizing sense: one that includes personal, governmental, militaristic, and corporate actions of adaptation to a changing climate. The adaptation frame may be most successful approach to communicating climate change because it provides the most relief from the failures of the previously discussed frames.

To start, a frame of adaptation pushes the discussion of climate change beyond frames that question its prevalence. The adaptation frame is enthymemic in its undisputed assumption that climate change exists. Frames that aim to prove climate change's prevalence through graphs and charts begin with the premise that climate change is under dispute. An adaptation frame, instead, starts with the premise that the prevalence of climate change is not under scrutiny.

Additionally, the adaptation frame looks beyond questions about the anthropogenic origins of climate change. Adaptation is more interested in solutions than causes. An adaptation frame is less interested in what's causing an unprecedented release of green-house gases and more interested in how humans can reduce those gases. An adaptation frame, for example, might encourage improved emissions policies regardless of climate change's natural or anthropogenic origins.

The adaptation frame invites citizens to negotiate personal, social, and ecological hierarchies in order to adapt. While governments and militaries begin making adaptations to a changing climate, individual citizens are likely to follow suit. When governmental entities take the lead in frames of adaptation, individuals are more likely to incorporate those frames into their personal, social, and ecological hierarchies as well. The result of framing climate change through adaptation is that climate change becomes the concern of everyone, not just environmentalists and environmental scientists.

# Conclusion:
# Moving Toward Broader Social Frames

Climate change researchers and communicators often seem perplexed by the public's resistance to understanding and acting upon the threat of climate change. Indeed, environmental scientists should be frustrated and outraged by the unethical manipulation and undermining of legitimate scientific research by think tanks, pundits, and public relations firms that are funded by the fossil fuel industry. However, climate change scientists and communicators also need to be mindful that they themselves don't unwittingly fall into the fossil fuel industry's negative framing of this issue.

In this article, our overall argument is that climate change scientists and communicators need to move away from traditional environmentalist frames that often put them at odds with broader social frames that the public finds more familiar. They should speak positively within social frames of progress, science, ethics, truth, problem-solving, and adaptation. Meanwhile, they should avoid frames that stress trade-offs, dominion, theory, catastrophe, and costs vs. benefits. Keep in mind that the "hired guns" of the fossil fuel industry are very savvy at boxing climate scientists in with environmental activists, which allows the public to ignore climate science as a "special interest" that is alarmist, extremist, and ultimately a matter of opinion.

We believe environmental scientists and science communicators have the power to re-frame these debates in terms that the broader public will find persuasive and appealing. In an age of rapid information exchange, the language in which scientific findings are framed may be equally as important as the findings themselves. Going forward, researchers and science communicators must actively and consciously work to frame how their research findings are communicated in the public sphere.

## References

1. ExxonMobil, *ExxonMobil's Response to Union of Concerned Scientists Report,* 2007. Available at http://abcnews.go.com/Technology/story?id=2768373andpage= 1andsinglePage=true

2. J. B. Fourier, Les Temperatures du Globe Terrestre et des Espaces Planetaires, *Mémoires de l'Académie des Sciences de l'Institut de France, 7,* pp. 569–604, 1827.

3. J. Tyndall, On the Absorption and Radiation of Heat by Gases and Vapours, and on the Physical Connexion of Radiation, Absorption, Conduction—The Bakerian Lecture, *The London, Edinburgh, and Dublin Philosophical Magazine and Journal of Science, 4*:22, pp. 169–194, 1861.

4. S. Arrhenius, On the Influence of Carbonic Acid in the Air upon the Temperature of the Ground, *Philosophical Magazine and Journal of Science, 5*:41, pp. 237–276, 1896.

5. D. Demeritt, The Construction of Global Warming and the Politics of Science, *Annals of the Association of American Geographers, 91*:2, pp. 307–337, 2001.

6. C. D. Keeling, The Concentration and Isotopic Abundances of Carbon Dioxide in the Atmosphere, *Tellus, 12*, pp. 200–203, 1960.

7. C. D. Keeling, The Influence of Mauna Loa Observatory on the Development of Atmospheric CO2 Research, in *Mauna Loa Observatory, A 20th Anniversary Report, National Oceanic and Atmospheric Administration Special Report, September 1978*, J. Miller (ed.), NOAA Environmental Research Laboratories, Boulder, Colorado, pp. 36–54, 1978.

8. Climate Change Foreseen, *The Science News-Letter, 62*:7, p. 103, August 16, 1952.

9. Warm Earth Man's Doing, November 18, *The Science News-Letter, 80*:21, p. 335, 1961.

10. W. A. Gamson and A. Modigliani, The Changing Culture of Affirmative Action, R. D. Braungart (ed.), *Research in Political Sociology, 3*, pp. 137–177, 1987.

11. J. B. Corbett and J. L. Durfee, Testing Public Uncertainty of Science, *Science Communication, 26*:2, pp. 129–151, 2004.

12. R. M. Entman, Framing: Toward Clarification of a Fractured Paradigm, *Journal of Communication, 43*:4, pp. 51–58, 1993.

13. K. Carragee and W. Roefs, The Neglect of Power in Recent Framing Research, *Journal of Communication, 54*:2: pp. 214–233, 2004.

14. T. C. Chamberlin, A Group of Hypotheses Bearing on Climatic Changes, *The Journal of Geology, 5*:7, pp. 653–683, 1897.

15. D. R. Kinder and T. E. Nelson, Democratic Debate and Real Opinions, in *Framing American Politics*, K. Callaghan and F. Schell (eds.), University of Pittsburgh Press, Pittsburgh, Pennsylvania, pp. 103–122, 2005.

16. G. Lakoff, *Don't Think of an Elephant: Know Your Values and Frame the Debate*, Chelsea Green Publishing, Vermont, 2004.

17. J. Davies and V. J. Mabin, Knowledge Management and the Framing of Information: A Contribution to OR/MS Practice and Pedagogy, *Journal of the Operational Research Society, 52*, pp. 856–872, 2001.

18. K. Burke, *A Grammar of Motives*, University of California Press, Los Angeles, California, 1969.

19. G. Morgan, *Images of Organisation*, Sage, Thousand Oaks, California, 1986.

20. United Press International, Scientists Caution on Changes in Climate as a Result of Pollution, *New York Times*, December 20, 1969.

21. Grim Effects Seen if Earth Warms Up, *The Milwaukee Sentinel*, p. 2, January 8, 1979.

22. L. Whitmarsh, What's in a Name? Commonalities and Differences in Public Understanding of "Climate Change" and "Global Warming," *Public Understanding of Science, 18*:401, pp. 401–420, 2009.

23. J. P. Schuldt, S. H. Konrath, and N. Schwarz, "Global Warming" Or "Climate Change"? Whether the Planet is Warming Depends on Question Wording, *Public Opinion Quarterly, 75*:1, pp. 115–124, 2011.

24. M. Nisbet, Communicating Climate Change: Why Frames Matter for Public Engagement, *Environment: Science and Policy for Sustainable Development, 51*:2, pp. 12–23, 2010.

25. A. McCright and R. Dunlap, Challenging Global Warming as a Social Problem: An Analysis of the Conservative Movement's Counter-Claims, *Social Problems, 47*:4, pp. 488–522, 2000.

26. A. McCright and R. Dunlap, Defeating Kyoto: The Conservative Movement's Impact on U.S. Climate Change Policy, *Social Problems, 50*:3, pp. 348–373, 2003.

27. A. McCright and R. Dunlap, The Politicization of Climate Change and Polarization in the American Public's Views of Global Warming, 2001–2010, *The Sociological Quarterly, 52*, pp. 155–194, 2011.

28. F. Baumgartner, J. Berry, M. Hojnacki, D. Kimball, and B. Leech, *Lobbying and Policy Change: Who Wins, Who Loses, and Why*, University of Chicago Press, Chicago, Illinois, 2009.

29. S. Pralle and J. Boscarino, Framing Trade-Offs: The Politics of Nuclear Power and Wind Energy in the Age of Global Climate Change, *Review of Policy Research, 28*:4, pp. 323-346, 2011.

30. M. T. Boykoff and J. M. Boykoff, Balance as Bias: Global Warming and the U.S. Prestige Press, *Global Environmental Change, 14*, pp. 125–136, 2004.

31. A. Leopold, *The Sand County Almanac,* University Press, Oxford, 1949.

32. T. Dillahunt, G. Becker, J. Mankoff, and R. Kraut, Motivating Environmentally Sustainable Behavior Changes With a Virtual Polar Bear, *Pervasive Computing Conference*, pp. 19–22, May 5, 2008.

33. National Academy of Sciences, *Science and Creationism: A View from the National Academy of Sciences* (2nd ed.), 1999.

34. J. deBoer, Framing Climate Change and Spatial Planning: How Risk Communication Can be Improved, *Water Science and Technology, 56*:4, pp. 71–78, 2007.

35. A. Gore and D. Guggenheim, *An Inconvenient Truth*, Paramount Home Entertainment, Los Angeles, California, 2006.

36. J. Nofsinger, Household Behavior and Boom/Bust Cycles, *Journal of Financial Stability, 8,* pp. 161–173, 2012.

37. R. Surette, *Media, Crime, and Criminal Justice* (4th ed.), Wadsworth, Belmont, California, 2011.

38. R. B. Howarth and A. Monahan, Economics, Ethics, and Climate Policy: Framing the Debate, *Global and Planetary Change, 11*, pp. 187–199, 1996.

# Chapter 2 ■ Framing and Re-Framing in Environmental Science

## Questions for Discussion

1. What is the difference between a *metaphoric frame* and a *paradigm*? Is there any overlap between these concepts? Discuss with a partner. Come up with your own definition for each, as well as an example that you will share with the class.

2. How could redirecting and reframing the problem help you better reach your patron and population? In what ways should your terminology be different while speaking to your patron, as opposed to speaking to your population? If your proposal uses a great deal of technical vocabulary, how do you plan on making your writing clear enough so that anyone can understand it, even if they do not have sufficient background knowledge?

3. Paraphrasing linguist George Lakoff, the authors explain how "For the most part people don't even notice their own frames . . . because their own frames express their cultural values. As a result, people accept their frame as true or common sense, while rejecting new frames or the frames of others as false." Do you anticipate any strong opposition from other cultures or disciplines in terms of how you plan to present your framework? List possible arguments of your opposition.

4. As a follow-up to question 3, list three counterarguments to the arguments you anticipate your opposition will assert. Make sure you are thinking about metaphoric framing as you do so. List these counterarguments below. Be sure to back your statements with viable evidence.

5. Do you think that reframing climate change will be beneficial in getting more individuals to acknowledge its existence and significance? Why or why not? Discuss the faults in how climate change is presented to the public now. List suggestions for how this information could be better presented.

6. In a small group, discuss which of the six guidelines you think will be most effective when it comes to reframing climate change. Once you choose one, write down ways in which you think it will be successful by giving concrete examples. Be prepared to share with the class in a discussion.

7. This article was chosen in part because it offers a good model of the type of reading you might find valuable as you write your own proposals. How is this piece different from more popular sources, such as newspaper and magazine articles? Do you think the article is persuasive? What factors contribute to its credibility? How might you use a source like this to develop your paradigm in your proposal?

# The 5 R's: An Emerging Bold Standard for Conducting Relevant Research in a Changing World

C. J. Peek, PhD[1], Russell E. Glasgow, PhD[2], Kurt C. Stange, MD, PhD[3],
Lisa M. Klesges, PhD[4], E. Peyton Purcell, MPH[5], and Rodger S. Kessler, PhD, ABPP[6]

■ ■ ■

## Abstract

Research often fails to find its way into practice or policy in a timely way, if at all. Given the current pressure and pace of health care change, many authors have recommended different approaches to make health care research more relevant and rapid. An emerging standard for research, the "5 R's" is a synthesis of recommendations for care delivery research that (1) is relevant to stakeholders; (2) is rapid and recursive in application; (3) redefines rigor; (4) reports on resources required; and (5) is replicable. *Relevance* flows from substantive ongoing participation by stakeholders. *Rapidity and recursiveness* occur through accelerated design and peer reviews followed by short learning/implementation cycles through which questions and answers evolve over time. Rigor is the disciplined conduct of shared learning within the specific changing situations in diverse settings. *Resource reporting* includes costs of interventions. *Replicability* involves designing for the factors that may affect subsequent implementation of an intervention or program in different contexts. These R's of the research process are mutually reinforcing and can be supported by training that fosters collaborative and reciprocal relationships among researchers, implementers, and other stakeholders. In sum, a standard is emerging for research that is both rigorous and relevant. Consistent and bold application will increase the value, timeliness, and applicability of the research enterprise.

Ann Fam Med 2014;12:447-455. doi:10.1370/afm.1688.

## The Need for Relevant Research in a Rapidly Changing Health Care World

Accelerated pressure for change in health care creates an exploding need for relevant and rapidly generated new information. A growing volume of care delivery experiments around the country pose questions that research can help answer: Which interventions or system changes improve care, access, safety, or quality—and for which populations, under what conditions? Which system changes reduce underuse, overuse, or misuse? Which approaches are implementable and engaging to clinicians and patients—and can be done at reasonable cost?[1,2]

From *Annals of Family Medicine*, September/October, 2014, Volume 12, No. 5 by C.J. Peek. Copyright © 2014 by American Academy of Family Physicians. Reprinted by permission.

[1] Department of Family Medicine and Community Health, University of Minnesota Medical School, Minneapolis, Minnesota

[2] Department of Family Medicine and Colorado Health Outcomes Program, University of Colorado, Denver, Colorado

[3] Department of Family Medicine & Community Health, Department of Epidemiology & Biostatistics, and Department of Sociology, Case Comprehensive Cancer Center, Cleveland Clinical & Translational Science Collaborative, Case Western Reserve University, Cleveland, Ohio

[4] School of Public Health, University of Memphis, Memphis, Tennessee

[5] Clinical Research Directorate/CMRP, SAIC-Frederick, Inc, Frederick National Laboratory for Cancer Research, Frederick, Maryland

[6] Department of Family Medicine and the Center for Clinical and Translational Science, University of Vermont College of Medicine, Burlington, Vermont

Evolving clinical, organizational, and business models for health care, such as patient-centered medical homes[3] and accountable care organizations[4] need rapidly generated research evidence in real-world experiments for multiple stakeholders: implementers who want to improve their practices; purchasers who want to pay for value; health plans that administer benefits and take risks for care provided; policy makers who are being asked to change "the rules of the game" to support new approaches; patients who wish to know their care is effective, safe, and worth their effort and money; and public health, community groups, and agencies who wish to see improved health at a societal level.[5,6]

The current research approach is not up to this challenge. Most recent research is slow to influence practice, does so only in pockets, or does not address practical needs for decision making.[7-9] Innovative ideas to remedy this situation have been proposed and some implemented. Yet the overall problem remains. It is time to pull together and implement changes in research paradigms and habits to better meet the research needs of changing health care delivery.[10-14]

The threads of a fresh research paradigm are already apparent, having been suggested separately in many publications,[15-17] but need to be woven together to form a picture—the whole cloth with which to tailor research to answer the important stakeholder questions. This article weaves those threads together in the form of an integrated set of "5 R's" to guide research.

# The 5 R's of Health Care Delivery Research

Below we articulate the issues and how they can be addressed through the 5 R's to generate health care research that (1) is relevant to stakeholders; (2) is rapid and recursive in application; (3) redefines rigor; (4) reports on resources required; and (5) is replicable. *Relevance* flows from substantive ongoing participation by stakeholders. *Rapidity and recursiveness* occur through accelerated design and grant reviews followed by short learning/implementation cycles through which questions and answers evolve over time. *Rigor* is the disciplined conduct of shared learning within the specific changing situations in diverse settings. *Resource reporting* includes costs of interventions and likely cost of replication in other settings. *Replicability* involves designing for the factors that may affect subsequent implementation of an intervention or program in different contexts.

# Relevant to Stakeholders

## *What Is the Issue?*

Perceived lack of relevance is cited as the primary reason practitioners do not use research.[18-21] Research must generate setting-based evidence designed to flow into practice realities and meet stakeholder needs; as has been stated, "If we want more evidence-based practice, we need more practice-based evidence."[22]

## *How Can It Be Addressed?*

*Involve end users meaningfully and continuously from the outset in forming research questions and selecting outcomes.*[2,5,15,16,18,21-24] Research agendas should have origins in need on the ground[16]—with stakeholders being not only customers for research, but also producers of meaningful questions. Questions come from implementers, policy makers, health plans, purchasers, and patients—with researchers who listen and translate different user concerns into researchable questions.[5,24] Such participatory, practice- or community-based "partnership research"[15] extends to all phases of research: question generation, designs and measures, implementation, interpretation, presentation, and application of results.

*Build an ultimate use perspective into all stages of the research process.* If research waits too long before considering sustainable real-world implementation, investment in the preceding research may prematurely "freeze" the intervention in ways not compatible with later use. Engaging stakeholders in how to implement at earlier phases may help avoid retooling and reduce the time to real-world application.

*Seek continuation, not only translation.* Health care practitioners are arguably more likely to apply and sustain what is learned from research in their own practices.[25] The question becomes not, "how do we translate this to our practice?" but, "how do we continue, adapt, and spread what we just learned in our practice?" If done widely, this continuation could make research relevant and make knowledge generation part of the fabric of practice.

# Rapid and Recursive in Application

## What Is the Issue?

It is not acceptable that it takes 17 years on average for a 14% uptake of funded research into practice.[7] In a rapidly changing environment, we need to find ways to accelerate the research enterprise.

## How Can It Be Addressed?

*Engage stakeholders in rapid-learning research systems.* In "rapid-learning health care," "routinely collected real-time clinical data drive the process of scientific discovery, which becomes a natural outgrowth of patient care."[26] Components may include databases or registries organized by populations, electronic health records, guidelines and clinical decision support, patient engagement, and multiple sponsors or research networks.[26,27] In "rapid-learning research systems"[21] researchers, funders, implementers, health systems, and community partners are brought together to develop questions, answer them, and then ask new questions of practical importance.

*Streamline review processes.* The health care delivery world moves on with new partners, questions, and technology, whereas traditional grant application and review often takes a long time.[21] Rapid review processes[26] that shorten the time from conception of a study to its approval, funding, and start can help keep studies timely and relevant.

*Pose research questions to multiple networked practices.* Practice-based research networks (PBRNs) are practices that work together to answer health care questions and translate findings into practice. PBRNs can generate relevant questions from stakeholders, design research, and collect data that result in rapid answers from large data sets, including deidentified data from clinical and financial records stored in electronic health records from natural experiments happening in real time, such as data for complex patients treated under real-world conditions by real-world clinicians. Some of these practice settings, as well as public health system research networks,[28] are becoming true "learning organizations"[27] where quality improvement research is included with, not separated from, more experimental findings.

*Allow discoveries within a study to influence the study.* Discoveries, sometimes unexpected, can modify subsequent data collection and measurement. Data collection is no longer only at fixed points, using static measures. Implementation or study processes are continuously improved along the way. This is a recursive and rapid learning situation.[27] When discoveries in a study begin to appear, they may reshape stakeholder questions or begin to answer others. The next set of questions may begin to emerge, along with energy for answering those reshaped or more insightful questions. As discoveries roll in, stakeholders, in partnership with researchers, guide these iterations.

# Redefines Rigor

## *What Is the Issue?*

Scientific rigor is essential, but common conceptions of rigor may limit the range of real-world situations that can be studied—and methods, settings, and populations with which to do so. The hallmark of rigor has been the "gold standard" efficacy randomized controlled trial (RCT) emphasizing internal validity.

## *How Can It Be Addressed?*

We suggest a modified version of rigor suited to broader questions meaningful to multiple stakeholders and answered in heterogeneous populations and settings with attention to transportability and sustainable implementation.

*Regard rigor as a property of a series of decisions, observations, and relationships rather than of techniques.*[29] Rigorous research (1) is systematic and organized about concepts, tools, data collection, measures, procedures, and analyses; (2) checks for superfluous connections and confounding variables; (3) has controls and conclusions justified by standards of evidence; and (4) uses transparent descriptions of what was done. Rigor is not defined as a list of certain techniques and exclusion of others. Particular experimental designs, data collection, or analysis techniques are not always considered more rigorous than others or that any one is the optimal design for all questions and all situations. Others have commented, "If techniques are tools in a researcher's toolbox, then this is like saying that 'A saw is better than a hammer because it is sharper.'"[29] Stated as a principle, "Research agenda determines the research methods rather than methods determine the research agenda."[16]

*Give attention to both external and internal validity.* Most methods developed to assess research quality focus predominantly or exclusively on internal validity. Rigor also implies attention to transparent reporting on issues related to generalizability.[16,30]

# Reporting on Resources

## *What Is the Issue?*

Use of health care resources is a major concern when a priority is to bend the cost curve. Stakeholders are making decisions among alternative care approaches based on the cost of interventions as well as on clinical effectiveness. Information on resources used to conduct or replicate interventions can be helpful in larger economic analysis, but is seldom well reported.[31]

## *How Can It Be Addressed?*

*Use a consistent vocabulary for reporting.* For example, measuring cost includes money, but also clinician and staff time and energy, plus intervention systems, infrastructure, or training costs. There are start-up costs, ongoing costs, and opportunity costs. There are costs of doing a study intervention, and likely costs of recreating it in another setting. Costs incurred in one place or to one stakeholder may save costs in some other place or for another stakeholder.

*Report on as many of the relevant costs of different interventions as possible and do so in a standard manner.*[14,32,33] For example, what did the program in question cost to promote and implement, and what are estimates of what it would cost to replicate a similar program under different conditions or settings? Such estimates do not require researchers to do complex economic or cost-benefit analyses, but reporting on resources is important to those who pay attention to *value* in health care. Although value may mean many things to many people, it is being defined and becoming part of efforts to be rigorous, transparent, and relevant to stakeholders,[34] including patients who have their own perspective on value.[35]

# Replicability

## *What Is the Issue?*

Research design can help address questions regarding how an innovation will perform in a new system with different contextual influences.[36] Replication of findings is increasingly recognized[37] as a major challenge across the translation spectrum from basic discovery (eg, genomewide association studies) to community interventions. The conditions under which a finding can be replicated are central to understanding robust effects that can be reasonably expected under various conditions. Hence, researchers must design for replicability and report results needed for reproducibility—either under the same or different conditions in which the findings are likely to be applied.

## *How Can It Be Addressed?*

*Design for sustainable implementation from the start.* This approach is arguably more efficient and effective if it saves rework for real-world application. We recommend asking 3 questions: (1) is the study designed to inform implementation—and re-invention in different settings? (2) is the "how" reported as well as the "what" of interventions, and to what extent are procedures replicable in similar or diverse settings? and (3) are contextual factors reported that are important to understanding what happened and why—for example, relevant policies, and inclusion and exclusion criteria for settings and staff as well as patients?

These strategies can go a long way toward making findings replicable, realizing that not every study can be transported to other settings. But such data will allow others to make reasonable judgments about what aspects to retain and what to change for replication or reinvention in a different time and place, using relevant domains for contextual factors.[38]

# Examples

Some of the 5 R's have found their way into research studies, networks, and tools. Table 1 describes a few examples. Readers can likely cite other examples or see other R's in these. The 5 R's are emerging not as a response to a *completed* record of implementation in full scope, but as a logical (and promising) *challenge* to package in application the separate elements already abundantly demonstrated in the literature, but not yet combined to full effect in more than a few examples. What is "bold" is the proposal to routinely apply the 5 R's as a package and to take on the substantial challenges of practical implementation and evolution. For inspiration, consider McDonnell Douglas' bold integration of 5 existing technologies for the first time in 1 airplane (the 1935 DC-3), the innovation that swept away the competition and opened the era of commercial air travel, when a plane with 4 of those technologies failed commercially the previous year.[51]

# Conclusions

Health care transformation needs the full benefit of research to inform decision making and discover new options. The research community owes it to its "customers" and the public to evolve its standards and methods for health care research. The 5 R's are offered as a next step in the developmental trajectory of an evolving field—a framework for a much needed discussion and adjustment of criteria for what is considered high-quality research.

| Example: Study/Project/Resource Title and Relevant R's | Study/Project/Resource Details |
|---|---|
| **Particular studies and programs**<br>DIAMOND (Depression Improvement Across Minnesota–Offering a New Direction)<br>1. Relevant to stakeholders<br>2. Redefines rigor<br>3. Replicability | The DIAMOND initiative for depression in primary care was a statewide collaborative of practices and health plans accompanied by a separately funded NIMH research study using a stepped wedge/phased intervention design.[15,25,39,40] Practices launched the DIAMOND care process in cohorts, 6 months apart, with baseline data collected for all. Outcomes that mattered to different stakeholders were compared before and after launch across the many practices launching at different times. Outcomes were tracked using both quantitative and qualitative measures, including clinical outcomes, health plan claims data, patient surveys, and practice leader surveys regarding implementation.<br><br>An explicit balance of fidelity and adaptation to local situations—specifics that practices had to tailor for themselves (eg, choice of discipline for care managers, specific workflow for PHQ-9, type of data tracking system)—helped practices implement the DIAMOND intervention.[41,42] |
| P4H (Prescription for Health)<br>1. Relevant to stakeholders<br>2. Recursive<br>3. Redefines rigor<br>4. Reports on resources | P4H was an initiative of The Robert Wood Johnson Foundation (RWJF) with the Agency for Healthcare Research and Quality (AHRQ) to fund a collaboration of 17 PBRNs that developed and evaluated strategies to improve health behavior changes for multiple behaviors through linkage to community resources.[43] Practices worked with researchers, and teams of researchers, and PBRN leaders worked with each other and with a cross-cutting research group to share evolving learning, and develop common measures and an evolving research agenda.[44]<br><br>Using mixed quantitative and qualitative methods (including researcher diary data and interviews)[45] and cost analyses, P4H showed that primary care practices have the ability to develop their linkages to connect patients with community resources[46] to improve practice processes,[47] health behavior counseling, and patient behavior change.[48] |
| ¡Viva Bien!<br>1. Relevant to stakeholders<br>2. Reports on resources<br>3. Replicability | ¡Viva Bien![32,33] was a randomized trial that provided a clear description of methods, implementation costs for a diabetes self-management program, and estimates of costs to replicate the program under different conditions, calculating incremental costs per behavioral, biologic, and quality-of-life change. It discussed how to separate the costs of development and research from implementation, and how to conduct relatively straight-forward sensitivity analyses to estimate costs of replicating a program or policy under different conditions. |
| MOHR (My Own Health Report)<br>1. Relevant to stakeholders<br>2. Rapid and recursive<br>3. Redefines rigor<br>4. Reports on resources<br>5. Replicability | MOHR[23,49] is a pragmatic participatory trial in which diverse primary care practices implement the collection of patient-reported information and provide patients advice, goal setting, and counseling in response—with deliberate diversity of settings and populations to ensure greater generalizability of results. Practices, patients, funding agencies, and content experts were engaged throughout the study to take into account local resources and characteristics in design, implementation, evaluation, and dissemination.<br><br>Core elements of the study protocol were identified, with local tailoring to ensure implementation was relevant to local culture and practice on issues such as workflows, eligible patients, when and where assessment would be completed, whether electronic or paper, and how clinicians would receive the feedback. The trial used mixed methods, including cost analyses. |
| **Research networks across studies**<br>PRC (Prevention Research Centers) of the Centers for Disease Control and Prevention<br>1. Relevant to stakeholders<br>2. Recursive<br>3. Replicability | PRC directs a national network of 37 academic research centers at public health or medical schools with a preventive medicine residency program, translating research results into policy and public health practice. Centers have capacity for community-based, participatory prevention research needed to drive community changes to prevent and control chronic disease.<br><br>Research involves collaboration among partners bringing different expertise to the table, identifies research needs of partners, conducts research that builds on previous evidence for promising interventions, and recommends how interventions can be packaged for replication and adoption (http://www.cdc.gov/prc/index.htm). |
| QUERI (Quality Enhancement Research Initiative)<br>1. Relevant to stakeholders<br>2. Rapid and recursive<br>3. Redefines rigor<br>4. Replicability | QUERI is a Veterans Affairs initiative that brings together operations with research staff to address key gaps in quality and outcomes. It has contributed to remarkable and rapid improvements in the quality of care received by veterans across 10 conditions deemed high-risk or highly prevalent.<br><br>This initiative uses a 6-step process to spot gaps in performance and to identify and implement interventions. QUERI studies and facilitates adoption of new treatments, tests, and models of care into routine clinical practice—feasibility, implementation, adoption, and impact (http://www.queri.research.va.gov/default.cfm). |
| **Research application tools and resources**<br>RTIPs (Research Tested Intervention Programs)<br>1. Relevant to stakeholders<br>2. Reports on resources<br>3. Replicability | RTIPs is a resource of the National Cancer Institute that provides information on the specific conditions under which each of their tested interventions has been evaluated and tools for addressing issues about applicability (http://rtips.cancer.gov/rtips).<br><br>New features related to external validity using the RE-AIM framework are included to help users better determine the likely public health impact of a given program if replicated in their setting. RTIPs also reports on the resources required to implement these programs. |
| PRECIS (Pragmatic Explanatory Continuum Indicator Summary)<br>1. Relevant to stakeholders<br>2. Redefines rigor<br>3. Replicability | PRECIS[50] is a graphic representation of the extent to which a study is pragmatic (testing effect in usual conditions) vs explanatory (testing effect in ideal conditions) on 10 key dimensions.<br><br>If used consistently, this tool could greatly help practitioners decide whether a study is likely to be reproducible in their setting and researchers to investigate the dimensions along which similarity is more vs less critical for replication. |

**Table 1** Examples of Projects Illustrating the R's

NIMH = National Institute of Mental Health; PBRN = practice-based research network; PHQ-9 = 9-item Patient Health Questionnaire; RE-AIM = Reach Effectiveness–Adoption Implementation Maintenance.

# Routinely Apply the Complete Package of 5 R's

As is the case for other models—for example, the Reach Effectiveness–Adoption Implementation Maintenance (RE-AIM) evaluation model,[52,53] the Chronic Care Model,[54] and the Institute of Medicine 6 quality aims[55]—the effect of the 5 R's model comes not from doing separate R's or even 2 or 3 of them, but from doing them all in an integrated fashion whereby each reinforces the others. The 5 R's are proposed to work together across stages of the research and dissemination process. Table 2 shows a research "preflight" checklist.

**Bold Standard 5 R's**

| Stage of Research | Relevant to Stakeholders | Rapid and Recursive | Refines Rigor | Report on Resources | Replicability |
|---|---|---|---|---|---|
| **Design** | End users of this research identified? Stakeholders who need to be involved identified? Plan in place to engage their perspectives? Plan in place to gather stakeholder questions and what is important to them? | Rapid cycle measurement and assessment built into the design? How? Approach in place to allow early discoveries to shape the study? | How is study systematic and pragmatic about concepts, measures, data collection procedures, and analysis plan? Multiple methods used? How? Internal and external validity balanced? How? | Intervention costs (monetary and other) measured? How? A standard vocabulary for reporting on resources in place? What? | Study designed to inform implementation and reinvention in different settings? How? Likely relevant settings for this research identified? |
| **Implementation** | Stakeholders involved in ongoing refinement? How? Changes they suggested along the way recorded? Changes suggested implemented? Which ones? | Short cycle learning taking place to refine design and measurement? Is learning influencing the study? How? | Systematic approach being followed to concepts, tools, data collection, measures, procedures, analyses? Checks for bias and superfluous connections in place? Clear description of what is being done recorded? | Cost data gathered on an ongoing basis? Using a consistent vocabulary for different kinds of costs? | Contextual factors documented that are important to understanding what happened (and why) in the study setting? |
| **Reporting** | Diverse stakeholders involved in interpreting and reporting findings? Their different interpretations reported? | Emergent findings shared on an ongoing basis throughout the study? Have adaptations made been reported? | Study methods reported transparently and thoroughly? Reported how study checked for potential biases and superfluous connections? Reported how conclusions are justified by standards of evidence? | Study reports useful cost data using a defined vocabulary for different kinds of costs? Estimates made for costs under different conditions? | Contextual factors relevant to reinvention in new settings reported, including variation across settings or within settings? |
| **Dissemination** | Target audiences, stakeholders, or likely users involved in next steps? Findings expressed in language and context that mean something to different stakeholders? | Guidelines provided for adaption and customization/tailoring for future use? | Description included for how internal and external validity findings support wider use? | Intervention cost data discussed as a factor in dissemination? | Data-supported suggestions included about the contexts for which program or intervention is relevant or reproducible? |

**Table 2**   Questions to Apply the 5 R's at Each Stage of the Research and Dissemination Process

## Overcome the Practical Challenges of Implementing the R's

There is little doubt that implementing the 5 R's on a meaningful scale will require continued changes in thinking and infrastructure pointed out in literature on the separate R's. Table 3 summarizes such changes.

Although many of these changes are under way in different places in different ways, considerable challenges remain. We believe that emerging stakeholder interests align well with the 5 R's and will drive such change. For example, the 2014 Academy Health report on improving the evidence base for Medicare policy making[56] interviewed leaders in health policy and care delivery for their most pressing health services research needs over the next 3 to 5 years; it was research that (1) aims at understanding the performance of new organizational forms such as accountable care organizations and Medicare Advantage plans; (2) uses comparable data sets for performance of physician practices and new organizational arrangements; (3) engages with the promises and pitfalls of electronic data, rapid cycle research, and comparative effectiveness research; (4) understands how the politics of evidence and policy affect research relevance and usefulness; and (5) builds relationships between researchers and policy makers, with study findings available at the time decisions were made—even if "best available" rather than "best" evidence. Although this study was focused on Medicare, we believe its lessons can be much more broadly taken.

In addition, we solicited feedback from a convenience sample of 8 stakeholders on the importance of research for practical decision making and on the 5 R's. Participants were balanced across practitioners, other implementers, and administrators. Responses indicated that *relevant* was the most important R, with *rapid* a close second, followed by other R's—none of which were considered unimportant. The most important role for research in practical decisions was testing viability of approaches in their own settings and available resources. Suggested reasons why research is often not useful were lack of relevance, rapidity, or good relationships with researchers. The 2 facets identified as making research more helpful were "faster turnaround" and building better relationships between researchers and clinicians; as one clinician put it, "Relationship is so important, you should put a 6th R in there!"

# Recognize the Wide Range of Application for the 5 R's

Admittedly aspirational, we do not expect every study to comprehensively address all 5 R's. We do not expect, for example, all epidemiologic research or basic mechanism studies to address all of them. Studies having as their long-term goal achieving translation to real-world settings or making a population impact, however, would benefit from considering each R, reporting on those most relevant, and discussing implications for the others. Examining the implications of all 5 R's should be useful in the vast majority of research studies, from efficacy to effectiveness to implementation and dissemination, not just for a few community translational "T4" studies, which are investigations of practice intervention effects on population health. This strategy would help align the pipeline of potential interventions with real-world pragmatic requirements.

# Build Better Relationships Using the 5 R's

Practitioners often experience research as interfering with practical procedures or believe that researchers just want study participants to address their own questions and further their careers. On the other hand, researchers often experience clinicians as not interested in research, resistant to research protocols, or not being ready to implement evidence-based findings. This is not a perceived relationship between researchers and practitioners or other stakeholders that will carry us into a successful future. The 5 R's proposed embody the terms of a new and more transparent win-win partnership between researchers and stakeholders with important questions that research can help answer.

| Challenges | Changes to Address Challenges |
|---|---|
| **Accelerating the pace and iterative nature of the research enterprise** | Harness stakeholder interest in timeliness to drive a cultural shift to shorten what is considered "rapid" or "timely" compared with present custom |
| Decision-maker needs outpace current speed of review cycles: grant review; funding decision; IRB approval and modification processes | |
| Study implementation time frames | Implement a variety of technical changes to research processes already suggested in literature[19,21,26,27,54] |
| Publication cycles not amenable to "just in time" decisions; slow review and release of findings (see more below on dissemination) | Use rapid-cycle testing of hypotheses, allowing ineffective ideas to "fail fast" and successful innovations to spread quickly |
| Low priority assigned to designs that can speed research | Link social media with traditional communications vehicles |
| **Expanding limited concepts of rigor (eg, preference for, confidence in, or insistence on certain designs such as RCTs) by:** | Among all parties, build awareness of and comfort with a broader "palette" of research designs, so that research design is driven by the questions, rather than research questions driven by designs |
| Funding agencies offering calls for proposals | |
| Grant application reviewers | Use professional meetings/training events to more clearly articulate features, pros/cons of different designs—their appropriate or promising scope of application |
| Researchers | |
| "Customers" of research (stakeholders who use the findings) | |
| **Ensuring a blend of research team skills and interests** | Propose an enhanced "job description" for research teams—a checklist of skills, interests, and relationships required for specific studies |
| Skill and interest in stakeholder involvement in generating questions, articulating ultimate use of study findings, study design, implementation, reporting, and dissemination | Beyond essential methodologic, data-gathering, and analytic skills, include "softer" skills and methods such as shown in left column |
| Awareness of and respect for political as well as scientific concerns of stake- holders such as policy makers | Build up those skills through examples, conferences, and training among both existing and new researchers |
| Skill and comfort in building relationships with clinicians and clinics—consultative, cooperative, problem solving | |
| Experience and confidence with the broader "palette" of research designs, including rapid learning in real-world experiments | |
| **Increasing clinician familiarity with being active research partners** | Provide examples and assistance through professional venues and practice facilitation or technical assistance that help clinicians and researchers adjust mindset, methods, and interactions to create practical research partnerships along the lines described in the literature[15,16,25] |
| Negative experiences or preconceptions about feasibility or practical value of doing research in the practice | |
| Few or no current relationships with researchers | |
| Unfamiliarity of working with researchers to turn practice concerns and curiosity into researchable questions | |
| Unfamiliarity with building research data gathering into routine clinic systems rather than being an effortful "add on" | |
| Not connecting research with more familiar quality improvement, rapid- cycle learning | |
| **Raising priority on collection and reporting on context and resources** | Adjust research announcements and grant review guidelines to ask for greater reporting on context and resources required; accompany by explanation of why |
| Limited researcher and reviewer expectation that data on resource use of interventions or on context information relevant to transportability or reinvention in new settings be gathered systematically or reported | For publication in limited space, consider other methods such as web supplements to access detailed context and resource use data if not in standard published article |
| Space limitations and/or customary priorities in journals that reduce additional context and resource data reporting | Publish replications (successful or not) in places where stakeholders will find them |
| **More powerfully bringing publication and dissemination to practical decision making** | Reward researchers via funding and career paths for key replications, not only for new positive results |
| Limited readiness to publish replications of key findings in original or new contexts or to publish negative results of replication | Create a stakeholder map—which stakeholders need what information from the study, in what form, and where it is most likely to be read |
| Reaching those stakeholders who want to make research-based decisions at the time and place decisions are made | Create stakeholder-specific versions of core journal publications to increase reach of the information |
| Limited dissemination in publications or forms in which stakeholders are already engaged, knowing that different forms of publication/dissemination reach different stakeholders | |

**Table 3**   Challenges and Changes for Routine Implementation of 5 R's
IRB= institutional review board; RCT= randomized controlled trial.

# Teach to This New Standard

This new standard (and its implicit partnership between stakeholders and researchers) is especially important for students and those early in their careers, whether clinicians, researchers, policy makers, or others wishing to develop or use research evidence. The 5 R's are offered as teaching tools as well as research tools—helping all stakeholders wear constructive "hats" with each other when addressing important questions. Over time, this approach may lead to an improved relationship between the research and health care enterprises—on behalf of the public they both serve.

# References

1. Smith JM, Topol E. A call to action: lowering the cost of health care. *Am J Prev Med.* 2013;44(1) (Suppl 1):S54–S57.

2. Patient-Centered Outcomes Research Institute (PCORI). Funding announcement: Improving healthcare systems. May 22, 2012. http:// www.pcori.org/assets/PFA-Improving-Healthcare-Systems-05222012. pdf. Accessed Jul 15, 2013.

3. Nutting PA, Crabtree BF, Miller WL, Stange KC, Stewart E, Jaén C. Transforming physician practices to patient-centered medical homes: lessons from the national demonstration project. *Health Aff (Millwood).* 2011;30(3):439–445.

4. Fisher ES, Shortell SM. Accountable care organizations: accountable for what, to whom, and how. *JAMA.* 2010;304(15):1715–1716.

5. Selby JV, Beal AC, Frank L. The Patient-Centered Outcomes Research Institute (PCORI) national priorities for research and initial research agenda. *JAMA.* 2012;307(15):1583–1584.

6. Stange KC. Refocusing knowledge generation, application, and education: raising our gaze to promote health across boundaries. *Am J Prev Med.* 2011;41(4)(Suppl 3):S164–S169.

7. Balas EBS. *Managing Clinical Knowledge for Health Care Improvement. Yearbook of Medical Informatics.* Stuttgart, Germany: Schattauer; 2000.

8. Brownson RC, Colditz GA, Proctor EK, eds. *Dissemination and Implementation Research in Health: Translating Science to Practice.* 1st ed. New York, NY: Oxford University Press, Inc; 2012.

9. Kessler R, Glasgow RE. A proposal to speed translation of health-care research into practice: dramatic change is needed. *Am J Prev Med.* 2011;40(6):637–644.

10. Moher D, Hopewell S, Schulz KF, et al; Consolidated Standards of Reporting Trials Group. CONSORT 2010 Explanation and Elaboration: Updated guidelines for reporting parallel group randomised trials. *J Clin Epidemiol.* 2010;63(8):e1–e37.

11. Schulz KF, Altman DG, Moher D, CONSORT Group. CONSORT 2010 statement: updated guidelines for reporting parallel group randomised trials. *BMC Med.* 2010;340:c332.

12. Higgins J, Green S. Cochrane Handbook for Systematic Reviews of Interventions. Updated 2011. http://www.cochrane-handbook.org.Accessed Jul 16, 2013.

13. Equator Network. Library for Health Research Reporting. EQUATOR Network Resource Center website. Updated 2013. http://www.equator-network.org/resource-centre/library-of-health-research-reporting. Accessed Jul 16, 2013.

14. Gold M, Siegel J, Russell L, Weinstein M. *Cost Effectiveness in Health and Medicine.* New York, NY: Oxford University Press; 2003.

15. Solberg LI, Glasgow RE, Unützer J, et al. Partnership research: a practical trial design for evaluation of a natural experiment to improve depression care. *Med Care.* 2010;48(7):576–582.

16. Kottke TE, Solberg LI, Nelson AF, et al. Optimizing practice through research: a new perspective to solve an old problem. *Ann Fam Med.* 2008;6(5):459–462.

17. Berwick DM. Broadening the view of evidence-based medicine. *Qual Saf Health Care.* 2005;14(5):315–316.

18. Rothwell PM. External validity of randomised controlled trials: "to whom do the results of this trial apply?" *Lancet.* 2005;365(9453): 82–93.

19. Glasgow RE, Chambers D. Developing robust, sustainable, implementation systems using rigorous, rapid and relevant science. *Clin Transl Sci.* 2012;5(1):48–55.

20. Kessler RS. The patient centered medical home: a great opportunity to move beyond brilliant and irrelevant. *Transl Behav Med.* 2012;2(3):311–312.

21. Riley WT, Glasgow RE, Etheredge L, Abernethy AP. Rapid, responsive, relevant (R3) research: a call for a rapid learning health research enterprise. *Clin Transl Med.* 2013;2(1):10.

22. Green LW. Making research relevant: if it is an evidence-based practice, where's the practice-based evidence? *Fam Pract.* 2008; 25(Suppl 1):i20–i24.

23. Krist AH, Glenn BA, Glasgow RE, et al. Designing a valid randomized pragmatic primary care implementation trial: the My Own Health Report (MOHR) project. *Implement Sci.* 2013;8:73.

24. Tunis SR, Stryer DB, Clancy CM. Practical clinical trials: increasing the value of clinical research for decision making in clinical and health policy. *JAMA.* 2003;290(12):1624–1632.

25. Solberg LI, Crain AL, Jaeckels N, et al. The DIAMOND initiative: implementing collaborative care for depression in 75 primary care clinics. *Implement Sci.* 2013;8(1):135.

26. Abernethy AP, Etheredge LM, Ganz PA, et al. Rapid-learning system for cancer care. *J Clin Oncol.* 2010;28(27):4268–4274.

27. Etheredge LM. A rapid-learning health system. *Health Aff (Millwood).* 2007;26(2):w107–w118.

28. Mays GP, Hogg RA. Expanding delivery system research in public health settings: lessons from practice-based research networks. *J Public Health Manag Pract.* 2012;18(6):485–498.

29. Ryan B. Data management and analysis methods. In: Denzin N, Lincoln Y, eds. *Handbook of Qualitative Research.* 2nd ed. Thousand Oaks, CA: Sage Publications; 2000:769–802.

30. Green LW, Glasgow RE. Evaluating the relevance, generalization, and applicability of research: issues in external validation and translation methodology. *Eval Health Prof.* 2006;29(1):126–153.

31. Glasgow RE, Klesges LM, Dzewaltowski DA, Bull SS, Estabrooks P. The future of health behavior change research: what is needed to improve translation of research into health promotion practice? *Ann Behav Med.* 2004;27(1):3–12.

32. Ritzwoller DP, Sukhanova A, Gaglio B, Glasgow RE. Costing behavioral interventions: a practical guide to enhance translation. *Ann Behav Med.* 2009;37(2):218–227.

33. Ritzwoller DP, Sukhanova AS, Glasgow RE, et al. Intervention costs and cost-effectiveness for a multiple-risk-factor diabetes self-management trial for Latinas: economic analysis of Viva bien! *Transl Behav Med.* 2011;1(3):427–435.

34. Porter ME. What is value in health care? *N Engl J Med.* 2010;363(26): 2477–2481.

35. deBronkart D. How the e-patient community helped save my life: an essay by Dave deBronkart. *BMJ.* 2013;346:f1990.

36. Cohn S, Clinch M, Bunn C, Stronge P. Entangled complexity: why complex interventions are just not complicated enough. *J Health Serv Res Policy.* 2013;18(1):40–43.

37. Ioannidis JP. Effect of the statistical significance of results on the time to completion and publication of randomized efficacy trials. *JAMA.* 1998;279(4):281–286.

38. Tomoaia-Cotisel A, Scammon DL, Waitzman NJ, et al. Context matters: the experience of 14 research teams in systematically reporting contextual factors important for practice change. *Ann Fam Med.* 2013;11(Suppl 1):S115–S123.

39. Crain AL, Solberg LI, Unützer J, et al. Designing and implementing research on a state-wide quality improvement initiative: the DIAMOND study and initiative. *Med Care.* 2013;51(9):e58–e66.

40. Glasgow RE, Magid DJ, Beck A, Ritzwoller D, Estabrooks PA. Practical clinical trials for translating research to practice: design and measurement recommendations. *Med Care.* 2005;43(6):551–557.

41. Cohen D, McDaniel RR Jr, Crabtree BF, et al. A practice change model for quality improvement in primary care practice. *J Healthc Manag.* 2004;49(3):155–168, discussion 169–170.

42. Allen J, Linnan L, Emmons K. Fidelity and its relationship to implementation effectiveness, adaptation and dissemination. In: Brownson R, Colditz G, Proctor E, eds. *Dissemination and Implementation Research in Health: Translating Science to Practice.* 1st ed. New York, NY: Oxford University Press; 2012:281–303.

43. Cohen DJ, Tallia AF, Crabtree BF, Young DM. Implementing health behavior change in primary care: lessons from prescription for health. *Ann Fam Med.* 2005;3(Suppl 2):S12–S19.

44. Cohen DJ, Crabtree BF, Etz RS, et al. Fidelity versus flexibility: translating evidence-based research into practice. *Am J Prev Med.* 2008;35(5)(Suppl):S381–S389.

45. Cohen D, Leviton L, Isaacson N, Tallia A, Crabtree B. Online diaries for qualitative evaluation: gaining real-time insights. *Am J Eval.* 2006;27(2):1–22.

46. Etz RS, Cohen DJ, Woolf SH, et al. Bridging primary care practices and communities to promote healthy behaviors. *Am J Prev Med.* 2008;35(5)(Suppl):S390–S397.

47. Balasubramanian BA, Cohen DJ, Clark EC, et al. Practice-level approaches for behavioral counseling and patient health behaviors. *Am J Prev Med.* 2008;35(5)(Suppl):S407–S413.

48. Cohen DJ, Balasubramanian BA, Isaacson NF, Clark EC, Etz RS, Crabtree BF. Coordination of health behavior counseling in primary care. *Ann Fam Med.* 2011;9(5):406–415.

49. Glasgow R, Kessler R, Ory M, et al. Conducting rapid, relevant research: lessons learned from the My Own Health Report (MOHR) project. *Am J Prev Med.* 2014;47(2):212–219.

50. Thorpe KE, Zwarenstein M, Oxman AD, et al. A pragmatic-explanatory continuum indicator summary (PRECIS): a tool to help trial designers. *J Clin Epidemiol.* 2009;62(5):464–475.

51. Senge PM. *Fifth Discipline: Mastering the Five Practices of the Learning Organization.* New York, NY: Doubleday & Co; 1990.

52. Gaglio B, Shoup JA, Glasgow RE. The RE-AIM framework: a systematic review of use over time. *Am J Public Health.* 2013;103(6):e38–e46.

53. Kessler RS, Purcell EP, Glasgow RE, Klesges LM, Benkeser RM, Peek CJ. What does it mean to "employ" the RE-AIM model? *Eval Health Prof.* 2013;36(1):44–66.

54. Wagner EH. Academia, chronic care, and the future of primary care. *J Gen Intern Med.* 2010;25(Suppl 4):S636–S638.

55. Committee on Quality of Health Care in America. *Crossing the Quality Chasm: A New Health System for the 21st Century.* Washington, DC: National Academy Press; 2001.

56. Gluck ME, Radomski L. The AcademyHealth Listening Project Report: Improving the Evidence Base for Medicare Policymaking. Academy-Health. Updated February 2014. http://academyhealth.org/files/publications/listeningprojectmedicare.pdf. Accessed Apr 4, 2014.

# Chapter 2 ■ The 5 R's: An Emerging Bold Standard for Conducting Relevant Research in a Changing World

## Questions for Discussion

1. How do the 5 R's help you maintain a clear focus on the 6 P's as you conduct your research? Explain the connection using a few sentences, a diagram, or an illustration.

2. How can you use the elements of your paradigm as a model to help you make a plan for how your research track and scope might change over the course of the semester?

3. Based on the definition given in "Redefines Rigor," give two examples of external validity that you might find useful when selecting paradigm research for your own project proposal.

4. Work with a partner or small group to analyze Table 2. Add one question per section that is relevant to your own research (Design, Implementation, Reporting, Dissemination). Be prepared to explain to the class (a) why you added each question and (b) how it relates to your research.

5. Map out how you can address all 5 R's in your own research. Then, list them in order of relevance. Are there any R's that do not specifically apply to your prospective proposal? If not, why is this the case?

# "I'm Ambivalent about It": The Dilemmas of PowerPoint

Andrea Hill[1], Tammi Arford[1], Amy Lubitow[2], and Leandra M. Smollin[1]

## Abstract

The increasing ubiquity of PowerPoint in the university classroom raises complex questions about pedagogy and the creation of dynamic and effective learning environments. Though much of the sociological teaching literature has focused on engagement and active learning, very little of this work has addressed the presence of PowerPoint in sociology classrooms. Teaching sociology requires discussion, critical thinking, and debate—characteristics many critics argue are at odds with PowerPoint's unique presentation style. Utilizing survey data from faculty and students at a private university, this research explores PowerPoint usage and the many ways it influences the learning environment of the sociology classroom.

## Keywords

technology, student engagement, active learning

Since its introduction in 1987, PowerPoint presentation software has become almost inescapable. Found on over 250 million computers worldwide, it is estimated that over 1 million PowerPoint presentations take place each hour (Mahin 2004; Parker 2001). While long present in corporate boardrooms, in recent years the technology has become entrenched in the academy. From accounting to geology, it is now a common feature of academic instruction (Cyphert 2004; Mackiewicz 2008). The increasing ubiquity of PowerPoint in the university has been accompanied by mounting concern over the ways it shapes learning environments. Though the matter has been addressed by other disciplines, sociological exploration of PowerPoint's influence on classroom culture has been sparse (Benson et al. 2002; Reinhardt 1999; Stoner 2007). This silence is particularly surprising because much of the sociological teaching literature is concerned with critical pedagogy—a goal seen as directly threatened by slide technology. It is essential for sociologists to concern themselves with "the culture, customs, and behavior that are dragged along with PowerPoint and how they affect the way we think" (Craig and Amernic 2006:158). Recognizing this need, our research explores PowerPoint and its implications for pedagogy and learning environments.

[1]Northeastern University, Boston, MA, USA
[2]Portland State University, Portland, OR, USA

From *Teaching Sociology,* Volume 40 (3), 2012, pp. 242–256. Copyright © 2012 American Sociological Association. Reprinted by permission of SAGE Publications.

# Previous Research

## *PowerPoint and Learning Outcomes*

Most of the sociological empirical work on technology in the classroom has been concerned with a variety of technologies, including Web sites, statistical software, Internet discussion groups, Blackboard, and other multimedia (Persell 1992; Susman 1988). This research has most often explored PowerPoint in combination with other instructional technologies. Hence, though these works have commonly concluded that technology in the classroom "makes possible and calls forth from students increased response to and interaction with the instructor and the course" (Koeber 2005:298), these assertions cannot be attributed to PowerPoint alone. In fact, research focused solely on the slide technology has produced decidedly mixed conclusions.

Most studies have found PowerPoint to have no measurable influence on course performance and a minimal effect on grades—concluding, as Levasseur and Sawyer (2006:111) do, the technology brings "no significant change in learning outcomes when instructors augment their lectures with computer-generated slides" (see also Dietz 2002; Howard 2005; Kunkel 2004; Susskind 2005). In the studies that found an association between slide usage and higher exam scores, students were exposed to slides during lecture and were also either given printed versions of slides prior to class or were able to access slides via the Internet. Thus, access to instructor-prepared, thorough class notes, in combination with PowerPoint, was the crucial factor in improving student performance (Levasseur and Sawyer 2006).

While its effect on student *performance* remains largely unclear, several studies have found that PowerPoint has a measurable influence on student *perception*. These works, which explore software and course experiences, find that students greatly enjoy slide technology. In their review of the research on reactions to PowerPoint in the classroom, Levasseur and Sawyer (2006) found that the majority of empirical research concludes that students view slide usage positively. For example, despite the fact that PowerPoint made relatively little difference in their grade outcomes, Susskind's (2005) students reported that PowerPoint positively impacted their learning, organization, and note taking. Similarly, Wilmoth and Wybraniec's (1998) social statistics classes had favorable perceptions of PowerPoint's ability to increase their interest in course material, promote learning, and improve their exam performance. Time and again, studies show that students favor slides over chalkboards or overhead projectors and feel that computer-generated slides improve course organization and note taking and make classes more interesting (Bartsch and Cobern 2003; Pippert and Moore 1999; Young 2004). Students also perceive PowerPoint-using instructors as more effective and are more likely to give these instructors favorable evaluations (Koeber 2005; Susskind 2005; Weinraub 1998). To date, there has been little research exploring the dynamics of PowerPoint classrooms and pedagogy, and most existing treatments of the subject are primarily theoretical. Despite a lack of empirical foundation, however, these treatments raise important debates regarding the ways that slide software shapes learning

## *PowerPoint and Learning Environments*

Critics observe that PowerPoint, which was created for business environments, has a style that is naturally suited for marketing and counterproductive for educating (Knoblauch 2008; Tufte 2003a, 2003b). According to Tufte (2003a:26), the software's best recognized and most vociferous detractor, it has a "definite, well-enforced, and widely-practiced cognitive style that is contrary to serious thinking." There is little question that slide software uses simplification to enable efficient and straightforward information dissemination. Though simplification is important for learning, when it becomes oversimplification, it can discourage and even derail critical thinking. Slide settings, which provide limited space for words, cultivate "oversimplification by asking presenters to summarize key concepts in as few words as possible" (Simons 2005:5). Critics charge that presentations transform content into overly simple snippets or buzz phrases that elide intricacy and nuance. This maximization of brevity trivializes and homogenizes knowledge (Adams 2006; Fendrich 2010; Norvig 2003). Further, critics note that minimally worded bullet-pointed content forced into outline form neglects context and fails to explore the multiple and complex relationships between concepts. The loss of breadth, depth, and complexity results in the transmission of material that is at best deficient and at worst so simple it belies the nature of course content.

PowerPoint's detractors also maintain that it is an impediment to fostering engaged student participants and active classrooms, noting that slides encourage students to passively consume information and make it possible to acquire knowledge at little cognitive expense. These critics charge that PowerPoint cheapens learning experiences by structuring the lecture hall in ways that discourage discussing, engaging, and interacting with instructors and peers. For example, they note that classroom lighting must be at least partially dimmed and seats must be arranged so that the projected images may be seen clearly by all. In essence, the screen becomes the focal point of the class, making the physical setup of a PowerPoint classroom much like that of a theater. Such a unidirectional environment is set up for one-way knowledge transmission rather than knowledge exchange and establishes "a dominance relationship between speaker and audience" (Adams 2006; Creed 1997; Tufte 2003a:13). The environment of the PowerPoint lecture hall creates "spectators rather than participants, in a classroom where the professor 'orchestrates' a multimedia presentation" (Reinhardt 1999:49). Critics argue that instead of a supplementing the educational experience, slideshows become a substitute for the lecturer.

Many also decry software's influence on pedagogy, noting that the PowerPoint-using instructor tends to proceed through class by following the pre-determined path established by slides. This pre-planned organization inhibits instructor digressions, anecdotes, and creativity—moments that often inspire student questions that are so vitally important for effective learning (Norvig 2003; Simons 2005). PowerPoint discourages teaching improvisation and in turn student questions, because "the slides tend to impel the lecture conversation along a pre-set unidirectional course, disregarding and sometimes blind to . . . the unbidden: the unsolicited question or unexpected comment" (Adams 2006:404). Thus, though the technology enables well-planned lectures, order may come at the cost of student engagement and instructor spontaneity. Rather than critically engaging with the meaning and context of materials, students simply copy the information they see in front of them each time they are presented with a new slide. As such, critics note that engagement with course content ends when projected information has been successfully copied into learners' notes.

While existing studies have been useful for understanding some aspects of the student PowerPoint relationship, they fail to address the nature of PowerPoint classroom environments. In turn, those works that do address behavior and interaction in slide-using classrooms tend to be somewhat speculative and lack empirical grounding. As Benson et al. (2002:145) note, "We need research that reveals how students use digital technology in a classroom setting and the extent to which this use affects learning in both planned and unplanned ways." In addition, there are no studies that explore how sociology instructors view the technology and its influence on learning environments (Koeber 2005; Pippert and Moore 1999). Recognizing these needs, we explore student and instructor perceptions of slide technology and classroom dynamics.

# Method

To explore PowerPoint classroom culture, we administered surveys to undergraduates enrolled in sociology courses and instructors from the sociology and anthropology department at a medium-sized private university in New England. The university's institutional review board (IRB) approved the study and the survey instruments prior to distribution. We chose to focus on PowerPoint because the overwhelming majority of presentations in higher education utilize the Microsoft software. Alternative presentation programs have emerged in recent years—one of the most commonly used alternative programs is Prezi, a software package with an interactive style that allows users to create nonlinear, nonhierarchical shows and manipulate projected content to move, flow, and connect. Although this and other similar technologies may combat many of the challenges posed by static slideware, existing critiques suggest that *all* presentational software is problematic for teaching and learning (Cooper 2009; Gries and Brooke 2010; Stryker 2010). Admittedly, the choice to limit our study to PowerPoint may neglect important developments that alternative programs have brought to the small number of classes in which they are used. However, our work will usefully inform much-needed future research on Prezi and other similar programs.

## Undergraduate and Instructor Surveys

Our undergraduate sample consisted of students enrolled in one of eight sociology classes during the summer and fall semesters of 2010. We distributed paper surveys to those enrolled in two sections of Introduction to Sociology and one section each of Deviant Behavior and Social Control, Drugs and Society, Family Violence, American Society, Environmental Sociology, and Social Theory. The sampled classes ranged in size from 9 to 113 students—five of the courses had more than 50 undergraduates and three had fewer than 30. In order to build understanding of how the average student enrolled in a sociology course experiences slide software, we did not restrict survey participation to sociology majors or minors. Although the 9 participants from the Social Theory class included in the study were primarily junior- and senior-level sociology majors, the other courses surveyed did not require prerequisites and thus contained a wide variety of majors and grade levels. The undergraduate survey consisted of 10 questions adapted from previous research on student perceptions of technology use in the classroom (Burke and James 2008; Nowaczyk, Santos, and Patton 1998). In addition to 9 fixed-choice questions regarding frequency and purpose of use, preferences, and impressions of the technology's effectiveness, the survey also included an open-response question that asked students to explain what they most like and dislike about instructional PowerPoint (contact authors for complete survey). A total of 384 students (approximately 87 percent of the sample) completed the survey.

Sociology instructors, including full-time faculty, graduate student instructors (teaching as adjunct lecturers or funded graduate instructors), and adjunct lecturers, were also surveyed. We administered questionnaires to graduate student and adjunct instructors through an online platform and distributed paper copies of the instrument to faculty during a department meeting. The nine-question survey administered to instructors included three fixed-choice questions assessing rank, teaching experience, and course load and a further three fixed-choice questions regarding frequency and purpose of instructional PowerPoint use. This survey also included three open-response questions that asked instructors to reflect on their perceptions of how students feel about PowerPoint and their personal impressions of its effects on the classroom environment and their own pedagogy (contact authors for complete survey). A total of 33 instructors (approximately 72 percent of sampled population) completed the survey.

## Data Analysis

After compiling and quantitatively analyzing responses to the fixed-choice questions for both the undergraduate and instructor surveys, we then inductively coded answers to the open-ended questions and analyzed them for recurrent themes and concepts. Using a multistep process of constant comparison to analyze the qualitative responses, the authors (1) read through the written survey answers to develop a series of thematic categories, (2) sorted the written data into emergent categories, (3) compared observations to confirm or disconfirm trends in the data, and (4) reviewed data to verify the accuracy and relevance of themes (Bogdan and Biklen 2007; Glaser and Strauss 1967; Strauss and Corbin 2008). We chose to use both open-response and fixed-choice survey questions to elicit quantitative and qualitative data and thus better explore students' and instructors' perceptions of PowerPoint.

# Findings

## Prevalence, Frequency, and Purpose of Use

We found PowerPoint to be a prevalent feature of undergraduate classes: 67 percent of students reported that all or most of their instructors use the software, and 23 percent reported that at least half of their instructors use it. According to respondents, not only are slide presentations present in the majority of their courses; they are also present in most individual class meetings: 95 percent of students reported that PowerPoint-using instructors use the software in all or most class meetings.

Sociology instructors reported similar usage prevalence: Approximately 91 percent use PowerPoint at least some of the time in their courses—76 percent of instructors use it in between one quarter and three quarters of their class meetings, while 55 percent use it in at least three quarters of their classes. Frequency of use differs by professional rank (see Table 1). Twenty percent of full professors report using PowerPoint frequently (more than three quarters of classes) or always, while 60 percent of associate and 50 percent of assistant professors use it that often. Graduate student instructors are the most frequent users of the technology—69 percent reported using slides frequently or always. Instructors' *lack* of PowerPoint use also differs by rank: 63 percent of full professors reported that they do not use it at all or do so in less than a quarter of class meetings, while no graduate student instructors gave that reply. Though our findings indicate that prevalence and frequency of use is significantly higher among graduate student instructors, we did not find a consistent rank/use relationship across the sample. Given the limitations posed by the size and nature of the sample, the relatively large dichotomy between the most (full professors) and least (graduate student) experienced instructors cannot be interpreted as anything more than a suggestive avenue for future research.

We also explored the purposes for which slideware is used. All PowerPoint-using instructors reported using slides to project lecture notes, charts, definitions, and explanations. Just over half (54 percent) of those surveyed also embed video clips in presentations, and 41 percent use slides to display discussion questions. Undergraduate answers confirmed that PowerPoint most often serves as a tool of information display; when asked what their instructors typically use PowerPoint for (e.g., to show pictures, play video clips, or project lecture notes), 95 percent answered that their instructors use slides for lecture notes most of the time.

## Student Perceptions

Undergraduates reported PowerPoint is a useful feature of classroom instruction that improves learning. When asked which of the software's functions they found most helpful, a small number of students chose "showing pictures" (16 percent) or "showing video clips" (4 percent) while the vast majority—approximately 80 percent—reported that slideware is most useful when it is used to outline lecture notes and information. Students' answers to the open-ended question, "What do you like most about PowerPoint?" support this finding (see Table 2): Over half (52 percent) of the responses to this query mentioned liking the software for its ability to outline lectures and point to important infor-

| | Grad Student | Assistant Professor | Associate Professor | Full Professor | All Instructors |
|---|---|---|---|---|---|
| Always/frequently | 68.7 | 50.0 | 60.0 | 20.0 | 54.5 |
| Moderately | 31.3 | 0.0 | 20.0 | 12.5 | 21.2 |
| Infrequently/never | 0.0 | 50.0 | 20.0 | 62.5 | 24.2 |
| Total | 100 | 100 | 100 | 100 | 100 |

**Table 1** Instructor Frequency of PowerPoint Use by Percentage

*Note:* Frequency of PowerPoint use was measured using the following scale: never, infrequently (less than 25 percent of class meetings); moderately infrequently (25 percent to less than 50 percent of class meetings); moderately frequently (50 percent to less than 75 percent of class meetings); frequently (75 percent to almost every class meeting); and always.

## What do you like most about PowerPoint?

### Outlines lectures and points to what is important (52 percent)

"how it shows you the information and makes it easier to outline what we will be learning that day and makes it easier to follow along."

"I like how it hits the key points our professors want us to know. And it gives a general outline of the reading."

"I like that I can focus more on what the professor is saying because I can add what the professor says in class but also already have the major points I need written down (because of the slides)."

"It shortens main points up and makes them easier to understand."

### Makes class interesting/keeps me awake (30 percent)

"How it keeps my attention and makes lecture easy to follow."

"When there are pictures it helps to keep my attention."

"Keeps me interested by giving me something to look at and focus on."

### Good for visual learners (10 percent)

"Because I am a visual learner, it makes it easier for me to comprehend material."

"I am a visual learner, so I like to see outlines as well as pictures and video clips. If I miss what the teacher says I can see it up on the slide."

## What do you dislike most about PowerPoint?

### Instructor reads verbatim off of slides (32 percent)

"I wish some professors wouldn't just read the Power Point word for word, I wish there was more discussion."

"How it encourages me at times to not come to class since some professors read directly from the PowerPoint and posts them online to easily access."

"When my professor reads directly off a slide, I would rather them not use it. It makes me feel as if class is optional."

### Lecturing too fast, not enough time to read/take notes (24 percent)

"Teachers switch too fast and can't copy everything. Sometimes just copy the PowerPoint and not what the teacher talks about."

"When a teacher puts too many words on the slides and you can't write everything down before they move to the next slide."

"If a professor doesn't give out the PowerPoint you have to keep up and try to copy the slides and still copy or listen to what the professor says."

### Discourages discussion (12 percent)

"It distracts from actual discussions . . . people are so busy trying to take down notes, no one's really paying attention."

"It monopolizes the class and leaves little opportunity for discussion or interaction. It also can be an excuse to not take notes and not pay attention as it can be accessed online whenever it is convenient for me."

"It encourages passive rather than active learning."

**Table 2**   Students' PowerPoint Likes and Dislikes

mation. As one student wrote, slideware is helpful because "it shows you the information and makes it easier to outline what we will be learning that day." This appreciation is manifest in students' self-reported classroom behavior, as the vast majority said that they regularly copy information from slides—82 percent report that they "always," "almost always," or "usually" do so, while only 5 percent answered that they "almost never" or "never" copy words from slides.

When evaluating PowerPoint's utility for improving several components of learning, students reported that it is "almost always" or "always" effective for aiding exam preparation (56 percent), enhancing comprehension of course material (52 percent), and improving attention in class (38 percent). Though

| | Exam Preparation | Paper Writing | Comprehension of Material | Paying Attention in Class | Engaging Discussion |
|---|---|---|---|---|---|
| Always/almost always | 56.1 | 25.3 | 52.3 | 38.1 | 24.5 |
| Often/usually | 38.1 | 50.5 | 43.7 | 49.6 | 55.4 |
| Sometimes | 1.6 | 14.6 | 3.2 | 9.9 | 17.9 |
| Almost never/never | 4.2 | 9.6 | 0.8 | 2.4 | 2.2 |
| Total percent | 100 | 100 | 100 | 100 | 100 |

**Table 3**  Student Perceptions of PowerPoint effectiveness for Learning Tasks by . . .

they found the software somewhat less useful for paper writing and engaging discussion (25 percent answered that it is "almost always" or "always" effective for both), only a minority of students (fewer than 10 percent) answered it was "almost never" or "never" effective for any of the learning tasks they evaluated (Table 3).

Written responses to the open-ended questions "What do you most like/dislike about PowerPoint?" support these findings. After projection of lecture outlines, the second most commonly mentioned advantage of slideware was its ability to make class more interesting. Approximately 30 percent of answers to the "like" question were a variation of one student's comment that PowerPoint "keeps me interested by giving me something to look at and focus on." Further, responses to the open-ended "dislike" question correspond to the previously mentioned finding that PowerPoint is less effective for encouraging discussion than it is for any other learning task. In discussing what they most disliked about the software, many students found fault with its tendency to discourage discussion—approximately 12 percent of these responses expressed sentiments along the lines of one student's observation that "[PowerPoint] monopolizes the class and leaves little opportunity for discussion or interaction." In addition, the more commonly cited failings—32 percent most disliked instructors reading from slides and 24 percent felt slides cause instructors to lecture too fast—are undoubtedly implicated in suppressing discussion, as one response illustrates: "I wish some professors wouldn't just read the PowerPoint word for word, I wish there was more discussion."

Given their perceptions of its usefulness, it is unsurprising that the undergraduates surveyed greatly enjoy classroom PowerPoint. Eighty-four percent of students agreed that the technology improves their overall classroom experience, and only a small minority (9 percent) reported that it does nothing to enhance their learning (Figure 1). Fully 69 percent of students expressed a preference for PowerPoint classes, while only 10 percent answered that they prefer classes without the technology.

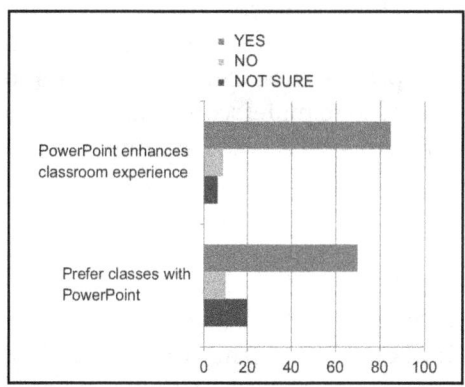

**Figure 1**  Percentage of students who believe PowerPoint enhances classroom experience and prefer classes with PowerPoint

## Instructor Perceptions

PowerPoint's popularity among undergraduates was not lost on sociology instructors, whose responses to the open-ended question, "What are your perceptions of students' expectations regarding PowerPoint?" reflected an awareness that students expect and greatly enjoy slide-supplemented lectures. While some instructors (30 percent) answered that they felt that at least some students dislike it, more than twice as many (65 percent) disagreed, reporting that students expect and/or like slides. As one explained, "Some of our students had PowerPoint in high school and have come to expect it." Instructors revealed a commonly shared explanation of why undergraduates favor slideware: Approximately 70 percent commented that students enjoy the technology because it simplifies information and makes class easier.

Responses to the question, "What are your reasons for using/not using PowerPoint?" indicated that instructors use the software for two primary reasons—to provide clarity for students and to improve their own teaching performances. Approximately 70 percent of responses to this question explained that slides are used because they help students by organizing information. As one instructor commented, "[they] can be helpful as a 'carry-all' for information that students can look back on while they study." In addition, 60 percent of the instructors who answered this question noted that they use slideware because it improves their teaching performance and helps them manage class. This, the second most commonly reported reason for using PowerPoint, was illustrated by one instructor's explanation that using it "allows me to move away from feeling like I'm reading from my lecture notes, but rather am able to have a more natural flow prompted by slides." Of those who answered that they rarely or never use it, 75 percent commented that they do not use slideware because it discourages student discussion—as one explained, slides put "students into passive 'audience' mode."

Answers to the open-response survey question, "Do you think that PowerPoint affects your teaching performance?" revealed that instructors recognize a significant relationship between the technology and pedagogy (Table 4). Every instructor who answered this question agreed that slideware has an impact on the way they teach. The majority—86 percent—noted that slides improve their organization and pacing by ordering lectures and keeping them on track, a function they greatly appreciate. In addition, approximately one third of instructors noted that PowerPoint alleviates performance anxiety, as one explained, it "gives me confidence, and gives me something to refer to if I have a moment of panic." Although instructors largely shared favorable impressions of the technology, a sizeable portion acknowledged that PowerPoint could negatively influence instruction. In fact, 43 percent of responses to this question mentioned that preset slideware can constrain teaching and limit interaction.

# Discussion: The Dilemmas of Instructional PowerPoint

PowerPoint is hailed as a tool for delivering information in an entertaining, quick, and efficient manner; the Microsoft Web site boasts: "Get your class to sit up and take notice! You can easily transform your presentation from boring lists and blocks of text to a vibrant and engaging slide show with images and video to underscore your main points" (Microsoft Corporation 2012). While the technology's core purposes and strongest selling points—simplifying information and making learning entertaining—are highly valued by students and instructors alike, they also pose serious dilemmas for educators. Our research revealed that the software's strengths are also sources of potentially detrimental influences on classroom environments. According to responses to open-ended survey questions, instructional use of PowerPoint raises three serious dilemmas: First, while students and instructors appreciated the technology's manifest function of clarification, their comments revealed anxiety regarding the software's latent tendency to oversimplify. In addition, although respondents reported that the software captures attention, some students and most instructors also acknowledged that it may often result in passivity and disengaged entertainment. Finally, sociology instructors' responses uncovered a tension between pragmatic career concerns and personal pedagogical philosophies. These dilemmas shed much-needed light on the complex experiential realities of PowerPoint in the sociology classroom.

## *Clarification and Oversimplification*

Survey responses indicate that instructional PowerPoint gives rise to a tension between clarification and oversimplification. The majority of undergraduates agreed that slides are most useful when they outline lectures, and their written comments repeatedly cited the technology's ability to organize and simplify course material as its greatest advantage. One student commented that PowerPoint "shortens up main points and makes them easier to understand," and another noted that it serves to "outline material so students know what info is important and what they can forget." In essence, the software allows learners to cut through complexity and focus on—as several put it—"only the important material." Instructors shared this appreciation for simplification—several noted that the technology

### *What are your perceptions of students' expectations regarding PowerPoint?*

**Students think it simplifies information and/or makes class easier (70 percent)**

"I think that students want an outline. They don't want every word the professor says. They want it before class so they know what to expect and can print it out and use the lecture to fill in the notes."

"That it simplified what they have to know for exams."

"Students like PowerPoint because it is a crutch."

**Students like or expect it (65 percent)**

"The students expect instructors to use PowerPoint."

"Some of our students had PowerPoint in high school and have come to expect it."

"They like it."

**Some or most students dislike it (30 percent)**

"I find that students are used to most of their sociology classes using PowerPoint, but are very divided about whether they like it or not."

"[Students] probably think it is boring and tedious."

### *What are your reasons for using, or not using, PowerPoint?*

**Organization and clarity for students (88 percent)**

"It can provide a path for the lecture to take which can be easily followed."

"PowerPoint helps to clearly follow the lecture use. It summarizes the lecture points."

"PowerPoint can be helpful as a 'carry-all' for information that students can look back on while they study."

"Helps to organize material."

**Improve teaching performance and classroom management (60 percent)**

"Allows me to move away from feeling like I'm reading from my lecture notes, but rather am able to have a more natural flow prompted by slides."

"I do think PowerPoint can be helpful in that I don't waste class time writing down extensive notes on the blackboard."

"It seems like a way to avoid my anxiety about teaching, particularly since I use it every day."

**Provide visuals and media (50 percent)**

"I find that it helps provide a visual guide for students who may be visual learners or who may benefit from seeing the outline of a lecture laid out."

"I also enjoy using PP to show my class various pictures and graphs to illustrate what I am lecturing about."

"Also to show images, maps, links to YouTube, etc."

**Reasons for not using: hampers discussion (75 percent of nonusers)**

"It oversimplifies complex info and puts students into passive 'audience' mode."

"I believe in the power of the presentation and class interactions. PowerPoint detracts."

### Do you feel that using PowerPoint affects your performance? If so, how?

**Organization and pacing (86 percent)**

"It does help with the organization and making sure that I and the students get the main points."

"Overall, I think it makes me more effective—keeps me on point, keeps the lecture structured and clear."

**Works to constrain performance and/or interaction (43 percent)**

"I am wary of being too tied to the slides, and therefore unwilling to veer from the presentation if the class wants to."

"[O]ccasionally, I discuss topics in a different order than I originally planned, which makes more sense in the context of a class discussion or a student question. That can be difficult to coordinate with the PowerPoint. Sometimes I feel like I have to 'teach to the PowerPoint.'"

**Relieves performance anxiety (33 percent)**

"It allows me to move away from feeling like I'm reading from my lecture notes, but rather am able to have a more natural flow prompted by slides."

"I think that PowerPoint makes me more effective in the sense that it gives me confidence, and gives me something to refer to if I have a moment of panic."

---

**Table 4**  Instructor Perceptions of PowerPoint

*Note:* Percentages are calculated from the number of responses to each open-ended question. Some respondents left one or more of the open-ended questions unanswered.

increases learning by "breaking down" course material and helping "students to clearly follow the lecture."

Instructors enjoyed that slides enable them to "communicate key points to students." This appreciation, however, was tinged by uneasiness with what they see as PowerPoint's tendency to dilute knowledge, and their explanations of their slide usage revealed tension between the value of clarification and the problem of oversimplification. Instructors were aware that students desire presentations with, as one explained, "not too much text on each slide," and most reported they use PowerPoint for overviews and outlines. Though distillation illuminates basic information, it may do so by oversimplifying complex material. Half of the instructors who praised clarity also worried that slideware breaks down information too much and were concerned that excessive parsimony could deter learning. They mentioned that slides can present information as misleadingly simple and uniform—one instructor wrote, "I sometimes have a concern that students will think that the takeaway from the content of the lecture can be distilled into the slides." Another frequent user expressed this tension:

> PowerPoint simplifies and dumbs down the info for them into neat little bullet points. The reality of our social world is often messier and more complicated than that which can be expressed by neat little bullet points. Because the info is already synthesized for them in PP slides, the students are less responsible for (and increasingly less capable of) picking out the crucial elements of a lecture, as they always have the slides to fall back on.

Of the majority who cited improved clarity as their primary reason for use, a significant portion also expressed concern that PowerPoint's inherent tendency to oversimplify could threaten learning.

## Education and Entertainment

According to survey responses, instructional PowerPoint gives rise to a second dilemma—a tension between entertaining and educating. Although the technology successfully captures learners' attention, some students and many instructors reported that this might prove to be more diversion than useful tool. The learning goals in sociological education typically extend far beyond knowledge transmission—in fact, because the discipline has a particularly powerful ability to inspire critical thinking, "teaching *only* the content of [the] discipline may do students a real disservice" (Fobes and Kaufman 2008; Roberts 2002:2). Thus, sociological learning objectives commonly include developing analytical reasoning abilities, inspiring creativity, and establishing the foundations necessary for critical intellectual growth—all vital parts of the sociological imagination. Learning experts maintain that these goals are best achieved through active learning that requires students to expend cognitive energy to reach understanding. Key features of active learning—discussions and exchanges, questions, improvisations, and off-the-map developments—ensure that learners actively participate in knowledge creation rather than simply passively consume information. When students reflectively engage by talking about what they know, questioning what they don't, and interacting with instructors and peers, they develop the ability to understand and apply what they have learned. In contrast, learning that consists of information consumption and little else may be more entertainment than education. Classrooms in which students take notes instead of actively engaging with material are little different from movie theaters—both are arenas of passive entertainment rather than active knowledge construction.

This education/entertainment dilemma plainly was apparent in survey responses. Students overwhelmingly reported that slideshow presentations capture their interest—most agreed that slides help them pay attention (Table 2), and 30 percent commented that they feel PowerPoint helps them, as several students put it, "stay awake" in class. One undergraduate explained that presentations are useful because "they give me something to look at so I don't get distracted by other things." Although slideware does the important job of capturing students' attention, it could discourage in-depth, reflective engagement. Responses from the undergraduate survey indicated that the technology is less useful for engaging discussion than for any other task. Students' written comments further illuminated this: Several noted that although graphics help them focus, they sorely missed the active discussions that they felt slideshows discouraged. According to one respondent, PowerPoint "monopolizes the class and leaves little opportunity for discussion or interaction."

Students frequently mentioned that PowerPoint "makes class less exciting" because it compels them to replicate what they see on slides, a task that they feel consumes their classroom experience. Indeed, the overwhelming majority of students (82 percent) answered that they focus on copying projected words into their notes. Although transcribing information requires students to focus to a certain degree, this type of attention can be mindless, unreflective, and even counterproductive. Many students were aware of this problem and admitted that copying slides negatively affects their learning, as one student explained:

> I frequently write down blindly anything that is written on the Power Point without absorbing it until studying for the test. Also, when I'm copying down the Power Point words I'm not usually listening to the instructor. Power Point minimizes the engagement I have with a class and instead condenses it into a few slides with bullet points.

Some undergraduates reported that focusing on copying projected words distracts them from the meaning and context of the topics being discussed; as another student commented, slides make it "easy to lose focus on the topic and JUST copy PowerPoints without engaging in the topic." These critiques make it clear that although slides capture notice, thoughtful engagement and attention are not one in the same.

The worry over entertainment and education was more troubling to sociology instructors. Their open-ended comments revealed a deep and broadly shared concern that PowerPoint distracts and fosters passivity among students. Those who never or infrequently use the software were most critical of the ways it shapes classroom dynamic; as one infrequent user noted, the technology "often makes class discussions less engaging. Students focus on 'writing notes' . . . instead of engaging in critical thought and discussion." In fact, passivity was the most cited reason that non- and infrequent users rejected slideware. Regular users of the technology were less critical, but did express anxiety over the disengaged, entertainment-like nature of slideshows. Many instructors expressed suspicion that students' copying of projected information may inhibit discussion, as one commented, "I do worry that they may become too reliant on [slides] (rather than paying close attention to the lecture and taking their own notes)."

Instructors were also highly critical of PowerPoint's influence on pedagogy—all agreed that the technology shapes instruction, and most commented that it does so in ways that inhibit engaged, interactive teaching. Again, non- and infrequent users were most critical of PowerPoint instruction. One non-using faculty member noted that it "has nothing to do with teaching and learning," and another remarked that it is "not as effective as raw teaching." While frequent users were most likely to report that slides improve teaching, many also conceded that streamlined lectures can sometimes make classes more like "entertainment" or a "show" and less interactive and spontaneous. These instructors worried that slides may create distance between themselves and their students. One reflected, "I feel PowerPoint lowers my engagement with students," and another admitted, "it takes away some of the spontaneous nature of class discussions, [and] limits students' active participation sometimes." Slide-using instructors also mentioned that PowerPoint can constrict creativity, as one explained, "[it] puts me in lecture mode [and is] less interactive." The majority of users noted that slides make ad hoc interactions and off-the-cuff examples a challenge, as another explained:

> Occasionally, I discuss topics in a different order than I originally planned, which makes more sense in the context of a class discussion or a student question. That can be difficult to coordinate with the PowerPoint. Sometimes I feel like I have to "teach to the PowerPoint."

Thus, on one hand, most students and instructors agree that slideware aids learning by capturing attention and organizing teaching. On the other, however, reports of disengaged teaching and learning behaviors indicate that the technology may be passively entertaining rather than actively educating learners.

## Career Pragmatism and Pedagogical Commitment

Finally, instructors' reflections unveiled a third dilemma brought forth by instructional PowerPoint—there exists a significant tension between career pragmatism and pedagogical commitments. Though the majority of sociology instructors expressed at least some unease regarding the technology's pedagogical merit, most use it regularly. Many instructors explained that they continue to use slideware in spite of their concerns because they know students expect and desire it, as one noted: "I think that students want an outline. They don't want every word the professor says." Awareness of and compliance with this expectation was most prevalent among graduate student instructors, as one explained:

> The first time I taught, I didn't use PowerPoint for the first half of the semester, and on my mid-semester evaluation (that I hand out to see how things are going generally for the students), there was such a big request for PowerPoint that I used it in every class after that.

Instructors' discussions of student expectations were marked by hesitation and concern over the true educational value of the technology. One commented, "I think unfortunately [students] expect it. . . . Also—it is contributing, sadly, to [an] atmosphere of each class meeting as a drop-in experience and really more like distance learning." Another instructor agreed that the student-PowerPoint relationship has become "a hugely problematic expectation" because "there are numerous situations in which . . . their education would be better served by digesting data in a less formalized or summarized manner."

Slideware-using instructors were conflicted over their decision to integrate PowerPoint into their classes. While many recognized the importance of teaching in ways that students enjoy, they also noted that slides might not always be best for learning. Instructors indicated that student preference for slide-augmented lectures had become so prevalent that it was now an expectation they felt pressured to conform to. A full professor with over 20 years of teaching experience demonstrated the strong pull of PowerPoint culture, remarking, "I believe in the power of the presentation and class interactions. PowerPoint detracts. Having said that, I will move toward PowerPoint in a major way next year, and use it quite a bit." For some instructors, when student expectations and teaching ideology are at odds, demand trumps philosophy.

Several of those most conflicted by this dilemma noted that the institutional pressure to receive positive student evaluations of teaching lay at the heart of their compromise. Teaching evaluations play a major role in career success—they are often the primary means by which schools evaluate teaching and are routinely used for hiring and promotion decisions (Delucchi and Smith 1997; Kulik 2001; Sojka, Gupta, and Deeter-Schmelz 2002). Given that instructors who meet student expectations receive better evaluations and that today's students expect PowerPoint, it is not surprising that instructors incorporate the technology to boost their evaluations (Greenwald and Gillmore 1997; Williams and Ceci 1997). In fact, this approach has proven rewarding, as "many lecturers, to their delight, discovered that teaching scores and student satisfaction improved with the use of PowerPoint" (Gabriel 2008:257; see also Delucchi 2000; Delucchi and Korgen 2002; Titus 2008).

The lure of tailoring teaching to meet student preferences is directly related to pragmatic concerns about career success. This may be even more powerful for newer instructors who do not have the security of tenure and are often adjunct or contingent lecturers. Indeed, we found graduate students were most vocal about the dilemma of pedagogical commitment and career pragmatism, as one noted:

> I am still inclined to use PowerPoint because my future career is dependent upon good teaching evals, which only happen when the students are happy with the class. They like and expect their profs to use PowerPoint. . . . Unfortunately, I also perpetuate the overuse of PowerPoint out of fear of being unfavorably compared to my colleagues who all use Power-

Point and post the slides online. I'm troubled by the fact that I often decide to use and post PP slides because my teaching evals would suffer if I didn't, not because I think PP is always the best thing for their intellectual development or understanding of the subject matter.

The software's ubiquity, popularity with students, and instructors' perceptions of student expectations speak to a growing PowerPoint culture in the university—it has become a normative feature of academic instruction. It is important to recognize that this norm carries several potentially problematic implications. While students enjoy slides and instructors continue to use them, both users and consumers recognize that PowerPoint can shape learning environments and experiences in positive and negative ways.

# Conclusion

The sociology instructor who concluded "I am ambivalent about PowerPoint. Sometimes it helps the quality of discussion tremendously and sometimes it is distracting" perhaps best summarizes our study. While the technology has a great many advantages, these advantages may also have negative consequences for lasting learning. The dilemmas identified by our research contribute to an ongoing debate in the academic scholarship surrounding PowerPoint pedagogy. While many have concluded that PowerPoint should be used in academia, others have expressed concerns about how it has transformed teaching and learning. Our exploration of the issues surrounding PowerPoint in the university provides support for both advocates and critics of the software. We found that undergraduates expect and enjoy instructional use of PowerPoint, and sociology instructors who use the software often find it to be a useful teaching tool. We also found that classroom slideshows may negatively influence-earning by encouraging mindless copying and discouraging questions and participation.

Future research comparing classroom dynamics and long-term learning outcomes of students in PowerPoint and non-PowerPoint courses would be useful for identifying the mechanics of how this technology influences learning. In addition, studies with larger and more diverse samples could answer important questions regarding the possible impact of class size (Are slideshows appreciated more in larger classes than smaller classes?), student demographics (Do factors such as student major, gender, or other characteristics influence how learners feel about the technology?), and course content (Are intro students more apt to enjoy slideware than upper-level students?). Finally, empirical evaluation of the various strategies instructors employ to make slides a tool for engaged learning would be enlightening for practice.

It would be a mistake to "overlook the over-whelming influence of this software presentation tool on today's educational culture, particularly in redefining what a lecture looks like, consists of, and how it is experienced" (Adams 2006:408). Whether one agrees that the technology is a tool for conveying information in a clear and engaging way or sees that even thoughtful use cannot escape an inexorable cognitive style that oversimplifies material and fosters passivity, it is impossible to deny that slide software has had transformative repercussions for education. Reflexively considering the costs and benefits of PowerPoint is essential for educators concerned with creating effective learning environments that inspire and nurture developing sociological imaginations.

# Note

Reviewers for this manuscript were, in alphabetical order, Anne F. Eisenberg and Karl R. Kunkel.

# References

Adams, Catherine. 2006. "PowerPoint, Habits of Mind, and Classroom Culture." *Journal of Curriculum Studies* 38(4):389–411.

Bartsch, Robert A. and Kristi M. Cobern. 2003. "Effectiveness of PowerPoint Presentations in Lectures." *Computers and Education* 41(1):77–86.

Benson, Denzel E., Wava Haney, Tracy E. Ore, Caroline Hodges Persell, Aileen Schulte, James Steele, and Idee Winfield. 2002. "Digital Technologies and the Scholarship of Teaching and Learning in Sociology." *Teaching Sociology* 30(2):140–57.

Bogdan, Robert and Sari Knoop Biklen. 2007. *Qualitative Research for Education*. Boston: Allyn and Bacon.

Burke, Lisa A. and Karen E. James. 2008. "PowerPoint-based Lectures in Business Education: An Empirical Investigation of Student-perceived Novelty and Effectiveness." *Business Communication Quarterly* 71(3):277–96.

Cooper, Elizabeth. 2009. "Overloading on Slides: Cognitive Load Theory and Microsoft's Slide Program PowerPoint." *Association for the Advancement of Computing in Education Journal* 17(2):127–35.

Craig, Russell J. and Joel H. Amernic. 2006. "PowerPoint Presentation Technology and the Dynamics of Teaching." *Innovative Higher Education* 31(3):147–60.

Creed, Tom. 1997. "PowerPoint, No! Cyberspace, Yes." *The National Teaching and Learning Forum*. Retrieved July 26, 2010 (http://www.ntlf.com/html/sf/cyberspace.htm

Cyphert, Dale. 2004. "The Problem of PowerPoint: Visual Aid or Visual Rhetoric?" *Business Communication Quarterly* 67(1):80–84.

Delucchi, Michael. 2000. "Don't Worry, Be Happy: Instructor Likeability, Student Perceptions of Learning, and Teacher Ratings in Upper-level Sociology Courses." *Teaching Sociology* 22(3):220–31.

Delucchi, Michael and Kathleen Korgen. 2002. "'We're the Customer—We Pay the Tuition': Student Consumerism among Undergraduate Sociology Majors." *Teaching Sociology* 30(1):100–07.

Delucchi, Michael and William L. Smith. 1997. "Satisfied Customers versus Pedagogic Responsibility: Further Thoughts on Student Consumerism." *Teaching Sociology* 25(4):336–37.

Dietz, Tracy L. 2002. "Predictors of Success in Large Enrollment Introductory Courses: An Examination of the Impact of Learning Communities and Virtual Learning Resources on Student Success in an Introductory Level Sociology Course." *Teaching Sociology* 30(1):80–88.

Fendrich, Laurie. 2010. "PowerlessPoint." *The Chronicle of Higher Education*, April 27. Retrieved July 27, 2010 (http://chronicle.com/blogs/brainstorm/powerlesspoint).

Fobes, Catherine and Peter Kaufman. 2008. "Critical Pedagogy in the Sociology Classroom: Challenges and Concerns." *Teaching Sociology* 36(1):26–33.

Gabriel, Yiannis. 2008. "Against the Tyranny of PowerPoint: Technology-in-use and Technology Abuse." *Organization Studies* 29(2):255–76.

Glaser, Barney and Anslem Strauss. 1967. *The Discovery of Grounded Theory: Strategies for Qualitative Research*. Chicago: Aldine.

Greenwald, Anthony G. and Gerald M. Gillmore. 1997. "No Pain, No Gain? The Importance of Measuring Course Workload in Student Ratings of Instruction." *Journal of Educational Psychology* 89(4):743–51.

Gries Laurie Ellen and Collin Gifford Brooke. 2010. "An Inconvenient Tool: Rethinking the Role of Slideware in the Writing Classroom." *Composition Studies* 38(1):9–26.

Howard, Jay R. 2005. "An Examination of Student Learning in Introductory Sociology at a Commuter Campus." *Teaching Sociology* 33(2):195–205.

Knoblauch, Hubert. 2008. "The Performance of Knowledge: Pointing and Knowledge in Powerpoint Presentations." *Cultural Sociology* 2(1):75–97.

Koeber, Charles. 2005. "Introducing Multimedia Presentations and a Course Website to an Introductory Sociology Course: How Technology Affects Student Perceptions of Teaching Effectiveness." *Teaching Sociology* 33(3):285–300.

Kulik, James A. 2001. "Student Ratings: Validity, Utility, and Controversy." Pp. 9–25 in *The Student Ratings Debate: Are They Valid? How Can We Best Use Them?*, edited by M. Theall, P. C. Abrami, and L. A. Mets. San Francisco: Jossey-Bass.

Kunkel, Karl R. 2004. "A Research Note Assessing the Benefit of Presentation Software in Two Different Lecture Courses." *Teaching Sociology* 32(2):188–96.

Levasseur, David G. and J. Kanan Sawyer. 2006. "Pedagogy Meets PowerPoint: A Research Review of the Effects of Computer-generated Slides in the Classroom." *The Review of Communication* 6(1/2):101–23.

Mackiewicz, Jo. 2008. "Comparing PowerPoint Experts' and University Students' Opinions about PowerPoint Presentations." *Journal of Technical Writing and Communication* 38(2):149–65.

Mahin, Linda. 2004. "PowerPoint Pedagogy." *Business Communication Quarterly* 67(2):219–22.

MicrosoftCorporation.2012. "Make Over a Presentation with PowerPoint 2010." Retrieved February 6, 2012 (http://office.microsoft.com/en-us/makeovers/microsoft-powerpoint-2010-class-presentation-makeover-FX10 2237806.aspx).

Norvig, Peter. 2003. "PowerPoint: Shot with Its Own Bullets." *The Lancet* 362(9381):343–44.

Nowaczyk, Ronald H., Lyndee T. Santos, and Chad Patton. 1998. "Student Perception of Multimedia in the Undergraduate Classroom." *International Journal of Instructional Media* 25(1):367–68.

Parker, Ian. 2001. "Absolute PowerPoint." *The New Yorker*, May 28. Retrieved July 28, 2010 (http://www.newyorker.com/archive/2001/05/28/010528fa_fact_parker).

Persell, Caroline Hodges. 1992. "Bringing PCs into Introductory Sociology Courses: First Steps, Missteps, and Future Prospects." *Teaching Sociology* 20(2):91–103.

Pippert, Timothy and Helen A. Moore. 1999. "Multiple Perspectives on Multimedia in the Large Lecture Classroom." *Teaching Sociology* 37(2):92–103.

Reinhardt, Linda. 1999. "Confessions of a 'Techno-teacher.'" *College Teaching* 47(2):48–50.

Roberts, Keith A. 2002. "Ironies of Effective Teaching: Deep Structure Learning and Constructions of the Classroom." *Teaching Sociology* 30(1):1–25.

Simons, Tad. 2005. "Does PowerPoint Make You Stupid?" *Presentations*. Retrieved July 26, 2010 (http://www.sociablemedia.com/PDF/press_presentations_ magazine_03_01_04.pdf).

Sojka, Jane, Ashok K. Gupta, and Dawn R. Deeter-Schmelz. 2002. "Student and Faculty Perceptions of Student Evaluations of Teaching: A Study of Similarities and Differences." *College Teaching* 50(2):44–49.

Stoner, Mark K. 2007. "PowerPoint in a New Key." *Communication Education* 56(3):365–81.

Strauss, Anselm and Juliet Corbin. 2008. *Basics of Qualitative Research: Techniques and Procedures for Developing Grounded Theory*. 3rd ed. Thousand Oaks, CA: Sage.

Stryker, Christian. 2010. "Slideware Strategies for Mathematics Educators." *Journal of Mathematics Education at Teachers College* 1:46–50.

Susman, Mary Beth. 1988. "Developing Computer-based Education and Self-pacing for Introductory Sociology: A Teacher's Perspective." *Teaching Sociology* 16(1):74–77.

Susskind, Joshua E. 2005. "PowerPoint's Power in the Classroom: Enhancing Students' Self-efficacy and Attitudes." *Computers and Education* 45(2):203–15.

Titus, Jordan J. 2008. "Student Ratings in a Consumerist Academy: Leveraging Pedagogical Control and Authority." *Sociological Perspectives* 51(2):397–422.

Tufte, Edward. 2003a. *The Cognitive Style of PowerPoint*. Cheshire, CT: Graphics Press.

Tufte, Edward. 2003b. "PowerPoint Is Evil." *Wired Magazine*. Retrieved April 21, 2010 (http://www.wired.com/wired/archive/11.09/ppt2.html).

Weinraub, Herbert J. 1998. "Using Multimedia Authoring Software: The Effects on Student Learning Perceptions and Performance." *Financial Practice and Education* 8(2):88–92.

Williams, Wendy M. and Stephen J. Ceci. 1997. "'How'm I Doing?' Problems with Student Ratings of Instructors and Courses." *Change* 29(5):12–23.

Wilmoth, Janet and John Wybraniec. 1998. "Profits and Pitfalls: Thoughts on Using a Laptop Computer and Presentation Software to Teach Introductory Social Statistics." *Teaching Sociology* 26(3):166–78.

Young, Jeffrey R. 2004. "When Good Technology Means Bad Teaching." *Chronicle of Higher Education* 51(12): 31–36.

# Bios

**Andrea Hill** is a PhD candidate at Northeastern University, where she teaches courses such as Research Methods in Sociology, Social Theory, and Introduction to Sociology. Her research interests include the cultural dynamics of neoliberalism and the ways it is lived and felt in the daily lives of U.S. workers. She is currently researching the relationship between economic crisis and neoliberal ideologies and practices.

**Tammi Arford** is a PhD candidate at Northeastern University, where she teaches courses such as Deviant Behavior and Social Control and Drugs and Society. Her research interests include punishment and social control, deviance, criminology, and social theory.

**Amy Lubitow** is an assistant professor of sociology at Portland State University, where she teaches courses related to environmental sociology, social movements, health, and gender. Her research focuses on the environmental health movement and public policy efforts to regulate toxic chemicals.

**Leandra Smollin** is a PhD candidate at Northeastern University, where she teaches courses in the Sociology and Women, Gender, and Sexuality Studies programs. She is also a lecturer at Tufts University, where she teaches about gender-based social inequalities and social change. Her research interests focus on the intersections of race, class, gender, and sexuality; health and violence; and feminist theory and methodologies.

# Chapter 2 ■ "I'm Ambivalent about It": The Dilemmas of PowerPoint

## Questions for Discussion

1. As mentioned in the article, according to some educators, "Slide settings, which provide limited space for words, cultivate 'oversimplification by asking presenters to summarize key concepts in as few words as possible'" and that "presentations transform content into overly simple snippets or buzz phrases that elide intricacy and nuance." As researchers, how can outlining key concepts and focusing on buzz phrases serve to lure your patron into following up with you for more information? Specifically, how might it be beneficial for you to not provide all of your information in your presentation? How can you use your presentation as a jumping off point for a meaningful discussion?

2. The article outlines how some educators feel as though the classroom is transformed into a theater-like setting when using PowerPoint. Although some educators feel as though "Such a unidirectional environment is set up for one-way knowledge transmission rather than knowledge exchange and establishes 'a dominance relationship between speaker and audience,'" how might treating your presentation as a performance make the endeavor more successful? In what ways might this technique elicit more interest from your patron?

3. Citing another criticism of PowerPoint, the article states, "pre-planned organization inhibits instructor digressions, anecdotes, and creativity—moments that often inspire student questions that are so vitally important for effective learning." As a presenter, how can you plan out meaningful pauses in your presentation where your audience might be able to ask a relevant question or share a personal anecdote? How can you strike a balance between reading from your prepared slides and adding information and/or personal stories as you go along? What potential pitfalls could you run into by not pre-planning enough for your presentation?

4. As Hill, et al. explain, "In discussing what they most disliked about the software, many students found fault with its tendency to discourage discussion—approximately 12 percent of these responses expressed sentiments along the lines of one student's observation that '[PowerPoint] monopolizes the class and leaves little opportunity for discussion or interaction.'" Discuss with a partner: How can you build small moments in your presentation when your audience can react to what you are saying? What questions might you include in your slides that prompt the audience to turn to a neighbor and discuss the information? What other techniques might you use to get the audience more involved in the presentation?

5. Many students explained that they found PowerPoint useful because it "shortens up main points and makes them easier to understand" and has the ability to "outline material so students know what info is important and what they can forget." How can you strike a balance between disseminating only the most important information while still prompting your audience to think deeply about the information that may come up later on in the research process? How might you be selective in choosing to share information that is both necessary *and* thought-provoking?

6. One critic of PowerPoint cited in the article argues, in reference to students, "there are numerous situations in which . . . their education would be better served by digesting data in a less formalized or summarized matter." Discuss with a small group: Is it important to have your presentation "feel" formal in order for your patron to take your work seriously? How can you be creative while still maintaining a professional tone? What activities might you be able to add into your presentation to make the process less passive?

# Organizing Data in Tables and Charts: Different Criteria for Different Tasks

Jane E. Miller

■ ■ ■

## Introduction

Tables and charts are efficient tools for organizing numbers. Too often, however, students and quantitative analysts do not give much consideration to the order in which they present data in tables or charts. This lack of thought means that the sequence of items may not be compatible with the author's objectives, whether testing a hypothesis, describing a pattern or reporting data for others' use. The appropriate criteria for arranging data in tables or charts often differ depending on whether they are to be used primarily with or without a prose description. Tables or charts intended to pre-sent numbers as evidence to address a specific question or to accompany a description of a pattern are usually best organized so that they coordinate with the associated narrative. On the other hand, tables intended to present data for reference use such as periodic series from the Bureau of Labour Statistics or a national census might work better if structured so that readers can find the numbers of interest to them with little written guidance. These two broad objectives suggest very different considerations for organizing variables or response categories.

No one of these purposes is inherently more important than the other, but in many cases a particular objective can be identified for reporting numbers in a given type of document. For example, numbers presented in a science laboratory report or a history essay are usually being applied as evidence for a particular hypothesis or to illustrate a trend or other pattern. In such cases, empirical or theoretical criteria are frequently a sensible basis for arranging the data because that is how they will be discussed in the accompanying prose. In contrast, detailed reference data on population or income for each of a dozen or more dates or places might not come with a written description, so using a self-guiding convention is well-suited to such tasks. This article uses data from the U.S. Consumer Expenditure Survey to illustrate four approaches to organizing data within tables and charts, discussing the situations for which each approach might be preferred.

Table 1 presents data on major categories of expenditures from the 2002 Consumer Expenditure Survey (CEX). The CEX is conducted annually by the Bureau of Labor Statistics (BLS) using a diary survey form to collect detailed information on expenditures (U.S. Department of Labor 2004a). The information is then coded into the

| Item | Expenditures ($) |
|------|------------------|
| Average annual expenditures | 42,557 |
| Food | 5612 |
| Alcoholic beverages | 415 |
| Housing | 13,481 |
| Apparel and services | 1872 |
| Transportation | 7984 |
| Health care | 2410 |
| Entertainment | 2167 |
| Personal care products and services | 562 |
| Reading | 145 |
| Education | 771 |
| Tobacco products and supplies | 334 |
| Miscellaneous | 846 |
| Cash contributions | 1366 |
| Personal insurance and pensions | 4593 |

**Table 1**  Average annual expenditures by major expenditure category, a U.S. Consumer Expenditure Survey, 2002

*Source:* U.S. Department of Labor, Bureau of Labor Statistics, 2004a. Table 1.

[a]For all households with complete income reporting.

From *Teaching Statistics*, Volume 29 (3), August 2007, pp. 98–101. Copyright © 2007 John Wiley and Sons. Reprinted by permission.

standard categories shown in Table 1, which retains the original order of major expenditure categories from a standard BLS report (U.S. Department of Labor 2004b).

## *Organizing Data to Accompany a Prose Description*

When testing hypotheses or portraying trends or other patterns, it is helpful to organize your data in tables or charts in the order you will describe them. For such purposes, alphabetical order and the sequence of items from the original data source are poor organizing principles because they rarely correspond to substantively interesting or empirically relevant patterns. Consider Figure 1, which presents the information from Table 1 in chart form, again preserving the order of expenditure categories from the BLS report. The heights of the bars and the conceptual content of adjacent categories vary erratically, requiring readers to zigzag back and forth across the axes to identify the rank order of expenditure categories by dollar amount or to compare categories of necessities to one another or to non-necessities.

For similar reasons, Figure 2—which sequences the expenditure categories alphabetically—would also be a poor choice to accompany a description of empirical rankings or a discussion of necessities versus non-necessities.

Instead, to complement a prose description of a pattern, it is often sensible to arrange your data so that the audience can easily follow the associated narrative using the well-established conventions of tracking left-to-right and top-to-bottom within the table or chart. Before creating the table or chart or writing the associated prose, consider which of the organizing principles described below best matches the main point you wish to make. Arrange the rows and columns (or axes and legend) accordingly, and then describe the numbers in the same order as they appear in the table or chart.

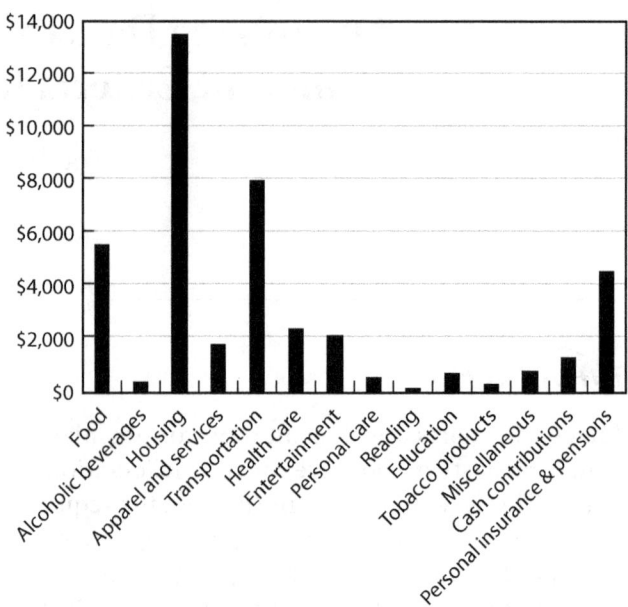

**Figure 1**   Major categories of expenditures, BLS ordering, 2002 U.S. Consumer Expenditure Survey

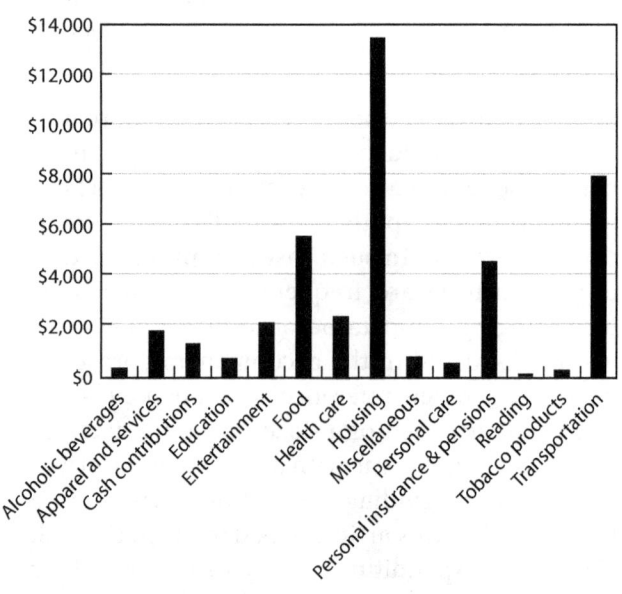

**Figure 2**   Major categories of expenditures, alphabetical order, 2002 U.S. Consumer Expenditure Survey

Which organizing criterion to use depends largely on the type of variables in question. When reporting results for ordinal variables such as age group or income quintile, the sequence of items in rows, columns or axes will be obvious. Likewise, it makes sense to follow the natural order of values for interval or ratio variables such as date, age in years or income in dollars or pounds.

For tables or charts that present nominal variables such as favourite flavour of ice cream, or items such as categories of consumer expenditures, the categories or variables lack an inherent order. In those instances, either empirical criteria or theoretical principles usually provide a good basis for deciding how to organize them.

## Empirical Ordering

For many tables or charts presenting distributions or associations, an important aim is to show which items have the highest and the lowest values and where other categories fall relative to those extremes. If this is your main point, it is often suitable to organize the categories in ascending or descending order of frequency or value. For example, Figure 3 shows major categories of consumer expenditures in descending order of dollar value.

## Theoretical Grouping

Arranging items into conceptually related sets can be very effective. For example, Duly (2003) reports statistics on consumer expenditures for necessities, which she defines as housing (including shelter and utilities but excluding other categories of housing-related expenses), food and apparel. To present the associated numbers, Figure 4 groups the expenditure categories into necessities on the left-hand side of the x-axis and non-necessities on the right-hand side, with axis titles to identify those classifications. A table version would comprise separate panels for necessities and non-necessities, each with rows reporting the respective component categories. The accompanying description could then contrast the relative shares of necessities and non-necessities without requiring the audience to meander all over the table or chart to find the pertinent numbers.

## Using Multiple Organizing Criteria

For tables or charts that present more than a few variables, a combination of approaches is often useful. For instance, consider grouping items theoretically and then arranging them within those groups in order of descending frequency or other empirical consideration. Figure 4 divides categories of consumer expenditures into necessities and non-necessities, and then organizes them in descending order of dollar value within each of those classifications, providing a useful structure for pointing out key patterns in the data.

Sometimes it makes sense to apply the same criterion sequentially, such as identifying major theoretical groupings and then minor topic groupings within them. Among the necessity categories of consumer expenditures are items related to housing, food and apparel, each with a major heading. Within each of those major categories would be minor categories and subcategories, such as shelter and utilities as subcategories under housing.

For charts or tables organized into several theoretically or empirically similar groups of items, alphabetical order can be a logical way to sequence items within those groups. For example, data on all the nations of the world might be grouped by continents, and then listed alphabetically within each continent. Alphabetizing within conceptual or empirical groupings also works well if several items have the same value of the statistics reported in the table (e.g., mean value or frequency).

## Writing a Narrative to Accompany the Table or Chart

Having created a table or chart that presents data in empirical or theoretical order, it is usually helpful to write the narrative to coordinate with that pattern, mentioning the organizing principle as you refer to the associated table or chart. For example, to describe the empirical pattern across categories of consumer expenditures, you might write:

> Figure 3 presents average consumer expenditures for the United States in 2002 in descending order of dollar value. Housing was the highest single highest expenditure category, followed by transportation, food and personal expenditures and pensions . . .

An analysis that compares necessities and non-necessities could read:

> Figure 4 shows average consumer expenditures for necessities and non-necessities in the U.S. in 2002. Among necessities, shelter was the highest. . . . Among non-necessities, transportation . . .

## *Organizing Data for Reference Use*

Reference documents typically include little if any prose description, so using a familiar convention or standard sequence is a sensible way to help readers find specific information quickly.

### Alphabetical Order

Alphabetical order is a widely understood organizing principle, commonly used in a variety of settings. For example, the daily stock market report of opening, closing, high and low prices effectively organizes thousands of numbers in a predictable format that readers can use without guidance.

### Order of Items from a Standard Document

Reference data from periodic surveys, censuses or surveillance systems are frequently best organized using the order of items from the original data collection instrument or following a standard coding or reporting scheme for that data source. People wishing to use those data often locate the variables

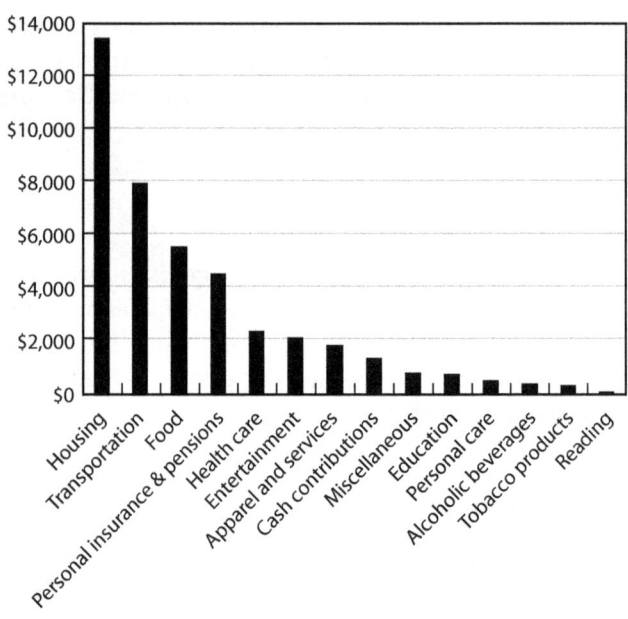

**Figure 3**   Major categories of expenditures, descending dollar value, 2002 U.S. Consumer Expenditure Survey

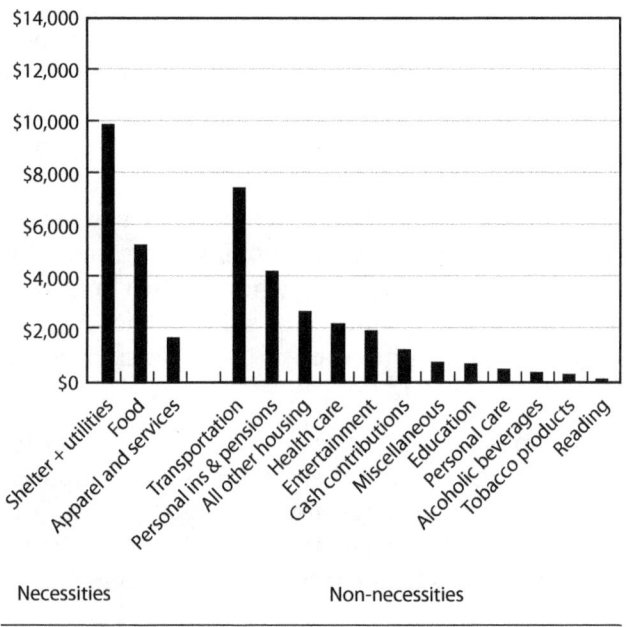

**Figure 4**   Descending dollar value of expenditures, necessities/non-necessities, 2002 U.S. Consumer Expenditure Survey

of interest using original documentation such as the code book, survey instrument or census form, or by consulting copies of earlier volumes of the same reference publication. Using that standardized approach to organize tables or charts of reference data facilitates users' collection efforts by maintaining consistency across sources. Table 1 above employs such an approach, presenting the expenditure categories in the standard order used in many BLS reports (U.S. Department of Labor 2004b). Having collected the data of interest to them, users can then organize those numbers to suit to their objectives, whether summarizing trends for a report or testing a hypothesis about relationships among variables.

## *Summary*

Using appropriate organizing principles can significantly enhance the efficacy of a quantitative description or increase the accessibility of reference data. Readers of this article who would like to go further into the issues explored here may find it useful to refer to Miller (2004).

## References

Duly, A. (2003). Consumer spending for necessities. *Monthly Labor Review,* **126**(5), 3. Available online at http://stats.bls.gov/opub/mlr/2003/05/art1full.pdf. Accessed June 2007.

Miller, J.E. (2004). *The Chicago Guide to Writing about Numbers.* The Chicago Guide to Writing, Editing, and Publishing. Chicago: University of Chicago Press.

U.S. Bureau of Labor Statistics (2004a). *Consumer Expenditure Survey, Diary Survey Form.* Available online at http://stats.bls.gov/cex/csx801p.pdf. Accessed June 2007.

U.S. Department of Labor, Bureau of Labor Statistics (2004b). *Consumer Expenditures in 2002.* Report 974. Available online at http://stats.bls.gov/cex/csxann02.pdf. Accessed June 2007.

# Chapter 2 ■ Organizing Data in Tables and Charts: Different Criteria for Different Tasks

## Questions for Discussion

1. In the introduction, Miller discusses the pros and cons of having figures integrated into the narrative of a document, as well as having them exist on their own so that readers can find the numbers they need with little written guidance. Consider each style. Which works better for your particular proposal? Why? Would your reader be able to understand the significance of your charts and graphs without any narrative guidance from you?

2. Many researchers choose to incorporate their charts and graphs directly into their narratives. How can the researcher introduce these text features in a way that provides just enough background information without making the charts and graphs seem superfluous?

3. Does your proposal more frequently discuss ordinal variables or nominal variables?

   a. If your proposal focuses mainly on ordinal variables, sketch out a few ideas for how you might be able to chart or graph this information based on Miller's guidelines on using rows, columns, and axes in clear sequences.

   b. If your proposal focuses mainly on nominal variables, the order in which you present your information may be a little less obvious. Create a plan for how this information could be presented in a way that seems logical and will be easy for the reader to follow.

4.  Miller discusses both empirical ordering and theoretical grouping as viable options for creating figures. Look back at Figures 3 and 4 and then list the pros and cons of each technique. As a researcher, which technique(s) do you intend implementing in your prospective proposal? Why?

5.  Figure 4 is useful in that it presents the information in a way that is organized both theoretically and empirically. Would any of your research be best understood if it was organized in this manner? Using your own research, create a rough draft of a figure that is organized in this way. Then, have a classmate read it to see if it is clear. Discuss the strengths and weaknesses of your figure.

6.  In what ways will you be more strategic about the presentation of your research after reading this piece? Will you focus more on simplifying your narratives so that your figures attract more attention? Will you better organize your figures so that they are easier to understand without a narrative introduction? Explain.

# The Missing Link: The Lack of Citations and Copyright Notices in Multimedia Presentations

Stephanie Huffman

## *Abstract*

Many of the projects and assignments we have our students complete for our classes include a multimedia presentation. Why are we not teaching our students how to cite their sources for these presentations? Writing style (APA, MLA, or Chicago) does not matter. Regardless of whether it is a paper or multimedia presentation students should always cite their sources, otherwise plagiarism is occurring. This is a skill we must teach and demand that our students take responsibility for when completing multimedia presentations. This article covers a brief overview of copyright law, provides helpful resources for students and teachers, and outlines a model that can be used in citing sources in multimedia presentations.

This model goes beyond the producer required credit slide to argue for the inclusion of "in product/ text" citations for multimedia presentations.

**Keywords:** Copyright, Fair Use, Intellectual Property, Multimedia

As part of our course requirements, we offer and encourage students to integrate technology within their assignments. One of the fundamental techniques is the multi-media presentation. We are excited by their use of images, text, video, and audio as a means of expression. Yet, we allow or overlook the fact that often they do not give credit for the use of others' work within the multimedia presentation. We set and demand high standards for our students concerning the papers they submit for evaluation. We would be displeased with, and likely not accept, work that was not formatted or appropriately cited for others' works.

Our students are not alone. As part of our scholarly activity, we present our research at professional conferences and attend sessions for professional development. This is a vital part of sustained professional growth, as well as serving as an avenue for contributing to the overall body of knowledge in academia. In addition, we use multimedia presentations as a guide for our classroom lectures. Yet, the lack of citations and copyright notices is glaring and shocking. We can and must hold ourselves to a higher standard.

## Why the Lack of Citations?

First, most do not understand that legally, regardless of the format used for expression or communication, credit must still be given to the authors/designers/photographers, etc., of works that are used as a foundation for professional presentations, classroom lectures, videos, teaching materials, and student work. Yes, we are made allowances under the *Copyright Fair Use Guidelines,* but *Fair Use* does not give us free reign. We must take responsibility. We must do everything within our power to ensure that proper credit is given.

Second, those faculty and students who do understand they should be citing sources do not know how to successfully accomplish this task or to what extent. There are numerous formatting guidelines for research papers and manuscripts (e.g., APA, MLA, Chicago), yet none of these publication manuals provide outlines or guidance in the realm of formatting "in product/text" citations for multimedia presentations. They do provide guidance in citing multimedia sources within a paper or manuscript and format of bibliographic citations listed on the reference page, works cited page, bibliography, etc. Scholars have written numerous articles about the necessity to cite sources when using these new media, the latest being the Code of Best Practices in Fair Use for Media Literacy published in November of 2008 in *Education Week.* "Whenever possible, educators should provide attribution for quoted materials, and of course they should use only what is necessary." (National Council of Teachers of English, 2008, p 11) Section 6.2 of, *The Fair Use Guidelines for Educational Multimedia* (1996), delineates the requirements for attribution and acknowledgments. Specifically, producers only require a credit slide for multimedia presentations. Should we not be doing more than this especially in regard to the text included within the multimedia presentation?

Therefore, the purpose of this article is twofold: 1) to provide some basic background information on intellectual property; and, 2) to share a guide/model for citing sources in a multimedia presentation; thus addressing the two major reasons for the lack of citations.

# Intellectual Property

Products developed as a direct result of human activity are intellectual property. These products might include songs, designs, clothing, and inventions. Intellectual property refers to any intangible asset. "Intellectual property establishes how and when a person and society as a whole can benefit and profit from someone's creation." (Waxer & Baum, 2006, p 5) The treatment of tangible property versus intangible ideas can be difficult to understand. Notwithstanding a natural disaster, tangible property passes from owner to heir, unless sold. Intangible property cannot disappear. Property rights extend to the owner's heirs for decades after death. This contentious aspect of intangible property inspires argument and litigation as the law evolves in a constantly changing world.

The origins of intellectual property law are outlined in the United States Constitution, Article 1, Section 8, and Clause 8. "Congress has the power to promote the progress of science and useful arts, by securing for limited time to authors and inventors the exclusive right to their respective writings and discoveries." (Waxer & Baum, 2006, p. 6) There are seven categories of Intellectual Property. Copyright is the one most familiar and applicable to educators. Copyright law protects the expression of an idea but not the underlying idea itself. For example, subject matter is not protected, but the matter in which it is expressed is protected. There are eight main categories of copyrighted works: 1) literary works, 2) musical works, 3) dramatic works, 4) pantomimes and choreographic works, 5) pictorial, graphic, and sculptural works, 6) motion pictures and audiovisual works, 7) sound recordings, and 8) architectural works.

Copyright in most instances is the life of the author plus 70 years. Joint authorship, corporate authorship, old law copyright extensions, and the rights of copyright heirs are a few exceptions that could affect the length of the copyright. For these instances further examination of copyright law is recommended, but for most purposes only a basic understanding is needed. At one time, it was life plus 50 years, but that changed in 1998 when Congress enacted the Sonny Bono Copyright Extension Act. (Underwood & Webb, 2006) A work enters public domain once the copyright lapses. The rights of the copyright owner are extended to five broad areas: 1) to reproduce the work, 2) to distribute the work publicly, 3) to make derivative works, 4) to display the work publicly, and to allow public performance of the work.

# Fair Use

"Fair use is an essential balance to the wide range of rights that copyright law grants to copyright owners. Remember, even simple quoting can constitute an unlawful reproduction of the original work." (Crews, 2004, p. 48) By simply citing our sources (giving the author credit and avoiding plagiarism), we are following fair use, although limits do apply. One must weigh four factors to determine if fair use is applied. For fair use to apply, the new work must be transformative, thus meaning the work is transformed into something new or of a new utility. For example, quoted text incorporated into a paper or pieces of mixed media put into a multimedia product for teaching purposes (Underwood & Webb, 2006). The second determining factor is nature. Nature refers to the characteristics of the work. Third, one must consider the amount of usage. Both quantity and quality define the amount of usage. The law does not outline an exact measure (quantity). The final factor is the potential impact on the market for, or value of, the original work; this directly links to the other three factors. The first three factors establish a baseline for the potential impact of the market place for the work. If the amount of the work used will influence the market value of the original work, then it is a copyright violation.

It is important to remember that copyright law is in constant flux, therefore, it is noted that the information previously outlined is a cursory treatment of copyright law and the Fair Use guidelines. It is recommended that every reader familiarize him or herself further with more detail. Listed below are excellent Web resources for information on fair use and copyright guidelines:

- Books, Periodicals, Music and Off-air Recordings http://www.musiclibraryassoc.org/copyright/
- Videotapes and Computer Software http://www.ifla.org/en/publications/the-ifla-position-on-copyright-in-the-digital-environment
- Visual Images, Distance Learning, and Multimedia http://www.uspto.gov/web/offices/dcom/olia/confu/conclu2.html
- Library of Congress: United States Copyright Office http://www.copyright.gov/
- Fair Use Guidelines for Educational Multi-media http://www.adec.edu/admin/papers/fair10-17.html
- A Proposal for Educational Fair Use Guidelines for Digital Images http://www.utsystem.edu/ogc/intellectual-property/imagguid.htm
- Copyright and Fair Use in the Classroom http://www.umuc.edu/library/copy.shtml
- Copyright and Other Legal Information http://www.libraries.psu.edu/mtss/resources/copyright.html

## Extending Accountability

As educational technology leaders we must first hold ourselves accountable for our work and second hold our students accountable for their work. Regardless of the vehicle with which our students or we choose to communicate, we must give respect to the work of others. Knowing the rules that govern copyright is just the beginning. The difficulty begins with explaining the importance of compliance to students who are lackadaisical in following any societal rule (Hoffman, 2001). So, why would they be concerned with copyright law? Extending accountability is essential to academic integrity, professionalism, and ethical behavior. Our expectations for students should be the same, as those we demand of ourselves. Educators need to be leaders, not followers in establishing best practices, holding themselves accountable, and extending that accountability to their students (NCTE, 2008).

As stated earlier the, *Fair Use Guidelines for Educational Multimedia* (1996), producers only require a credit slide for multimedia presentations. We should at least include a credit slide (reference slide) for our multimedia presentations and for those of our students. An argument can be made and should be made for extending accountability beyond this point. When requiring our students to write a paper or when developing a manuscript for publication, accountability is extended beyond the reference page. Within the body of the paper, "in text" citations are required and provide a *link* to copyrighted material listed on the reference page. These "in text-citations" distinguish the work of others from our work. When using photos, images, or figures created by others in a paper or manuscript a caption is required. Multimedia presentations have become extensions or substitutions (in some cases) to the term paper required of our students and for our research and manuscripts.

Why should these fundamental guidelines not be extended to the multimedia presentation? They should be. Otherwise, how are we distinguishing our work from the work of others within the presentation itself? Is plagiarism not occurring? Anyone might be accused of plagiarism if he or she only included a reference page for a paper and did not include in text-citations. As outlined by the, *Publication Manual of the American Psychological Association, 5th Edition,* "psychologists do not claim the words and ideas of another as their own; they give credit where credit is due. Quotation marks should be used to indicate the exact words of another. Each time you paraphrase another author, you will need to credit the source in the text." (American Psychological Association, 2001, p. 349) Ethical principles are imperative in ensuring the integrity of knowledge and to protect the intellectual property rights of others.

Thus, the main thrust for this article, which is to share a model for citing sources in multimedia presentations. The model goes beyond the mere producer requirement of a credit slide to include in-product/text citations, captions for images, figures, audio clips, and video clips, and an appendix slide for documenting free sources. There is a missing link between the content slides and the reference slide in multimedia presentations.

It should be noted that this model is specifically designed for multimedia presentations. It does not lend itself to other forms of multimedia. Although an argument can be made for the creation of models for the other various forms of multimedia. As was done in the past for written forms of communications, the links between the content of the product and the reference page should be included in order to remove all doubt as to the author of the ideas used to generate the product.

## Huffman Multimedia Presentation Model for Citing Sources

This model was developed by reviewing the current literature on citing sources, applying the formatting and design principles used in Microsoft PowerPoint, and applying guidelines outlined in the, *Publication Manual of the American Psychological Association (APA).* (Huffman & Rickman, 2008) Unless the information included within the multimedia presentation is one's original work, then the following set of basic components should be included.

1. General Guidelines

   a. "Use only lawfully acquired copyrighted works or self created works." (Simpson, p. 10, 2005)
   b. All pictures, files, or text taken from the Internet must be from a free site, found in public domain, or authorized by a webmaster/author. APA recommends obtaining written permission for reuse (for both print and electronic form) from the copyright holder.
   c. One may not modify scanned images, video clips, or audio clips without permission. (Walter, 1998) One must note all alteration in an appendix.
   d. Select a publication style to use as a guide for formatting citations (e.g., APA, MLA, Chicago).

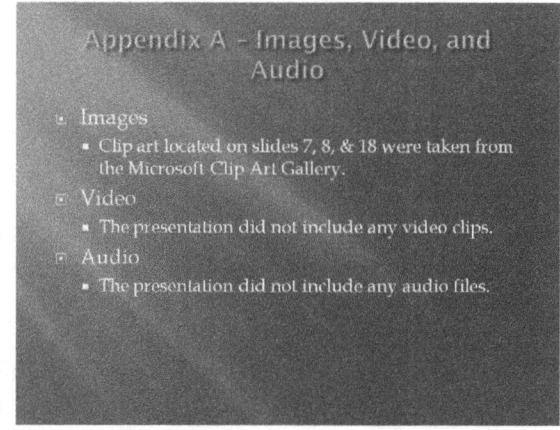

**Figure 1** Appendix Slide from the Digital Responsibility presentation delivered by Stephanie Huffman and Wendy Rickman at the Southeast Regional Association of Teacher Educators Annual Conference in November of 2008.

2. Specific Formatting Guidelines

   a. The basic sequence of screens/slides is as follows: 1) title slide, 2) content slides, 3) reference slide, and 4) appendix.

   b. Place a copyright notice on the opening screen or slide. (Walters, 1998) For example, "Notice: Certain materials are included under the Fair Use exemptions of U.S. copyright law, and have been prepared according to the Educational Multimedia Fair Use Guidelines and are restricted from further use."

   c. Acknowledge all sources used to create a screen or slide with a bibliographic citation, with an in product/text citation. Follow the rules outlined by the publication manual for specific format. The example demonstrates APA format for the in product/text citation.

   d. Single Column Layout

      i. If only one source is used for that screen or slide, then the citation is placed at the bottom of the slide aligned with the text. Placement of the citation in this location allows for maximum use of space on the screen/slide (see Figure 3).

      ii. If multiple sources are used for the content of the screen/slide, the citation is placed immediately following the text. If the text is directly quoted from the source, it is placed in quotation marks and a page number is included within the citation.

      iii. If the text is original (i.e., one's own thoughts & ideas), then no citation is necessary.

Figure 2   Title Slide from the Digital Responsibility presentation delivered by Stephanie Huffman and Wendy Rickman at the Southeast Regional Association of Teacher Educators Annual Conference in November of 2008.

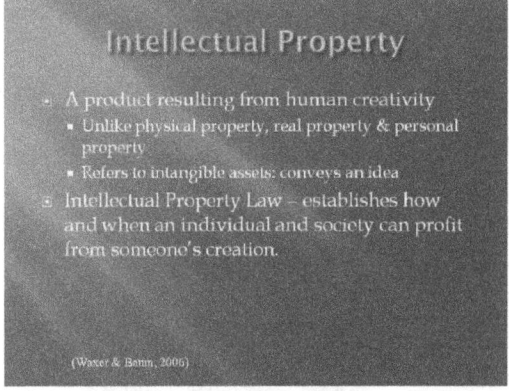

Figure 3   Intellectual Property Slide from the Digital Responsibility presentation delivered by Stephanie Huffman and Wendy Rickman at the Southeast Association of Teacher Educators Annual Conference in November of 2008.

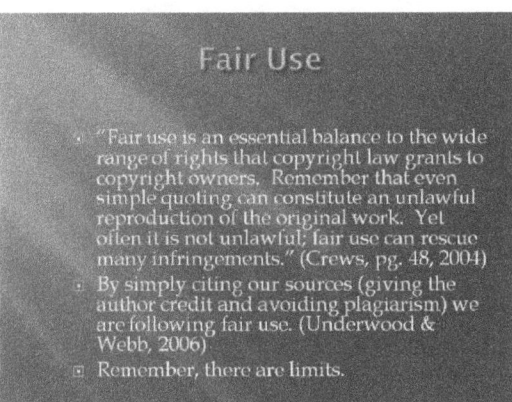

Figure 4   Fair Use Slide from the Digital Responsibility presentation delivered by Stephanie Huffman and Wendy Rickman at the Southeast Association of Teacher Educators Annual Conference in November of 2008.

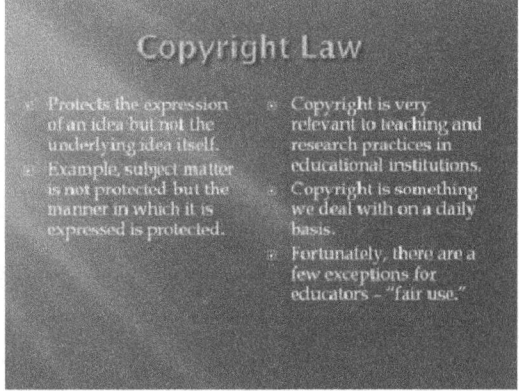

Figure 5   Copyright Law Slide from the Digital Responsibility presentation delivered by Stephanie Huffman and Wendy Rickman at the Southeast Association of Teacher Educators Annual Conference in November of 2008.

e. Multiple Column Screen/Slide Layout

   i. The same rules apply as outlined for single column layout.

   ii. Each column should be treated as a separate unit.

   iii. If only one source is used for the contents of the column, then the citation is placed at the bottom of the column aligned with the text.

   iv. If multiple sources are used for the content of the column, the citation is placed immediately following the text.

   v. If the text is quoted directly from the source, it is placed in quotation marks and a page number is included within the citation.

   vi. If the text is original, no citation is necessary.

f. Images (including tables and illustrations), Video, and Audio

   i. Images

      1. APA requires that a caption be created and that the author and copyright holder be acknowledged. "Any reproduced table (or figure) must be accompanied by a note at the bottom of the reprinted table (or in the figure caption) giving credit to original author and to the copyright holder." (American Psychological Association, 2001, p. 174)

      2. Due to limited space on a slide/screen, modifications to this rule are necessary. A brief caption is included along with an in product/text citation on the slide/screen in which the image appears. A full bibliographic citation is placed on the reference slide.

   ii. Video clips and Audio clips

      1. APA requires an in product/text citation and a full bibliographic citation on the reference page for papers and manuscripts. Because of the nature of multimedia presentations (icons used as placeholders for clips), this rule has been modified.

      2. Since the icon (placeholder for the clip) becomes an image, the same format discussed above should be utilized for giving credit to the author of the clips. A brief caption is included along with an in

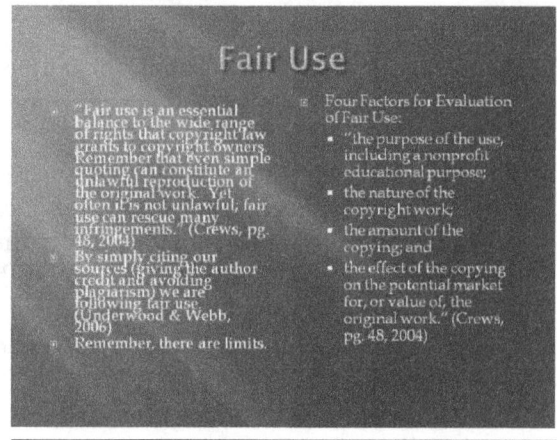

**Figure 6** Fair Use Slide from the Digital Responsibility presentation delivered by Stephanie Huffman and Wendy Rickman at the Southeast Association of Teacher Educators Annual Conference in November of 2008.

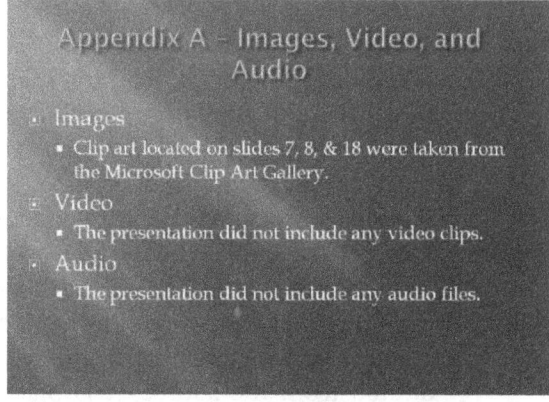

**Figure 7** Appendix Slide (Version #2) from the Digital Responsibility presentation delivered by Stephanie Huffman and Wendy Rickman at the Southeast Association of Teacher Educators Annual Conference in November of 2008.

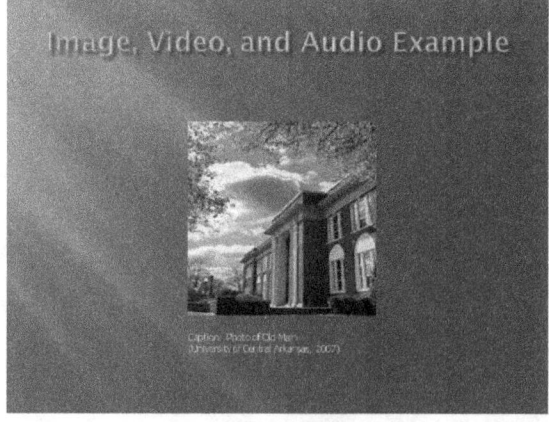

**Figure 8** Image Slide from the Digital Responsibility presentation delivered by Stephanie Huffman and Wendy Rickman at the Southeast Association of Teacher Educators Annual Conference in November of 2008.

product/text citation on the slide/screen in which the audio or video appears. A full bibliographic citation is placed on the reference slide.

iii. Any image, video clip, or audio clip that is from a free source should be acknowledged by listing the source(s) in an appendix. This demonstrates a commitment to high ethical standards by documenting all sources. It also provides instructors with a way to check the integrity of the students' work with minimal effort.

iv. Any image, video clip, or audio clip that is not from a free source, should include a caption.

1. Due to space limitation, the caption should only include the title of the work. An abbreviated title can be used for works containing long titles.
2. The caption is place under the image, video icon, or audio icon, and should be aligned with the left most edge of the icon or image. The in product/text citation should be listed under the caption.
3. A caption is not included for any audio clip that plays in the background and/ or is part of the time sequencing of the presentation. If taken from a free source, it should be listed in the appendix. If not taken from a free source, a full bibliographic citation should be included with the references.
4. A full bibliographic citation for all images, video, and audio should be included with the references.

   a. The following is an example of a bibliographic citation for both audio and video clips.
   b. For more examples, consult the APA manual.

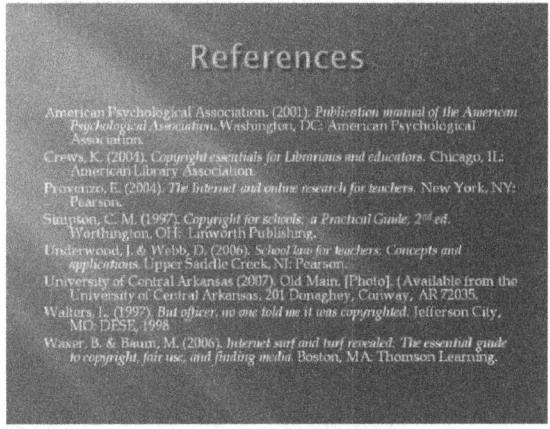

**Figure 9** APA Slide from the Digital Responsibility presentation delivered by Stephanie Huffman and Wendy Rickman at the Southeast Association of Teacher Educators Annual Conference in November of 2008.

**Figure 10** Reference Slide from the Digital Responsibility presentation delivered by Stephanie Huffman and Wendy Rickman at the Southeast Regional Association of Teacher Educators Annual Conference in November of 2008.

g. References

i. Include a reference slide, works cited page, or a bibliography slide at the end of the presentation.
ii. For more examples, consult the APA manual.

# Conclusion

Technology has drastically changed the way in which we share ideas and information. Faculty and students have unparalleled access to all types and forms of information (text, images, sound, and video). This level of access combined with the simplicity in which people can publish their work, presents a new level of complexity to the relevance of copyright law (Provenzo, 2004). In creating multimedia products, faculty and students may use lawfully acquired copyrighted works as long as proper credit and citations are included in the multimedia product. Care should be used in downloading material from Internet sites. Faculty and students should be aware that some copyrighted works have been posted to the Internet without authorization of the copyright holder. Therefore, it is vital that they contact the primary source to get permission to use the material.

The Huffman Multimedia Presentation Model provides a structure for citing sources that goes beyond the producer requirement of a credit slide (outlined in the Fair Use Guidelines for Educational Multimedia). It establishes a set format for "in product/text" citation placement and for the essential components necessary to insure that the Fair Use Guidelines of Copyright Law are being followed. Without structure, links between sources cited on the reference screen/slide and actual content are missing. Whether paraphrasing or quoting an author directly, one must give credit to the source; otherwise, plagiarism is occurring (American Psychological Association, 2001).

**Dr. Stephanie Huffman** is an Associate Professor of Library Media and Information Technologies at the University of Central Arkansas. She has published research on technology planning and leadership, distance education, and information literacy.

# References

American Psychological Association. (2001). Publication manual of the American Psychological Association. Washington, DC: American Psychological Association.

Crews, K. (2004). Copyright essentials for Librarians and educators. Chicago, IL: American Library Association.

Fair use guidelines for educational multimedia. (1996). Consortium of College and University Media Centers. Retrieved from http://www.adec.edu/admin/papers/fair10-17.html.

Hoffman, G. M. (2001). Copyright in cyberspace: questions and answers for librarians. NY: Neal-Schuman.

Huffman, S., & Rickman, W. (2008, November). Digital responsibility: Citing sources in multimedia presentations. Paper presentation for the 55th Annual Conference of the Southeastern Regional Association of Teacher Educators, Myrtle Beach, SC.

National Council of Teachers of English. (2008). Code of best practices in fair use for media literacy. Education Week, 1–20.

Provenzo, E. (2004). The Internet and online research for teachers. New York, NY: Pearson.

Simpson, C. M. (2005). Copyright for schools: a practical guide, 2nd ed. Worthington, OH: Linworth Publishing. Underwood, J. & Webb, D. (2006). School law for teachers: Concepts and applications. Upper Saddle Creek, NJ: Pearson.

University of Central Arkansas (2007). Old Main. [Photo]. (Available from the University of Central Arkansas, 201 Donaghey, Conway, AR 72035.)

Walters, L. (1997). But officer, no one told me it was copyrighted. Jefferson City, MO: DESE, 1998.

Waxer, B. & Baum, M. (2006). Internet surf and turf revealed: The essential guide to copyright, faire use, and finding media. Boston, MA: Thomson Learning.

# Chapter 2 ■ The Missing Link: The Lack of Citations and Copyright Notices in Multimedia Presentations

## Questions for Discussion

1. List, define, and explain the four characteristics of fair use.

   1.

   2.

   3.

   4.

2. a. In what ways will you ensure that the work you do with your sources is transformative?

   b. Based on the requirements of the final proposal, how will you make sure that your use of sources is balanced and fair? How can you make sure that the research you've done is backed by your own analysis in order to reasonably present your own proposal?

3. Have you discovered any models of success (songs, designs, clothing, inventions) in your research that would need to be protected by the intellectual property law? If so, explain how you will be able to employ this paradigm to shape your own plan without violating this law.

4. As you compile a number of sources, how do you plan on holding yourself accountable for making sure that you are using them fairly? How will you regulate using your resources to *guide* your plan rather than fully *dictate* it?

5. Review the section titled "Huffman Multimedia Presentation Model for Citing Sources." Create a list of guidelines that could potentially be problematic for you. Then, jot down ideas for possible solutions to these problems. If you are stuck, reach out to a fellow classmate or your instructor for feedback.

6. Define and discuss the following terms with a partner or small group:

   a. Intellectual Property

   b. Fair Use

   c. Accountability

   d. Copyright

   e. Plagiarism

   Make sure that everyone is clear about the definitions of each term and how they pertain to the research being done in this class.

7. Are you aware of the penalties associated with plagiarism at your university? Familiarize yourself with your school's academic integrity policies. Be sure to also check the policies of the department that is offering your course. List the guidelines you find for submitting original, research-based papers. Be prepared to discuss this with the class.

# The Job Search
# Assignment

*Chapter*

## The Assignment

Prepare a cover letter and résumé in response to a specific published job posting or advertisement. You will want to use a posting in a newspaper or online so that you can offer a print copy. You will want to have a copy of the job listing for peer review day and hand it in with your final draft.

Unless your instructor chooses to set forth more specific guidelines, this is the assignment:

- Each document must be one page only.

- You must submit the job announcement with your assignment.

- These documents need to be prepared according to standards discussed in class.

- They should be proofread closely so that there are no errors in either document.

- The assignment and any drafts discussed in class must be turned in according to the schedule set by your instructor.

The job advertisement must accompany the other documents on the day of peer review, since without it peers and instructors cannot judge audience expectations. The résumé should be ordered in a way that best responds to the potential employer's needs, and the cover letter should offer significant details distinguishing the candidate and highlighting aspects of the résumé in a way that clearly responds to those needs. Normally, all qualifications, activities, and experiences are listed in *reverse chronological order* in the résumé. The cover letter should offer a high level of detail and should interpret the résumé for the potential employer.

The résumé ought to have absolutely no errors of syntax, grammar, or consistency. Errors in consistency (in spacing, parallel form, layout, and capitalization) are especially prevalent. General carelessness or failure to adhere to accepted principles (such as using *active verbs*) will definitely factor into your level of success with this assignment.

# Sample Job Search Assignment

What follows is a sample Job Search Assignment, in response to an current advertisement for employment, from an actual student. The cover letter and résumé have been annotated with comments based upon the general requirements of the assignment.

The format and content of the Job Search Assignment will vary greatly with each instructor's specific requirements, as well as the demands of the position for which the student is applying, and the amount and type of experience and education offered by the applicant.

123 Elm Street
New Brunswick, New Jersey 08901

Return address

September 1, 2022

Today's date

Ms. Christine Mazza
Professional Engineering Intern Manager
T&M Associates
98 Tindall Road
Middletown, New Jersey 07784

Inside address, including contact person's name, job title, organization, and mailing address

Dear Ms. Mazza,

Salutation

Your engineering firm recently hosted an open house at T&M Headquarters in Middletown, New Jersey, related to Site Civil and Municipal Engineering internships. As a Civil Engineering Major at Rutgers University, I am eager to gain experience in a position related to these fields. Since my strong work ethic and goal of repairing coastal infrastructure align directly with the work of T&M, as described in your employment posting, I know that I can help your company achieve its goals.

First paragraph of body, expressing familiarity with the organization and the anticipated responsibilities of the position

As a freshman honors student at Rutgers, I have acquired many technical skills relevant to this position. My proficiency in AutoCAD and Building Information Modeling (BIM) allows me to prepare and understand floor plans, elevation models, and intricate isometric drawings. I also have programming experience in MatLAB that strengthens my ability to process, visualize, and present data in a professional format. I have strong presentation and communication skills which I have perfected through public demonstrations of the NextDorm Web App that I co-developed. This project included live demos for multiple judging panels that have exposed me to professional critique and bolstered my experience with public speaking.

1-2 additional body paragraphs, developing connections between the specific details in the résumé and the anticipated position

Due to my 46 AP credits and accelerated honors coursework, I have already mastered skills intended for students much older than me. This has allowed me the extra time to pick up additional qualities, such as a minor in Public Policy, and obtain the expertise necessary to manage both the relational and technical skills of an upper-level engineering position.

My attributes are a testament to my hard work and discipline across multiple fields. This internship would be an extension of my dedication to everything I am currently involved. Please review my enclosed résumé and feel free to reach out to me at (732) 555-1234 or at dragon@rutgers.edu to arrange an interview at your earliest convenience. Thank you for your consideration.

Cordial closing, including contact information

Sincerely,

*Luke Dragon*

Luke Dragon

Signature in ink above typed name

**Luke Dragon**
**123 Elm Street**
**New Brunswick, New Jersey 08901**
**732-555-1234**
**dragon@rutgers.edu**

## EDUCATION

Rutgers, The State University of New Jersey: New Brunswick, New Jersey
Civil Engineering Major, Public Policy Minor          *Expected Graduation May 2023*
GPA: 4.0, Dean's List Fall 2019

## EXPERIENCE

**Chadwick Beach: Toms River, New Jersey**          *June 2019-September 2019*
*Beach Lifeguard*
- Lifeguarded 45 hours per week during summer months and participated in Chadwick Beach tournament team. Performed multiple successful rescues

**Frankie's Bar and Grille: Point Pleasant, New Jersey**     *June 2016-June 2019*
*Line Cook*
- Prepared food, trained new kitchen employees, and cooked as a line chef
- Worked 8 hours per week during the school year and 40 hours per week during the summer months

## ACTIVITIES

**Rutgers Engineering Honors Council**          *January 2020–Present*
- Elected as Class Representative and chosen to organize events for the honors community.
- Attend weekly meetings, coordinate with other officers, and operated within a budget

**American Society of Civil Engineers**          *September 2019–Present*
- Member of the Sustainable Solutions Team which created a model for using recycled plastic as a modular construction material to build a small-scale structure

**NextDorm**          *September 2019–Present*
- Selected to present at Junior Science and Humanities Symposium at Rutgers University.
- Organized, programmed, and demoed a Web App that improved trading of goods between students through a virtual marketplace and included safety features

**St. Martha's Holiday Meals**          *November 2012–Present*
- Volunteer to arrange the delivery of 1,200 meals each Easter, Thanksgiving, and Christmas for the needy in Ocean County
- Oversaw the preparation of the largest order of 300 meals and led youth volunteers

## HONORS

**Rutgers Engineering Honors Academy**          *September 2019*
**Point Pleasant Borough High School Salutatorian**          *June 2019*

## SKILLS

**Technical:** AutoCAD, MatLAB, Building Information Modeling (BIM), Microsoft Office
**Certifications:** New Jersey Spanish Seal of Biliteracy, Red Cross CPR and First Aid for Professional Rescuers

# Chapter 3 ■ The Job Search Assignment Peer Review Workshop

Please fill out the following form for your partner. Feel free to write comments on the drafts as well.

Does the cover letter . . .
1. directly address the employer? _____ yes _____ no
2. respond to a specific, published job posting? _____ yes _____ no
3. explain why the job candidate is best suited to this job? _____ yes _____ no
4. include a high level of detail concerning the strengths
   of the job candidate? _____ yes _____ no
5. appear in full block form and include all six elements
   (return address, date, recipient's address, salutation, body, closing)? _____ yes _____ no

Is the cover letter . . .
1. signed? _____ yes _____ no
2. free of all grammatical and typographical errors? _____ yes _____ no
3. no more than one page in length, single-spaced in 12-point
   Times New Roman font with one-inch margins? _____ yes _____ no

Does the résumé . . .
1. catch the attention of the reader? _____ yes _____ no
2. include specific, active language? _____ yes _____ no
3. list and describe relevant work and/or academic experience? _____ yes _____ no
4. list and describe relevant extracurricular interests and/or activities? _____ yes _____ no
5. list all experiences and/or activities in reverse chronological order? _____ yes _____ no
6. provide appropriate contact information? _____ yes _____ no

Is the résumé . . .
1. visually appealing and appropriately formatted? _____ yes _____ no
2. free of all grammatical and typographical errors? _____ yes _____ no
3. no more than one page in length, in a professional font size and style? _____ yes _____ no

1. What parts of the drafts are most effective?


2. What parts of the drafts need the most improvement?


3. What three suggestions could you provide to strengthen this Job Search Assignment?

# Chapter 3 ■ The Job Search Assignment Peer Review Workshop

Please fill out the following form for your partner. Feel free to write comments on the drafts as well.

Does the cover letter . . .
1. directly address the employer?                                           _____ yes _____ no
2. respond to a specific, published job posting?                            _____ yes _____ no
3. explain why the job candidate is best suited to this job?                _____ yes _____ no
4. include a high level of detail concerning the strengths
   of the job candidate?                                                    _____ yes _____ no
5. appear in full block form and include all six elements
   (return address, date, recipient's address, salutation, body, closing)?  _____ yes _____ no

Is the cover letter . . .
1. signed?                                                                  _____yes _____ no
2. free of all grammatical and typographical errors?                        _____yes _____ no
3. no more than one page in length, single-spaced in 12-point
   Times New Roman font with one-inch margins?                              _____yes _____ no

Does the résumé . . .
1. catch the attention of the reader?                                       _____yes _____ no
2. include specific, active language?                                       _____yes _____ no
3. list and describe relevant work and/or academic experience?              _____yes _____ no
4. list and describe relevant extracurricular interests and/or activities?  _____yes _____ no
5. list all experiences and/or activities in reverse chronological order?   _____yes _____ no
6. provide appropriate contact information?                                 _____yes _____ no

Is the résumé . . .
1. visually appealing and appropriately formatted?                          _____yes _____ no
2. free of all grammatical and typographical errors?                        _____yes _____ no
3. no more than one page in length, in a professional font size and style?  _____yes _____ no

1. What parts of the drafts are most effective?



2. What parts of the drafts need the most improvement?



3. What three suggestions could you provide to strengthen this Job Search Assignment?

# Chapter 3 ■ The Job Search Assignment Peer Review Workshop

Please fill out the following form for your partner. Feel free to write comments on the drafts as well.

Does the cover letter . . .
1. directly address the employer?                                                        _____ yes _____ no
2. respond to a specific, published job posting?                               _____ yes _____ no
3. explain why the job candidate is best suited to this job?            _____ yes _____ no
4. include a high level of detail concerning the strengths
   of the job candidate?                                                                   _____ yes _____ no
5. appear in full block form and include all six elements
   (return address, date, recipient's address, salutation, body, closing)?  _____ yes _____ no

Is the cover letter . . .
1. signed?                                                                                          _____yes _____ no
2. free of all grammatical and typographical errors?                      _____yes _____ no
3. no more than one page in length, single-spaced in 12-point
   Times New Roman font with one-inch margins?                           _____yes _____ no

Does the résumé . . .
1. catch the attention of the reader?                                              _____yes _____ no
2. include specific, active language?                                              _____yes _____ no
3. list and describe relevant work and/or academic experience?  _____yes _____ no
4. list and describe relevant extracurricular interests and/or activities?  _____yes _____ no
5. list all experiences and/or activities in reverse chronological order?  _____yes _____ no
6. provide appropriate contact information?                                  _____yes _____ no

Is the résumé . . .
1. visually appealing and appropriately formatted?                        _____yes _____ no
2. free of all grammatical and typographical errors?                      _____yes _____ no
3. no more than one page in length, in a professional font size and style?  _____yes _____ no

1. What parts of the drafts are most effective?


2. What parts of the drafts need the most improvement?


3. What three suggestions could you provide to strengthen this Job Search Assignment?

# Researching Your Topic

*Chapter* 4

Research work is like any other work students encounter: a little basic knowledge makes the process more efficient. There are basically five things students need to know to be successful doing research for this course:

- When to use **primary** and **secondary** sources.
- How to judge among **scholarly**, **professional**, and **popular** publications.
- How to research **patrons**, **problems**, and **paradigms**.
- How to find **books**, **journal articles**, and other library resources.
- The proper way to cite sources according to **APA Style**.

These five aspects of research are covered in the paragraphs that follow.

## Primary and Secondary Sources

How will you show that your topic is important and needs to be addressed? It will not be enough to rely on an emotional appeal or to expect people to take you at your word. Research will be required to demonstrate the nature and extent of the problem in a logical way. Your instructor may require primary research as well as secondary research, but knowing how and when to use them is important.

### Primary Research

Primary research, sometimes called fieldwork, is data that you personally collect about the topic. Experiments, surveys, questionnaires, direct observations with note keeping, and interviews are typical examples of primary research. Data you collect in experiments, observations, and surveys can be presented in charts or graphs to quantify the problem. Questionnaires and interviews can be helpful when opinions are important.

### Secondary Research

Even if you do collect your own research, you will need other research to interpret your data for others. That is why it is necessary to look at published sources. Secondary research is the term used to describe the search for published information, which you must take at secondhand. The value of secondary sources depends a lot on their credibility.

For your proposal, you might do both primary and secondary research to introduce the problem, but you must do secondary research for the literature review (or paradigm) that helps interpret the problem and explain your solution. Each proposal stands or falls on the quality of its research, and all need a solid foundation of published and authoritative research to support their claims. Without published sources you will be very hard-pressed to develop a justification for your plan of action.

# Scholarly, Professional, and Popular: Evaluating Secondary Sources

If there is one thing that students should learn in college, it is that not all information is equally valid or credible. When evaluating sources, students need to keep in mind the types of sources they are, since that will greatly affect the power they have to persuade the reader. Three terms are key: scholarly, professional, and popular.

## *Scholarly Sources*

Scholarly sources are articles and research studies published in peer-reviewed journals or books. They show what scholars in a particular discipline are thinking about topics based on their research. In the scholarly journals, you will see that discussions reference accepted concepts and models. These readings can be difficult because the contributors to these journals use specialized vocabulary that someone outside of or fairly new to the discipline may not quickly comprehend. Realizing that these sources are the strongest authorities you will have for your proposal should help you persevere even when the reading is challenging. Scholarly sources are found in college and university libraries. Many journals are now in electronic form and accessible on the web, but many are still only in print form. When you access your university library, you will see whether articles you need can be downloaded or whether you need to go to the library and photocopy or take notes on the information.

## *Professional Sources*

Newsletters, journals, magazines, and websites that are used by the practitioners of a given profession or discipline are known as professional sources. They include up-to-date information about existing and new products, business applications, and commonplaces of the profession. You might find articles there about successful companies or methods written by respected people working in that field. These sources have some authority and can be excellent places to look for models of success. But because the writers of these publications often do not do research themselves and because they often do not take a critical perspective on their specialty or on companies in their industry (where these writers might be employed), professional sources are not considered quite as authoritative as scholarly sources. These publications can often be found in your university library or through internet sources.

## *Popular Sources*

Newspapers, magazines, and websites that are readily available to the public and written to a broad audience are generally called popular sources. While they are the easiest sources to find, they have the least value when authority is being established for a proposal that requests funding. Popular sources can, however, supplement the scholarly and professional sources and show how your topic is of general social interest. Many internet sources would fall under the category of popular.

Based on this brief discussion of the three types of sources, you can see that often the more easily obtained the information is, the less authority it has. The most authoritative sources are generally written for a specialized audience. Recognize the category of the sources you use so you can judge how well they bolster your own authority. Each proposal stands or falls on the quality of its research, and all need a solid foundation of published and authoritative studies, theoretical works, and other documents.

# Researching the Patron, Problem, and Paradigm

Often when students begin their research, they see their job as finding out as much as they can about the problem that they want to address. While this can be a good way to start your research, you need to recognize that finding information about the problem is only part of your task. You will also have to do research on funding sources (the patron) and ways of solving the problem (the paradigm). Each part of the project will require different types of research.

## *Patron*

How will you find a funding source? And how will you pitch your project to them? You will have to do research to find the best patron for your project and to learn more about what interests them. Often this research is not directly cited in your paper, but it is among the most important in making your paper realistic.

Even if the organization that will be funding your project is the company you currently work for or the school you attend, you will still want to do some research to find out how your project fits with their mission and values. Look at your company website. Look at what is online about your school or about the specific department in your school you are going to ask for funding. How can you connect your project with the issues and problems that concern them?

If there are no local sources of funding for your project, you will need to do some research to see what organizations (including government agencies, private philanthropies, and corporations) share your interests. Here are three good methods for getting started finding a funding source:

### Method 1: Go to the Library

University libraries have a wealth of print sources that can help you find funding. These sources are often more complete than sources you find on the web, though they might not be as current or quick to browse. Ask the reference librarians for help getting started.

### Method 2: Check Out Online Clearinghouses

There are a number of grant clearinghouse websites, where you can quickly access many groups that provide funding for projects. Some good websites to start your search for funding include the following:

*The Foundation Center*
http://foundationcenter.org/ and http://foundationcenter.org/findfunders/
This is the best clearinghouse for charity and private philanthropy information.

*Catalogue of Federal Domestic Assistance*
http://www.cfda.gov/
The official government clearinghouse for all types of funds.

*Grants.gov*
http://www.grants.gov/
A clearinghouse for different granting agencies of the U.S. government.

*Community of Science*
http://www.cos.com/
A clearinghouse for science-related projects.

*National Science Foundation*
http://www.nsf.gov/funding/
The NSF sponsors theoretical research in the sciences.

*Environmental Protection Agency*
http://www.epa.gov/epahome/grants.htm
The EPA sponsors environmental projects.

*National Institutes of Health*
http://grants1.nih.gov/grants/oer.htm
The NIH sponsors health and health education grants.

*U.S. Department of Education*
http://www.ed.gov/fund/landing.jhtml
A resource for educational projects.

**Method 3: Browse the Web**

Since most organizations who might fund your project probably have a website or are listed on the web, a search engine, such as Google, is not a bad initial search tool. Try entering your keywords for your topic, perhaps along with the words "grants" or "funding," and you should at least get some hints about who is interested in your subject area. This method involves a lot of trial and error, and you are better off starting with Method 1 and Method 2. However, when looking for some initial guidance, doing a general web search should at least give you a better sense of your topic and who is interested in it.

## Problem

How can you prove that there is a problem? And how can you emphasize its importance? To make a good case, you will have to do some research on your topic with the goal of finding numbers or of defining your problem well enough to understand its scope.

Before you begin your research on the problem, it's a good idea to think about the specific information that would be useful to your case. Some questions to consider:

- What are the most important numbers needed to convince your patron that this problem is important to address? How can you quantify its scope and scale?

- Can you conduct some of this research yourself, or use research that you have already done? Or will you need to rely on secondary sources of research?

- In order to quantify the problem, what are your best sources of documented evidence? What secondary sources might have information that can help your case?

- Which groups or organizations might have already studied the problem? And where might they publish their findings?

If you can get good numbers, you will be able to make especially powerful visual aids.

## When You Can't Find the Numbers You Need

- *Keep trying.* Often, especially with online research, key information is hidden behind the keywords that you haven't tried. For instance, say you are writing a project on making a community service project mandatory at a local high school. You need to find information about teens and community service or volunteering. A search in *Statistical Universe* using the keywords "teens" and "community service" or "volunteerism" will get you nowhere. The perfect graph for your project can only be found under "surveys—opinions and attitudes, by age." Start early and be persistent. Don't do your research when you are pressed for time.

- *Try extrapolating.* Often it is possible to take percentages from national studies and use them to make educated guesses as to how many people will be affected by an issue on a local level. In order for this to work well, your local population must be entirely typical with the rest of the larger area. For instance, if you absolutely can't find rates of smoking for your town, you could use state or local averages and then work out the equation. If 30% of people in New Jersey smoke, one might assume that 30% of people in Paterson smoke. However, if your local area is different in some significant way from the larger population, you should not rely on extrapolation.

  A town populated by a significant number of young families cannot be compared to a town with several senior citizen retirement villages. If you are reduced to documenting your local problem by extrapolating from national statistics, you must be honest about it and clearly show how you have arrived at the figures you are using.

- *Fill in the gaps with primary research.* Sometimes a problem is so new or so local that there is not a large amount of hard data to draw from. In that case, you will have to do some surveys or other primary research. Make sure that your surveys are legitimate and convincing. Your sample size must be large enough and varied enough to be representative. The fact that 20 of your friends say they dislike Economics 101 is not good evidence that a university should drop the course. As you survey, keep track of what day and time you did the survey, how many people responded, how many of each gender, age, and so on, depending upon the subject of the survey. You should also ask your survey questions in such a way that they will generate good statistical responses. If you conduct your surveys well and present them carefully, they can enhance your credibility. For example, which of the following two statements seems most convincing and why?

  - Fifty percent of the people I surveyed disliked Economics 101.

  - Out of 1,000 students, 50% stated that they ranked Economics 101 (on a scale of 1–10, 1 being the lowest) at 3 or below.

- *Use uncertainty to your advantage.* Sometimes a lack of knowledge is the best evidence you have that a problem exists. Scientists use uncertainty all the time in order to show that more research must be done. If you are writing a research proposal, you should use the lack of statistical information as part of your documentation of the problem. Be sure to discuss the possible dangers or lack of opportunities that result from "not knowing." Perhaps a central part of your project could be to gather data.

## Paradigm

How do you support your claim that your plan is the best way to address the problem? A paradigm gives you that support. You should think of it as the research-based rationale for your plan. It authorizes your claims about the problem and justifies your methods.

If you are doing a scientific research project in any given field, your paradigm will derive from previous research. That previous research offers you both examples of practice (what experimental methods did they use?) and a way of understanding the results (how did the experiment support the hypothesis based on previous theory?). Defining your paradigm outside of the hard sciences is not as straightforward, because there is usually not as strong a consensus as there is in the sciences about which methods and theories are best. However, you can still use the model of the sciences to guide you in researching support for your plan.

You need to think of paradigms as ideally having two parts, along the scientific model: a **theoretical frame** and **models of success**. A model of success is an example of how others have successfully addressed the problem in some other context. A theoretical frame is a language for explaining how a certain solution will work.

# Searching for a Theoretical Frame

Let's say that you wanted to take on the problem of crime on campus. To find research to justify a plan of action, you would want to find a theoretical frame and search for models of success. Both parts of your paradigm must be developed through the use of scholarly research.

If you were studying sociology or law enforcement, it would be logical for you to take on the problem of campus crime since your previous studies had already prepared you for the issue. You might already have an idea, in fact, of what theoretical frames might relate to the issue. If you don't, then at least you would know where to look to find out. You could talk to professors. You could look in your textbooks (especially in their bibliographies). Ultimately, though, you will need to do some research to see what others have written in journal articles and in books about ways of addressing the problem. That's where you will find your theoretical frame and the language you will need to explain it.

To address the problem of campus crime, you would want to look at what researchers have written in the areas of sociology or law enforcement (the fields that seem most applicable to your problem—though other fields might offer ideas as well). One theory of crime you might encounter in your reading is the "broken windows theory," which suggests that if you address small crimes (such as broken windows) you will be addressing the larger issue because, for one thing, small crimes and big crimes are committed by the same group of offenders.

# Searching for Models of Success

If you wanted to address the problem of crime on campus, you would logically look at programs at other schools that helped to reduce crime. You would probably also want to look at towns and cities, since they are also potentially good models. You could look for these models in a number of ways.

- You might look in professional or popular sources, such as college journals or newspapers and magazines, which might have stories about successful crime-stopping initiatives.

- You could look on the web, where schools might have posted information about their programs (especially those that proved successful).

- You might ask experts in law enforcement who they look to for models, and then try to interview people involved with the programs they suggest.

- If you have already begun your theoretical research, you may have come across some examples in scholarly sources that you can then try to find out more about.

Once you found those models of success, you would want to repeat the research process to see what specific information you could turn up about how and why those programs worked. The more information you could turn up the better, since you will need that research to justify your own choices in constructing a plan.

# Merging Theory and Practice

To construct a coherent project, you will need to merge theory and practice so that your theoretical frame explains the model of success you are using to justify your plan. A good example of this merging of theory and practice in the case of campus crime would be to use the model of the New York Police Department who made their city the safest in the nation by cracking down on low-level street crime (from petty theft to vandalism), following the logic of the broken windows theory. You could use the NYPD as your model and draw examples of good practice from them and explain them using the language of theory.

# The White Paper Assignment

A white paper is a document which describes a current problem. Your white paper will help you begin documenting and quantifying an actual problem in anticipation of the midterm letter. In addition, you will have the opportunity to present information in light of the needs of your chosen funding source.

The white paper should help you collate and organize information and test the viability of your topic. Pay close attention to the **scope** of your potential project. This is the time when you should be aware of your ability to fully address the problem identified. Upon further review, if the problem still requires additional narrowing or framing, this is the time to consider the possibilities. Your white paper should be brief (one to two pages) and include a significant amount of **fieldwork**. When drafting your white paper, consider whether a possible proposal does all of the following:

1. **Identifies with people**: Does the writer have a particular reader (or funding source) in mind? Does the writer's approach seem appropriate to the reader's concerns? Should the writer imagine a different reader for the idea or find out more about the reader's concerns? Does the project address the needs of a particular population? Might the interests of the reader differ from those of the population to be served? How so?

2. **Points to a problem**: Does the writer demonstrate a need for this proposal? Has he or she discussed a problem that could be researched and documented? How might the writer find out more about the problem? What sources of information might be helpful? What types of evidence would help illustrate the problem better?

3. **Faces complexity**: Is the idea of sufficient complexity to require a detailed proposal? If not, can you suggest ways to develop the project so that it would be adequately complex? Has the writer considered all the major problems here, or is there something he or she is avoiding?

4. **Suggests lines of research**: Does the topic lend itself to library research (a course requirement)? What other kinds of research should the writer consider? How might the writer support his or her claims about the problem suggested by the proposal?

5. **Positions the work within a paradigm**: Does the writer have a definite approach to the problem or issue? How might the writer position him or herself within a discipline or field of study in approaching the topic? What disciplines might be helpful? What research might the writer pursue in developing the paradigm?

6. **Demonstrates originality**: Is the specific work proposed at least somewhat original? Has this idea been tried before? What could make this idea more innovative? Are there other ways of approaching the problem?

7. **Stays within reach**: Is the proposed idea manageable? In other words, is the scope of the proposed work something that can be done well, given the time frame and resources? Is the student remaining within his/her reach, if not his/her grasp? Is the idea focused enough in terms of population, location, or issue? Is it something that could actually get done? Can you see this student actually taking on such a project now or being able to do so within the next few years?

Follow your instructor's directions about format and use of sources for this assignment.

# Sample White Paper

What follows is a sample White Paper for a prospective project proposal, with respective comments based upon the assignment's guidelines. The format and content of The White Paper Assignment will vary greatly with each instructor's specific requirements. As you work through the proposal writing process in this text, you will follow the progression of this student's project. In all of your assignments requiring cited research, be sure to follow the current APA formatting guidelines. Consult your instructor for the most recent standards.

## Program to Improve College Readiness for First-Generation High School Students in Ocean County, New Jersey

Title for prospective project

Luke Dragon
White Paper Assignment
September 15, 2022

Section providing background of problem and documentation/quantification of current status

### The Issues With College Readiness in Ocean County

College readiness is a prevalent issue faced by many disadvantaged populations, including first-generation high school students. According to the Center for First-Generation Student Success, 24% of college applicants nationwide have parents with no postsecondary education and 56% have parents without a bachelor's degree (RTI International, 2019). This lack of experience within immediate family puts these students at a distinct disadvantage when familiarizing themselves with the jargon, culture, and application process of an institute for higher education. This creates a burden on first-generation students to learn this system and the financial aid process on their own which leads to them missing information crucial to their success. Many high school districts in Ocean County, especially those which are underfunded, have few resources dedicated to educating parents and students to account for this gap. Many minorities are overrepresented in first-generation demographics and Ocean County districts including Lakewood and Brick have high rates of minorities enrolling in postsecondary education (NJ School Performance Report: Ocean County High Schools, 2019). Given this, it is highly probable that there is a population of first-generation students in Ocean County who would benefit from a college preparedness program. However, it is essential to initiate primary research to discern exactly where they are. My study will provide insight on which Ocean County district would benefit the most from a first-generation college preparedness program, assess which topics are most necessary to cover, and how to educate on them.

Section presenting and connecting prevailing research to the issue

### Research Concerning First-Generation Students

Given the strong correlation between a bachelor's degree and increased lifetime earnings, putting an emphasis on first-generation students is crucial for the financial mobility of disadvantaged populations (Byrd & Macdonald, 2005). However, according to a 2015 Gallup-Purdue poll, it is evident that first-generation students are 10% more likely to graduate with debt which lessens the positive economic impact brought about by continued education (Gallup-Purdue, 2015). A cause for this disparity could be the confusing and cumbersome nature of financial aid applications, like the Free Application for Student Aid or FAFSA. Research conducted in 2018 found that a significant portion of adult aged first-generation students struggled to understand financial aid vocabulary specifically related to the FAFSA (Taylor et al., 2019). Considering that many first-generation high school students have even less experience than their adult-aged counterparts, it is reasonable to conclude that this issue applies to them as well. Current models suggest that the inclusion of partnered dual-enrollment programs substantially increases college confidence amongst disadvantaged high school students (Roughton 2016). Finding a way to adapt this model to increase confidence and familiarity with financial aid applications will serve as the initial goal for my research. My study will also seek to demystify college culture and make sure students know exactly what resources are available to them.

Section suggesting potential plan of action based upon research completed up to this point

## The Potential Program for Ocean County

Through my research, I will investigate the most prominent issues surrounding college preparedness and make them accessible for both students and parents. The end goal is to create a low cost and easily comprehensible program to fill this lapse in the current college readiness system within specific district. Funding for this program will be sourced from the participating district as well as grants from organizations, such as the College Futures Foundation, which support financial literacy for first-generation students. Initial field work will include interviewing Ocean County high school principals and superintendents about what supports they already have in place. Additional surveys for first-generation students and their families to classify the aspects with which they struggle the most will also be required.

# References

Byrd, K., & Macdonald, G. (2005). Defining college readiness from the inside out: First-generation college student perspectives. *Community College Review, 33*(1), 22–37.

Gallup-Purdue. (2015). Student loan debt incurred as undergraduates among alumni who graduated between 2006 and 2015. Retrieved February 16, 2020, from https://www.gallup.com/services/185924/gallup-purdue-index-2015-report.aspx

NJ School Performance Report: Ocean County High Schools 2017–2018. (2019). Retrieved February 17, 2020, from https://rc.doe.state.nj.us/report.aspx?type=-school&lang=english&county=29&district=2520&school=050&SY=1718&-schoolyear=2017-2018

Roughton, D. (2016). Addressing college access and success gaps in traditionally underrepresented populations: The North Carolina early college high school model. *Higher Education Politics & Economics, 2*(1), 82–93.

RTI International. (2019). First-generation college students: Demographic characteristics and postsecondary enrollment. NASPA. Retrieved February 16, 2020, from https://firstgen.naspa.org/files/dmfil e/FactSheet-01.pdf

Taylor, Z., Bicak, I., Egetenmeyer, R., & Osborne, M. (2019). What is the FAFSA? An adult learner knowledge survey of student financial aid jargon. *Journal of Adult and Continuing Education, 25*(1), 94–112.

# Chapter 4 ■ The White Paper Assignment Peer Review Workshop

Please fill out the following form for your partner. Feel free to write comments on the draft as well.

Is the White Paper . . .

1. one to one and a half pages in length, not including the list
   of References?                                            _____ yes _____ no
2. double-spaced, with a brief heading at the top?           _____ yes _____ no
3. in 12-point Times New Roman font, with one-inch margins?  _____ yes _____ no
4. free of all grammatical and typographical errors?         _____ yes _____ no

Does the White Paper . . .

1. identify with *people*?                                    _____ yes _____ no
2. point to a *problem*?                                      _____ yes _____ no
3. face *complexity*?                                         _____ yes _____ no
4. suggest lines of *research*?                               _____ yes _____ no
5. position the work within a *paradigm*?                     _____ yes _____ no
6. demonstrate *originality*?                                 _____ yes _____ no
7. stay within *reach*?                                       _____ yes _____ no
8. address all *Six P's* to some degree?                      _____ yes _____ no
9. include *headings* to help guide the reader?              _____ yes _____ no
10. include a list of *References*?                           _____ yes _____ no
11. refer to at least *three sources*, cited in-text?         _____ yes _____ no
12. adhere to *APA format*, in-text and in the list of References?  _____ yes _____ no

1. In your own words, what is the *problem* addressed in this White Paper?

2. To what extent do you feel that this White Paper is successful in achieving its goals? Why?

3. What three suggestions could you provide to strengthen this White Paper?

# Chapter 4 ◼ The White Paper Assignment Peer Review Workshop

Please fill out the following form for your partner. Feel free to write comments on the draft as well.

Is the White Paper . . .

1.  one to one and a half pages in length, not including the list
    of References?                                                _____ yes _____ no
2.  double-spaced, with a brief heading at the top?               _____ yes _____ no
3.  in 12-point Times New Roman font, with one-inch margins?      _____ yes _____ no
4.  free of all grammatical and typographical errors?             _____ yes _____ no

Does the White Paper . . .

1.  identify with *people*?                                       _____ yes _____ no
2.  point to a *problem*?                                         _____ yes _____ no
3.  face *complexity*?                                            _____ yes _____ no
4.  suggest lines of *research*?                                  _____ yes _____ no
5.  position the work within a *paradigm*?                        _____ yes _____ no
6.  demonstrate *originality*?                                    _____ yes _____ no
7.  stay within *reach*?                                          _____ yes _____ no
8.  address all *Six P's* to some degree?                         _____ yes _____ no
9.  include *headings* to help guide the reader?                  _____ yes _____ no
10. include a list of *References*?                               _____ yes _____ no
11. refer to at least *three sources*, cited in-text?             _____ yes _____ no
12. adhere to *APA format*, in-text and in the list of References?  _____ yes _____ no

1.  In your own words, what is the *problem* addressed in this White Paper?

2.  To what extent do you feel that this White Paper is successful in achieving its goals? Why?

3.  What three suggestions could you provide to strengthen this White Paper?

# Chapter 4 ■ The White Paper Assignment Peer Review Workshop

Please fill out the following form for your partner. Feel free to write comments on the draft as well.

Is the White Paper . . .

1. one to one and a half pages in length, not including the list
   of References?                                                    _____ yes _____ no
2. double-spaced, with a brief heading at the top?                   _____ yes _____ no
3. in 12-point Times New Roman font, with one-inch margins?          _____ yes _____ no
4. free of all grammatical and typographical errors?                 _____ yes _____ no

Does the White Paper . . .

1. identify with *people*?                                           _____ yes _____ no
2. point to a *problem*?                                             _____ yes _____ no
3. face *complexity*?                                                _____ yes _____ no
4. suggest lines of *research*?                                      _____ yes _____ no
5. position the work within a *paradigm*?                            _____ yes _____ no
6. demonstrate *originality*?                                        _____ yes _____ no
7. stay within *reach*?                                              _____ yes _____ no
8. address all *Six P's* to some degree?                             _____ yes _____ no
9. include *headings* to help guide the reader?                      _____ yes _____ no
10. include a list of *References*?                                  _____ yes _____ no
11. refer to at least *three sources*, cited in-text?                _____ yes _____ no
12. adhere to *APA format*, in-text and in the list of References?   _____ yes _____ no

1. In your own words, what is the *problem* addressed in this White Paper?



2. To what extent do you feel that this White Paper is successful in achieving its goals? Why?



3. What three suggestions could you provide to strengthen this White Paper?

# Finding Books, Journal Articles, and Other Sources at the Library

Today there can never be the excuse that you "couldn't find any research" on something. You will see, in fact, that there is usually too much information on any topic. Just try a search on the Index called *Business Source Premier* at your university library. Enter keywords about your topic and you should find that there is a lot of information out there (much of which is accessible online in full-text format). And if you try a search at *Google*, it is likely you will get too many hits to look through in a sitting. You must learn to be selective, have confidence in your ability to analyze what you read, and just simply get to work.

The only way to learn how to use your university library or its home page is by using it. But if you have trouble getting started, there are tutorials online. Remember the reference librarians can be the best teachers of library skills; the library is their classroom, and you are their students. Show them what you have done; ask them questions; seek their advice whenever you get stuck looking for information. The more specific your question, the better the help you will receive.

If you can't locate a source at your university library, you can order any book or journal article through interlibrary loan, usually very quickly (no more than 2 weeks). If you start your research early, you should be able to get all the information you need. Be careful, however, to continue your research efforts while awaiting sources you have ordered. The deadline for completing an assignment will not change if your ordered source does not arrive on time or proves less than helpful.

## Some Advice on Searching the Internet

You should never rely upon general internet searching as your main source of information. Internet sources tend to be too simplified and too much driven by self-interest to serve as the basis for your research. You should always seek a wide variety of sources, using books for depth of coverage, peer-reviewed journals for thinking in your field, and periodicals for timely coverage of recent events. The internet should be only a supplement to these sources. These suggestions are, therefore, intended to give you some ideas about using the internet as an assistant rather than a crutch.

- Often web searches can help you most in developing a list of keywords that you can use later in searching through databases and books. Try putting quotes around specific phrases, like "binge drinking" rather than binge AND drinking, since this will help narrow your search to only sources that use those words together. Remember the basics of Boolean logic: use "and" to narrow and "or" to expand categories.

- An increasing number of statistical sources are available online. You can also use *Statistical Abstracts of the United States* and *Statistical Reference Index*, which are available in the reference section of most campus libraries. If you are seeking government statistics, check out "thomas," the government center for information at http://www.thomas.gov/. For New Jersey information, try http://www.state.nj.us/. For census information, go to http://www.census.gov/. If you were looking for statistics on campus crime (as in our example above), you would definitely need to visit the Office of Postsecondary Education's Campus Security Statistics website at http://ope.ed.gov/security/.

- If you find a good website, see if it contains links to others or lists of references you can find in the library. Often, web sources are abstracted versions of much better journal articles or books. Go to the original source!

# A Brief Guide to Using APA Style, Seventh Edition

The following guidelines are not intended to be all-inclusive but merely to help you avoid typical pitfalls in citation. For the purposes of this class, you should use citation format as given by the American Psychological Association. You will need to know APA Style for both in-text citation and your References page. The following are guidelines based on current APA recommendations. For more information on the intricacies of APA citation, consult the *Publication Manual of the American Psychological Association* (available in the reference section of all campus libraries). For the latest recommendations on electronic references, go to the frequently updated APA website at http://www.apastyle.org/elecref.html. The following examples of format are all based on those sources.

## In-Text, Parenthetical Citation

The main purpose of in-text citation is to link information in your text with entries on your References page. For that reason, you need to make the connection between citations and sources clear by using the same primary name in your text as the primary identifying reference in your References. Because science is rapidly evolving, APA citation emphasizes the date of publication by placing it second to the author's name. Therefore, when using APA Style the two most important pieces of information you should have in a textual reference are the last name of the author(s) and the date. The APA suggests that you include a page number (or paragraph number if no page number exists, as on a web source) only if you are using a direct quotation from the text. If you mention the author(s) in your sentence, then you should only put the date in your parenthetical citation. Three examples:

> According to J. Q. Wilson and G. L. Kelling (1982), "at the community level, disorder and crime are usually inextricably linked, in a kind of developmental sequence" (p. 33).

> According to a classic study of the "broken windows" theory, "at the community level, disorder and crime are usually inextricably linked, in a kind of developmental sequence" (Wilson & Kelling, 1982, p. 33).

> According to the classic study of the "broken windows" phenomenon, disorder leads inevitably to crime (Wilson & Kelling, 1982).

For a work with 3 or more authors, include the name of only the first author plus et al. in the citation:

> (Johnson et al. 2006)

> In a study done by Johnson et al. (2006), . . .

> OR

> In a study done by Johnson and colleagues (2006), . . .

If the source has no discernable author, then use the title. And be sure to use the title for reference both parenthetically and in your References:

> *Parenthetical citation for unpaginated, non-authored source:*
> Safir's first action was to focus on the seemingly "trivial" crime of jumping subway turnstiles to avoid paying the fare (Commissioner describes NYPD 'success story,' 2000).

> *References listing for unpaginated, non-authored web source:*
> Commisioner describes NYPD 'success story.' (2000, January 28). *Yale Bulletin and Calendar,* 28(18). Retrieved March 3, 2009, from http://www.yale.edu/opa/v28.n18/story4.html

## Non-Accessible Sources

Since the whole purpose of including citations and references is to provide your reader with the means of finding the same sources themselves for future research, you should not include the following as part of your list of references: email, personal interviews, phone communications, references to non-published lectures or speeches, and surveys or other original research you have done gathering information about the problem you are addressing in your proposal. You should, however, mention them in your text. Original research that you have done to find information about your project should especially be explained clearly. Here are some examples of how you might cite this material:

> A survey of 45 Busch campus students conducted at the Busch Student Center on April 1, 2003 (see Appendix I for questionnaire and results), showed an overwhelming number avoided taking Friday classes.

> In an interview on January 12, 2003, Robert Spears, the Director of Parking and Transportation for the Rutgers, New Brunswick campus, discussed some of the problems that made additional parking spaces on College Avenue Campus impractical.

> In a March 10, 2003, email response to my inquiries, Professor Dowling said that he thought student evaluations "put pressure on faculty to do the popular thing rather than the right thing" and therefore ought to be replaced by another system.

## Your References Page

A References page is just that: it reflects the works that you have actually referenced in your text, not works that you consulted for background information but did not cite, with a hanging indent. You must list your sources in alphabetical order, either by the author's name or the title. If you have two or more sources by the same author, list them by year and use the author's name for each. Where the author has two entries for the same year, add lowercase letters ("a," "b," etc.) to the date. Do not number your entries on the page—alphabetical order and indentation will separate one entry from the next.

The following examples will give you some idea of format; for more complete information, consult your instructor or the seventh edition of the *APA Handbook*.

**Books**

Jacobs, J. (1961). *The death and life of great American cities*. Random House.

**Books with more than one author**

Wilson, J. Q., & Herrnstein, R. (1985). *Crime and human nature: The definitive study of the causes of crime*.

    Simon & Schuster.

**Book chapters**

Wilson, J. Q., & Kelling, G. Broken windows: The police and neighborhood safety. In J. Q. Wilson (Ed.),

    *Thinking about crime* (pp. 77–90). Vintage Books.

### Periodical articles

If the periodical is paginated continuously throughout the year, only the volume number is needed. If each issue begins with page 1, include the issue number after the volume number, with the issue number in italics and the volume in parentheses. For example, for "volume 17, issue 4," use $17(4)$.

Brown, L., & Wycoff, M. A. (1987). Policing Houston: Reducing fear and improving service. *Crime and*

   *Delinquency, 33*(1), 71–89.

Strecher, V. (1991). Revising the histories and futures of policing. *Police Forum, 1,* 1–9.

### Newspaper articles

Remember to introduce page numbers with "p." or "pp." in the case of newspapers.

Campbell, G. A. (1997, October 14). Crime is down all over. *New York Times,* p. D14.

### Unpublished, in-house documents

Brown, M. (1997). Log of daily accounts. (Available at Bryan Dentistry, Westerly Place, West Park, NY 02984).

### Web references

For referring to documents on the web, please check the APA website http://www.apastyle.org/elecsource.html for the latest recommendations. For most web documents, you can use the same format as non-web sources, but you then need to add "Retrieved Month Day, Year, from the website: http://etc.org/whatever.html." Differences arise because of the impermanence of web sources and the fact that many do not have clear authors or titles on their pages. The impermanence of Web sources makes it necessary to add the date you retrieved it. In the case where there is no listed author, then use the title as your main listing, and only if there is no author or title should you merely list the source (such as the sponsor of the website). In any case, be sure to list the web address of the actual article or page you are using, not simply the address of the website you accessed first. Do not expect your reader to be able to follow all of the links you followed to find the article. If you are only referring to a website in general, and not a specific article or page on the site, you can just record the name and web address in your text without including any specific listing in your References. Do not include a period after web addresses.

Muzzey, E. H. (2001). Biochemical reactions in toddlers: The effects of television on the lymphatic system.

   *Journal of Northeastern Medicine, 36,* 90–123. http://www.jnm.org/journal/muzzey/23000.html

# The Annotated Bibliography Assignment

An annotated bibliography is simply a preliminary References page to which notes (or "annotations") have been added after each entry. For this assignment, you will provide one or two paragraphs briefly summarizing the information provided in the source and explaining how you expect to use this material in your project proposal. You might also want to say whether you will be using the source to quantify the problem or to set up the research paradigm for your project.

# Sample Annotated Bibliography

Luke Dragon
Annotated Bibliography
September 15, 2022

## Improving College Readiness for First-Generation High School Students in Ocean County, New Jersey

## Annotated Bibliography

Byrd, K., & Macdonald, G. (2005). Defining college readiness from the inside out: First-generation college student perspectives. *Community College Review, 33*(1), 22–37.

This paper provides insight on the social aspects of college preparation through interviewing first-generation college juniors and seniors. The survey attempts to draw connections between student background and academic success in their first 2 years of college. The majority of students surveyed remarked that self-advocacy and time management were key skills they needed to master for success in college. This led to the conclusion that recognizing nonacademic factors when guiding first-generation students is crucial as it enables them to recognize their strengths as they take more rigorous courses. This article is one of the first to qualify the extra needs of first-generation students, aside from academics, and thus will serve as a keystone component to support the creation of a college preparedness program.

Gallup-Purdue. (2015). Student loan debt incurred as undergraduates among alumni who graduated between 2006 and 2015. Retrieved February 16, 2020, from https://www.gallup.com/services/185924/gallup-purdue-index-2015-report.aspx

This data set includes valuable information related to first-generation students compared to other disadvantaged, majority, and minority groups. It shows that nationally, first-generation students take on more debt compared to Hispanic and White students. These statistics will work in tandem with the source related to FAFSA jargon as evidence that first-generation students are disadvantaged in the financial aid system. The source will also be used to create a connection to how this confusion mitigates the positive impact of higher education on financial mobility.

NJ School Performance Report: Ocean County High Schools 2017–2018. (2019). Retrieved February 17, 2020, from https://rc.doe.state.nj.us/report.aspx?type =school&lang=english&county=29&district=2520&school=050&SY=1718& schoolyear=2017-2018

The New Jersey Department of Education mandates that every public school report a standard set of data related to their demographics, academic performance, and post-graduation plans at the end of each year. Each district has its data compared directly

*Annotation note:* Properly and consistently formatted APA-style reference page

*Annotation note:* Annotation following source information, briefly summarizing the material, and identifying how it will likely be used in the prospective proposal

to state averages and how these schools have set goals to improve certain weaknesses. The most important data for each school lies on pages 26 and 27 which display enrollments in continuing education rates broken down by minority participation. This data is crucial for comparison with national statistics on the correlation between first-generation and minority students. This suggests the existence of a problem in Ocean County, establishes a specific population, and aids in the identification of a district.

Roughton, D. (2016). Addressing college access and success gaps in traditionally

underrepresented populations: The North Carolina early college high school

model. *Higher Education Politics & Economics, 2*(1), 82–93.

This study developed a model for increasing college preparedness using disadvantaged districts in North Carolina with low rates of graduation and continuing education as compared to the national average. They found that the implementation of "the early college high school" model which includes subsidized dual enrollment and lessons on college culture improved readiness in underrepresented populations. Also mentioned is the impact of a bachelor's degree on financial mobility and how its value should be viewed as a return on investment for social capital. This source will contribute to the model for implementing specific features of the program including workshops with the school guidance department and how to directly connect with students.

RTI International. (2019). First-generation college students: Demographic

characteristics and postsecondary enrollment. NASPA. Retrieved February 16,

2020, from https://firstgen.naspa.org/files/dmfile/FactSheet-01.pdf

This fact sheet includes a series of statistics and graphs comparing first-generation students to continuing-generation students from 2012 to 2014. The definition of a first-generation student is well articulated and will serve as the basis for the population of my research. Featured statistics include the percent of first-generation students at different minority serving institutions and the median income disparity between first- and continuing-generation students, which is about $50,000. This document serves as a source for many academic and financial figures that will justify workshop topics and areas of focus for research.

Taylor, Z., Bicak, I., Egetenmeyer, R., & Osborne, M. (2019). What is the FAFSA?

An adult learner knowledge survey of student financial aid jargon. *Journal of*

*Adult and Continuing Education, 25*(1), 94–112.

Despite this study primarily targeting adult aged college students, the majority (64%) of those surveyed were first-generation and the analysis specifically considers their results relative to continuing-generation students. The testing method involved participants reading two texts related to financial aid and having participants report on the words they did not understand. The survey concluded that first-generation students may be at a significant disadvantage with financial literacy compared to other demographics. This study provides invaluable evidence to support the need to educate parents as well given that high school students require their assistance to fill out financial documents.

# Chapter 4 ■ The Annotated Bibliography Peer Review Workshop

Please fill out the following form for your partner. Feel free to write comments on the drafts as well.

1. Is the document clearly labeled as an Annotated Bibliography
   at the top of the page?                                                   \_\_\_\_\_ yes \_\_\_\_\_ no
2. Does the document contain a minimum of six sources?                       \_\_\_\_\_ yes \_\_\_\_\_ no
3. Are there various types of sources represented (books to develop a
   theoretical framework, scholarly journals for detailed models, etc.)?     \_\_\_\_\_ yes \_\_\_\_\_ no
4. Are at least 50% of the references cited from scholarly sources?          \_\_\_\_\_ yes \_\_\_\_\_ no
5. Is the document formatted in proper APA citation style
   (alphabetized, indented after first line, publication elements
   ordered correctly, etc.)?                                                 \_\_\_\_\_ yes \_\_\_\_\_ no
6. Is the document correctly spaced, in 12-point
   Times New Roman type, with one-inch margins?                              \_\_\_\_\_ yes \_\_\_\_\_ no
7. Is each entry annotated and detailed in describing how the
   corresponding source would be useful to the plan?                         \_\_\_\_\_ yes \_\_\_\_\_ no
8. Is each annotation 100–150 words in length, single-spaced,
   and presented in a clear, readable form?                                  \_\_\_\_\_ yes \_\_\_\_\_ no
9. Do the bibliographic entries suggest a theoretical framework
   for the plan?                                                             \_\_\_\_\_ yes \_\_\_\_\_ no
10. Do the bibliographic entries include models of success appropriate
    to the plan?                                                             \_\_\_\_\_ yes \_\_\_\_\_ no
11. Based upon the entries, is there evidence of a recognizable
    paradigm (or rationale) for the plan?                                    \_\_\_\_\_ yes \_\_\_\_\_ no
12. Is the document free of errors in grammar, usage,
    and/or sentence structure?                                               \_\_\_\_\_ yes \_\_\_\_\_ no

1. What is the one part of the draft you liked the most?

2. What is the one part of the draft that needs the most improvement?

3. What three suggestions could you provide to strengthen this Annotated Bibliography?

**Reader:** _____  **Author:** _____

# Chapter 4 ■ The Annotated Bibliography Peer Review Workshop

Please fill out the following form for your partner. Feel free to write comments on the drafts as well.

1. Is the document clearly labeled as an Annotated Bibliography at the top of the page? _____ yes _____ no
2. Does the document contain a minimum of six sources? _____ yes _____ no
3. Are there various types of sources represented (books to develop a theoretical framework, scholarly journals for detailed models, etc.)? _____ yes _____ no
4. Are at least 50% of the references cited from scholarly sources? _____ yes _____ no
5. Is the document formatted in proper APA citation style (alphabetized, indented after first line, publication elements ordered correctly, etc.)? _____ yes _____ no
6. Is the document correctly spaced, in 12-point Times New Roman type, with one-inch margins? _____ yes _____ no
7. Is each entry annotated and detailed in describing how the corresponding source would be useful to the plan? _____ yes _____ no
8. Is each annotation 100–150 words in length, single-spaced, and presented in a clear, readable form? _____ yes _____ no
9. Do the bibliographic entries suggest a theoretical framework for the plan? _____ yes _____ no
10. Do the bibliographic entries include models of success appropriate to the plan? _____ yes _____ no
11. Based upon the entries, is there evidence of a recognizable paradigm (or rationale) for the plan? _____ yes _____ no
12. Is the document free of errors in grammar, usage, and/or sentence structure? _____ yes _____ no

1. What is the one part of the draft you liked the most?

2. What is the one part of the draft that needs the most improvement?

3. What three suggestions could you provide to strengthen this Annotated Bibliography?

# Chapter 4  ■  The Annotated Bibliography Peer Review Workshop

Please fill out the following form for your partner. Feel free to write comments on the drafts as well.

1. Is the document clearly labeled as an Annotated Bibliography at the top of the page? _____ yes _____ no
2. Does the document contain a minimum of six sources? _____ yes _____ no
3. Are there various types of sources represented (books to develop a theoretical framework, scholarly journals for detailed models, etc.)? _____ yes _____ no
4. Are at least 50% of the references cited from scholarly sources? _____ yes _____ no
5. Is the document formatted in proper APA citation style (alphabetized, indented after first line, publication elements ordered correctly, etc.)? _____ yes _____ no
6. Is the document correctly spaced, in 12-point Times New Roman type, with one-inch margins? _____ yes _____ no
7. Is each entry annotated and detailed in describing how the corresponding source would be useful to the plan? _____ yes _____ no
8. Is each annotation 100–150 words in length, single-spaced, and presented in a clear, readable form? _____ yes _____ no
9. Do the bibliographic entries suggest a theoretical framework for the plan? _____ yes _____ no
10. Do the bibliographic entries include models of success appropriate to the plan? _____ yes _____ no
11. Based upon the entries, is there evidence of a recognizable paradigm (or rationale) for the plan? _____ yes _____ no
12. Is the document free of errors in grammar, usage, and/or sentence structure? _____ yes _____ no

1. What is the one part of the draft you liked the most?

2. What is the one part of the draft that needs the most improvement?

3. What three suggestions could you provide to strengthen this Annotated Bibliography?

# The Letter of Inquiry    *Chapter* 5

## The Assignment

Write a four- to five-page business letter or memo, single-spaced, not including the list of references, that accomplishes the following:

- Represents the first point of contact and initial correspondence to your patron
- Addresses a specific person by name
- Explains a current problem
- Explains at least some of your initial research toward a solution (your paradigm)
- Cites your research clearly (according to APA Style)
- Gives a sense of your plan of action and associated costs
- Closes with an invitation to your oral presentation
- Appends a list of references of at least eight sources, cited in APA Style (remember, though, that at least 10 sources are required for the project proposal)

The letter of inquiry (LOI) should be written as a **letter of persuasion,** and as such it carries the added burden of addressing a particular reader and using some of the means of persuasion available to you for appealing to him or her (with special attention to rational or logical appeals).

## Requirements

This assignment will be graded according to how well it does the following:

- Adheres to proper letter or memo format
- Discusses, documents, and quantifies the problem
- Highlights the reader's concerns about that topic
- Cites specific facts and examples from your research
- Briefly proposes a plan and provides a rationale for it

- Convinces your reader to hear more
- Provides a list of references in APA Style
- Is proofread for errors and appearance

# Purpose

The letter of inquiry serves the following purposes:

- As a draft of the project proposal, it provides you an opportunity to organize your research toward a practical goal and to begin presenting your information clearly.

- As an evaluative tool, it allows you to receive feedback on your work thus far, so you can have a sense of where you stand with your proposal and in the class.

- As an exercise in persuasive writing, it gives you practice in the most valuable form of professional correspondence.

# Typical Pitfalls and Problems

Students typically go wrong with this assignment in the following ways:

- They do not address a specific person capable of funding the project.
- They fail to provide evidence of the problem or trend they seek to address.
- They fail to explicitly cite their research.
- They assert things without evidence.
- They fail to attach a list of references.
- They use insufficient or inappropriate sources.
- They are poorly proofread for errors and appearance.

# Some General Advice, or "14 Steps to a Strong Letter of Inquiry"

You have already gained some practice in writing the letter of persuasion when you wrote the cover letter with your résumé. Here you are also making a sales pitch, but in a much more detailed way. There are 14 things you will want to consider as you write it. Obviously, each situation should dictate the type of approach you take. Also, these ideas should not limit your creativity. Remember that the audience should always direct your approach. Who will read your letter? What are your reader's concerns and interests? How can you appeal to this reader most powerfully? How can you explain your evidence? The answers to these questions should guide the way you write the letter of inquiry, and they will always vary from situation to situation. What follows, generally speaking, are 14 essential elements to a persuasive letter of inquiry:

1. **Know your audience.**

   Knowing your audience will require some preliminary primary research, or fieldwork. If you are responding to a specific request for a proposal (commonly called an RFP), then you will know some of what your audience expects. You will usually be addressing someone you do not know very well at all. Find out what you can. What is the corporate culture like at your reader's organization? What is their motto or corporate philosophy? What image do they project in their advertising? What recent endeavors have they undertaken? What problems are they facing?

What is their competition up to? Find out about your reader's general interests so that you can know better how they might fit with your idea. What specific benefits can the individual or organization you plan to address gain from solving the problem or responding to the trend you are considering?

2. **Get the right name, and get the name right.**

Address your letter to a specific person. How many times have you seen a letter that opens, "Dear Sir or Madam"? Does that inspire much interest in you? Not only is a letter addressed to a specific person bound to generate a more positive response, it will more certainly be read—and it will more likely be read by that specific person capable of making a decision on your project. (The success of annoying ads like Publisher's Clearinghouse is due in no small way to the appearance of personal interest: even the most cynical readers are unconsciously and unavoidably flattered by the fact that Publisher's Clearinghouse knows their name.)

How do you find out the person to whom you should address the letter?

This is another one of those "legwork" things, but fortunately these days it doesn't require any walking around: usually a simple telephone call or a "visit" to the company website is all you need. This is part of the fieldwork, or primary research, discussed in Chapter 4.

When in doubt, just ask! Call up the company and ask a receptionist. Talk to a few people— maybe even speak to the person you plan to address (that will give you a better sense of his or her style and will provide a good introduction to your letter). Just ask, and be nice about it. Who would handle the sort of project you have in mind? What department? What person in that department?

Once you know who you should address, find out how you should address that person. How do you spell his or her name? For purposes of the oral presentation, you will want to know how it is pronounced. Does he or she have a title? Does she prefer Ms., Mrs., or Dr.? Is there a middle initial? A Jr., Sr., or Roman numeral? Find out.

3. **"Dear" is never wrong as an address.**

"Dear" is the expected mode of address. Though you may have struggled in personal correspondence over whether or not to write "Dear" to your reader, in business correspondence it is simply a standard formality.

4. **Make a strong first impression.**

How you open your letter will depend upon the specific audience and the specific appeal you want to make. If you know the addressee, you will likely want to remind him or her of that fact and allude to your most recent or most positive interaction. If you don't know the addressee personally, you'll have to be more creative. You can rarely go wrong by trying to open with a confident and definitive statement, and you should open emphatically whenever possible. Point to the problem or need you seek to address, or state the sort of vision you will provide in responding to this need. Get this person to read further.

5. **Show that you identify with your reader's concerns.**

Explicitly state what you know about your audience's interest in the idea you will propose or the problem you seek to solve. Explain why this person is the most appropriate addressee. Show that you can see things from the reader's perspective, and that you see the proposal as a win-win situation. Your funding source will want to know what is in it for them.

6. **Specify and quantify the problem or need you seek to address.**

If you can quantify the problem, you can show its magnitude and importance. Alternately, you might give an anecdote or example that helps highlight the importance of this problem to your audience.

7. **Get to the point.**

There are some cases where you may wish to enigmatically string your reader along before revealing your specific project. Usually, though, readers in business don't have time to read a mystery novel. So don't keep your reader waiting too long for your discussion of how you intend to solve the problem or respond to the recent trend you have identified. If you offer a deal, be up front about it. What are you offering? What do you want in return? Give your reader a forecast of what to expect.

8. **Provide evidence and examples.**

This is the key to a successful letter for this course. You must cite your research. You must also show that you can use the information you have collected to construct an effective argument for action. You might say that it requires putting information into action. Evidence is always logically persuasive.

9. **Activate your reader's imagination.**

Invite your reader to engage with your idea, perhaps by using rhetorical questions. Get your reader to participate in your text.

10. **Encourage empathy.**

Now that you have shown your reader that you see things from his or her perspective, start to turn the tables a bit. Get the reader to identify with your reasons for being involved in this project, and present your reasons in the best light possible. If your ethos is key to your appeal, you may consider highlighting it earlier in your letter.

11. **Close with a call to specific action and further contact.**

Make sure that the reader sees this as a pressing need, with a deadline for action. For the purposes of your letter of inquiry for the class, you must invite your reader to hear your presentation, listing the specific date, time, and location.

12. **Make contact easy.**

It is always a good idea to provide a way for your reader to contact you easily, either by phone or email. Don't forget to put that down, usually in the last paragraph—especially if it isn't clearly printed on the stationery you use.

13. **Sign off "Sincerely."**

Don't get fancy with the closing address, unless it is especially appropriate to offer "Best wishes." Like "Dear" at the outset, "Sincerely" is the standard close.

14. **Follow up and be persistent.**

Many times you will discover that your letter has languished in the wrong department or that a busy addressee has failed to take any action because the letter has gotten buried under more pressing work. Follow up your letter after a reasonable interval, perhaps with a phone call or another method of contact. Don't give up.

# Sample Letter of Inquiry

The sample paper that follows is rather typical of the work that students turn in at this point in the proposal-writing process. However, in line with the chronology of assignments, they all require a significant amount of additional work to make them more coherent and turn them into fully developed projects. Again, the sample assignment is annotated with comments based upon the assignment's guidelines.

Since the Six P's represent the process of writing the proposal, in order, it is not surprising that most letters of inquiry do a good job of identifying an appropriate patron to fund the project, defining a population to be served, and trying to understand the problem they want to address, but that they also might be rather vague about their paradigm and the plan. Of course, the price can never be definitive until the plan is sufficiently detailed. Some vagueness is natural, but the better assignments will still suggest a more coherent sense of project and will do more not only to describe a paradigm but also to show how that paradigm informs the plan. Since each element of the plan must be justified by published research, you can't possibly have all of the parts of your plan in place until you have identified and integrated all of your sources. However, in the letters of inquiry all of the Six P's must be represented in some way.

123 Elm Street
New Brunswick, New Jersey 08901

October 15, 2022

Rebecca Villarreal
Director of Education Grantmaking
Education Philanthropy Division of Ascendium Education Group
2501 International Lane
Madison, Wisconsin 53704

**Re: College Preparedness Among First-Generation Students in Lakewood, New Jersey**

Dear Ms. Villarreal,

Ascendium Education Group is a leader on the front of removing systemic barriers to postsecondary educational success of disadvantaged groups. Your organization has granted millions of dollars to projects dedicated to serving underrepresented demographics which have achieved progress around the country. One of the key populations Ascendium seeks to aid is first-generation high school students and their access to resources necessary for their success. Given that minorities are generally overrepresented in first-generation statistics, I conducted research into school districts in Ocean County, New Jersey, and found relevant data related to continued education of minorities. I identified Lakewood High School, which is a Title I district with a large population of first-generation and minority students, as a population which would benefit greatly from a dedicated college preparedness effort. This school has roughly 1,100 students of which 95% are minorities and only 20% attend four-year postsecondary institutions (NJ School Performance Report: Ocean County High Schools, 2019). This is significantly below the state average and, with their recent $30 million budget cut, there are few resources aside from guidance counselors dedicated to helping these students (Barchenger, 2019). Given Ascendium's outstanding grant history, there is no doubt that your organization would be the best patron to support my plan for first-generation preparedness in a community that desperately needs it. Together we share a goal of improving economic and social equity amongst disadvantaged populations through promotion of higher education to those with the least access.

**The Issue Under Investigation Among First-Generation Students**

Since the passage of the Federal Higher Education Act in 1965, there has been a deliberate emphasis to support first-generation students and other disadvantaged groups in postsecondary education (Bowden & Belfield, 2015). Without the pre-exposure brought about by being raised with at least one parent who has been through the college system, these students are at a distinct disadvantage when familiarizing themselves with the jargon, culture, and application process of educational institutes (Byrd & Macdonald, 2005). According to the Center for First-Generation Student Success, 24% of college applicants nationwide have parents with no postsecondary experience and 56% have parents without a bachelor's degree (RTI International, 2019). These percentages increase when certain racial minorities are isolated, which suggests that many first-generation students must also overcome racial inequalities in order to succeed (First-Generation Students in Higher Education, 2018). Alongside this, research shows that first-generation students access academic resources, like tutoring, less frequently which contributes to significantly lower college GPA's (Holmes & Slate, 2017). Other factors that amplify this situation include that first-generation students have a lower average household income which has been shown to contribute to a 44% lower degree completion rate through their first 6 years of postsecondary education (First-Generation Students in Higher Education, 2018). These circumstances prove that first-generation students struggle on a national scale which requires direct intervention in order to accelerate their performance.

> Documentation and quantification of problem

Lakewood Township is in a very disadvantaged and impoverished situation that does not lend well to the production of college graduates. The town has a median household income of $44,708 and a 37% poverty rate which is significantly worse than the national average of $61,372 and 12%. Pairing this with over 30% of the population being between the age range of 5–17, the township is in a precarious economic situation, but has significant potential with a sizeable upcoming generation (Lakewood, NJ Census Data, 2010). Given the strong correlation between a bachelor's degree and increased lifetime earnings, putting an emphasis on first-generation students is crucial for the financial mobility of disadvantaged populations, like Lakewood (Byrd & Macdonald, 2005). However, according to a 2015 Gallup-Purdue poll, it is evident that first-generation students are 10% more likely to graduate with debt which lessens the positive economic impact brought about by continuing education (Gallup-Purdue, 2015). This is where the essential problem exists, that economically distressed communities remain in the cycle of poverty because the benefits that should come immediately after obtaining a degree wind up being delayed, or "sticky." This higher frequency of loans and "stickiness" is directly related to the confusing and cumbersome nature of financial aid applications, like the Free Application for Student Aid or FAFSA. A 2019 experiment tested the financial literacy of adult aged first-generation students and found that they performed significantly worse and missed more critical information as compared to continuing generation students. The study concluded that "financial wellness and knowledge programming should focus on adults in poverty to bolster their sense of financial wellness and knowledge and assist during the federal student aid application process" (Taylor et al., 2019). This conclusion applies to parents of first-generation high school students as it suggests that they will have equal or less knowledge than the adult aged students surveyed and thus provide less effective advice to their children. A weaker understanding of the financial aid system leads to less aid awarded, greater and more frequent loans, and the perpetuation of income inequality amongst disadvantaged populations.

> Documentation and quantification of population

Within the last 2 decades, a shift in the perspective of qualifying this problem has occurred. Originally the problem was quantified by a plethora of statistics related to the lower academic performance of first-generation students. Early efforts sought to improve standardized test scores as the most common solution. However, in 1999 there was a shift toward studying the more interpersonal and social aspects of the high school to college transition. A keystone paper by Kathleen Byrd and Ginger Macdonald published in 2005 began to qualify issues outside of academics through interviewing first-generation juniors and seniors in college. They found that the most challenging self-identified learning curve was not a student's scholastic abilities, but rather absent experience with college and inability to self-advocate. Self-advocacy was noted as particularly important given their missing background knowledge of "the college system to understand resources such as advising, financial aid, and student-professor relationships" (Byrd & Macdonald, 2005). This puts many students behind and contributes to a psychological trend that they have "internalized the view that they are inadequate for college" (Byrd & Macdonald, 2005). Since this article's publication, there has been a significant increase in case studies to support a more holistic approach when serving first-generation students.

**Ineffective and Costly Measures Taken in the Past**

In terms of pre-existing federal programs that support first-generation students and their access to college, there exists a trend of low or even negative benefit to cost ratio. One specific study on the "Talent Search" approach created by the United States Department of Education found that the program offers too much variety. "Talent Search" seeks to provide counseling to high school students only when they need assistance rather than attempting to adapt the community or school culture. This led to implementation sites having either average or inconsistent results due to resources not being properly allocated. The observed cost per student in the program was $3,580 which led to cumulative expenses becoming out of control. Research concluded that there is no discernible evidence to decide whether this "blanket" method of college preparedness is effective (Bowden & Belfield, 2015). From this model it is clear that simply throwing money at this problem does not directly solve anything, but rather an intricate solution tailored to the specific district is needed in order to be cost-effective.

Presentation and analysis of at least one guiding theory to support the paradigm

While the aforementioned "Talent Search" model is too broad to be effective, it is also possible for models to treat preparedness as an indirect benefit of other changes. The "High Schools That Work" model represents a low-cost approach that attempts to expose students to a rigorous college-based math and science course progression, known as a pipeline. The goal is that this curriculum will strengthen academic skills through a "student effort-based" method. This method eliminated a progression tracking system in favor of sheer repetition in hopes that students will learn lessons through their own experience. However, a 10-year cycle of the model showed that there was no significant improvement in college readiness or pipeline progression. Reasons for this suggest that the program's reliance on outside consultants thwarted faculty development and thus the intended cultural shift was missed (Miller & Mittleman, 2012). The takeaway from this model is that college preparedness cannot be relied on as a side effect of solely academic improvement. Instead, it requires a much more deliberate combination of targeted areas including adaptation of school culture.

**The 4-Dimensional College and Career Readiness Model**

One of the most prevalent studies of the most effective college preparedness programs was a comprehensive research effort that investigated 38 high schools across the nation. Site visits were employed to accurately assess how students responded to and performed in different types of programs in districts that varied in socioeconomic settings. Each program was coded with at least one of 50 different identifiers such as "Parent Involvement," "Financial Aid/College Cost," and "Academic Rigor" which assisted in drawing broader conclusions related to categorial success. The study found seven principles that defined every successful preparedness program and broke them down into a 4-dimensional model for high schools to bolster college readiness.

Presentation and analysis of multiple models of success to support the paradigm

Principles one, two, and five are centered around constant promotion of a "pre-college" culture and a progressive increase in academic rigor that eventually meets college standards. One key takeaway from the initial principles is the need for faculty to discuss how students should prepare for college before focusing on whether they should attend or not. Self-management skills are the core of the third principle and findings display that districts that make a deliberate effort to highlight and reward strong organizational skills achieve success. Other notable attributes related to this principle include isolating students on the border of success to take "foundation courses designed to reinforce self-management and self-advocacy skills." This is especially important for underfunded and economically strained districts where a higher portion of students remain in this border state. The fourth principle includes directing students through the college application process by making it a part of their curriculum. Outstanding results were achieved when application tasks like writing one's Common App essay or filling out the FAFSA were made into school assignments. One district in New Mexico published a monthly newsletter named the "Counselor's Corner" which was highly effective at informing parents of important "deadlines, developments, and recommendations regarding college, scholarship, and financial aid applications" (Conley et al., 2010). Principle six is perhaps the most applicable to this specific problem given it is a result significantly amplified amongst first-generation and low-income students. This issue revolves around the tendency of high school seniors to stop challenging themselves. The study found that schools that deliberately engaged seniors with a capstone project and simulated college seminars had better postsecondary performance. The final principle of partnering with a local postsecondary program was highly effective at bridging the gap between academic expectations and enabling students the opportunity to have a full immersion experience.

These seven principles and techniques for successful college readiness have contributed to a 4-dimensional model on what high schools without an existing program should focus on in order to improve preparedness. They are academic behaviors, contextual skills and awareness, key content knowledge, and key cognitive strategy. Academic behaviors include training students to overcome obstacles and encourage self-perseverance through adversity. Contextual skills and awareness refer to correcting the gap displayed in students who are "raised outside of the college-bound cultural or social capital network and must rely more heavily on their high schools to provide access to both" (Conley et al., 2010). Essentially the study found that schools that could achieve this had the highest success rates for first-generation students across the board. The latter two dimensions of this model draw on using "human-centered learning" as a means of reinforcing a consistent learning structure through "foundation courses." This implements an interdisciplinary psychological approach to learning theory in which thinking skills and intelligence are considered teachable through a standard structure of processing and retaining information (Conley et al., 2010).

**The Plan for Lakewood**

In order to improve first-generation college preparedness at Lakewood High School, a program similar to the "4-Dimensional College and Career Readiness" model will be implemented with the faults of the "Talent Search" and "High Schools That Work" models in mind. This model is well supported within the literature backing college readiness and will suit this first-generation student rendition excellently.

When considering Lakewood's low-income economic situation, there must be certain adaptations made in order to keep renewing costs low so that the program lasts past its initial funding. To achieve this, each of the seven principles will be rooted in the aforementioned "foundation courses" which will serve as the basic structural unit of the program. Given that the population at hand is statistically predisposed to unpreparedness, "foundation courses" should be applied across the board as basic college knowledge cannot be assumed. Each of the remaining six principles will have their own "foundation courses" with some of them being directly applied to students while others are used as training opportunities for Lakewood faculty. For example, the first principle related to creation of a "college-like" culture would be faculty oriented given that it was used to change school atmosphere and attitude when initiated by guidance counselors (Conley et al, 2010). On the other hand, principle four about bringing the application process to first-generation students would be better served by a "foundation course" in which application completion events are held for students. Principle seven falls slightly outside of these restrictions as it will include partnering with Georgian Court University, a small private postsecondary institution less than 2 miles from Lakewood High School. This bridge between Georgian Court and Lakewood High School would prove invaluable in bolstering primary experience with first-generation students as its "foundation course" would be straight from a 4-year university. This could include "spend a day" events where interested high school students would be able to shadow a Georgian Court student and be exposed to their daily schedule.

More primary research in the form of surveys is required to grasp a deeper understanding of exactly what problems Lakewood's first-generation students face. The most common issues will be addressed in the curriculum of each "foundation course." Contact with the most successful districts in the 4-Dimensional model will be established in order to gain direct guidance on certain aspects, like how to effectively write a parent newsletter. The goal is to have one current faculty member lead and direct the progress of the program for its 5-year pilot. With many students speaking Spanish as a second language, it is crucial for this person to be bilingual in order to communicate with parents and technologically savvy in order to leverage online resources. A strong proposal will need to be presented to the Board of Education in hopes that the program will begin in the 2023–2024 school year. 

*Current plan of action*

## The Prospective Budget

The costs associated with this program include supplemental funding necessary to run a 5-year pilot of this preparedness model at Lakewood High School. To obtain the most accurate estimates for this budget, a public high school accountant with more than 20 years of experience was consulted. Expenses are expected to be highest during September through December when college applications are due. Cumulative cost for 5 years is $39,700 which is significantly less than average for similar federally funded projects:

*Discussion and delineation of current budget*

- Train 4 faculty members how to promote college culture from other programs.
  - $1,200 upfront at 10 hours per each faculty member
- Yearly stipend for Program Director, equivalent to two seasons of sports coaching.
  - $6,000 per year for 5 years

- Purchasing "foundation course" materials and preexisting program licensing.
  - $1,000 per year for 5 years
- Transportation and chaperone to Georgian Court for 4 visits per year for up to 52 students
  - $400 per year for 5 years
- Yearly event budget to host parents and build relationships
  - $300 per year for 5 years

## A Call to Action

College preparedness of first-generation students is a solvable problem that plagues many underrepresented districts around the country. Lakewood itself is in dire need of economic support and any contribution, especially in the form of social capital, will go a long way to improving financial mobility of subsequent generations. Hopefully the research and plan outlined above have convinced you of the urgency of this situation and you see the promise in this solution. I would like to invite you to my oral presentation of this research on November 1, 2022, at 3:20 p.m. in Tillett Hall, Room 253 on Livingston Campus at Rutgers, The State University of New Jersey, New Brunswick. Please feel free to reach out to me at (732) 555–1234 or email me at dragon@rutgers.edu to discuss this in more detail. Thank you for your time and I hope to hear from you soon.

Cordial invitation to oral presentation, indicating a specific time, date, and location

Sincerely,

*Luke Dragon*

Luke Dragon

# Appendix

**Benefit to Cost Ratio:** summarizes the overall relationship between relative costs and benefits of a proposed project. Can be expressed in monetary or qualitative terms. If the ratio is greater than 1.0, the project is expected to deliver a positive net present value to a firm and its investors. Required for a project to receive federal funding (Taylor et al., 2019).

**First-Generation:** students that are pursuing a postsecondary education and their parent(s)/ guardian(s) do not have a bachelor's degree (RTI International, 2019).

**Foundation course:** a college or university level course that introduces students to a subject and prepares them for studying it at a higher level (Foundation Course, n.d.).

**Title I:** a federally funded supplemental program to assist school districts with the highest concentrations of student poverty to meet educational goals (Title I School, n.d.).

**Sticky:** a general economic theory that can apply to any financial variable that is resistant to change (Taylor et al., 2019).

# References

Barchenger, S. (2019). Lakewood schools' $30M promised by Murphy cut from new Sweeney budget. Retrieved March 5, 2020, from https://www.app.com/story/news/education/2019/06/19/lakewood-nj-schools-lose-30-million-funding-lawmakers-budget/1483070001/

Bowden, A. B., & Belfield, C. (2015). Evaluating the talent search TRIO program: A benefit-cost analysis and cost-effectiveness analysis. *Journal of Benefit-Cost Analysis, 6*(3), 572–602.

Byrd, K., & Macdonald, G. (2005). Defining college readiness from the inside out: First-generation college student perspectives. *Community College Review, 33*(1), 22–37.

Conley, T., McGaughy, D., L. Kirtner, C., Valk, J. der, Adrienne Martinez-Wenzl, & Theresa, M. (2010). College readiness practices at 38 high schools and the development of the CollegeCareerReady school diagnostic tool. Retrieved March 2, 2020, from https://eric.ed.gov/?id=ED509644

First-Generation Students in Higher Education. (2018). Retrieved March 2, 2020, from https://pnpi.org/first-generation-students/

Foundation Course. (n.d.). In Cambridge Dictionary Online. Retrieved March 2, 2020, from https://academicanswers.waldenu.edu/faq/73139

Gallup-Purdue. (2015). Student loan debt incurred as undergraduates among alumni who graduated between 2006 and 2015. Retrieved February 16, 2020, from https://www.gallup.com/services/185924/gallup-purdue-index-2015-report.aspx

Holmes, L., & Slate, D. (2017). Differences in GPA by gender and ethnicity/race as a function of first-generation status for community college students. *Global Journal of Human Social Science Research, 17*(3), 1–5.

Lakewood, NJ Census Data. (2010). Retrieved March 2, 2020, from https://datausa.io/
profile/geo/lakewood-nj/

Miller, L., & Mittleman, J. (2012). High schools that work and college preparedness:
Measuring the model's impact on mathematics and science pipeline progression.
*Economics of Education Review, 31*(6), 1116–1135.

NJ School Performance Report: Ocean County High Schools 2017–2018. (2019).
Retrieved February 17, 2020, from https://rc.doe.state.nj.us/report.aspx?
type=school&lang=english&county=29&district=2520&school=050&SY=
1718&schoolyear=2017-2018

RTI International. (2019). First-generation college students: Demographic characteristics and postsecondary enrollment. NASPA. Retrieved February 16, 2020, from
https://firstgen.naspa.org/files/dmfile/FactSheet-01.pdf

Taylor, Z., Bicak, I., Egetenmeyer, R., & Osborne, M. (2019). What is the FAFSA? An
adult learner knowledge survey of student financial aid jargon. *Journal of Adult
and Continuing Education, 25*(1), 94–112.

Title I School. (n.d.). In US Legal Definitions Online Dictionary. Retrieved March 2,
2020, from https://definitions.uslegal.com/t/title-1-school/

# Chapter 5 ■ The Letter of Inquiry Peer Review Workshop

Please fill out the following form for your partner. Feel free to write comments on the draft as well.

Does the document . . .

1. directly address the funding source? _____yes _____no

2. catch the attention of the reader? _____yes _____no

3. discuss why the reader is appropriate? _____yes _____no

4. include specific and descriptive headings to help guide the reader? _____yes _____no

5. express a clear command of population and problem? _____yes _____no

6. adequately define and document a problem for a specific location and population? _____yes _____no

7. appropriately quantify the problem? _____yes _____no

8. argue in a way that would appeal to the audience? _____yes _____no

9. refer to specific evidence? _____yes _____no

10. offer examples and/or details from sources? _____yes _____no

11. cite each source in-text according to APA format? _____yes _____no

12. describe a particular paradigm? _____yes _____no

13. offer a researched rationale for the plan? _____yes _____no

14. present a plan which follows logically from the research? _____yes _____no

15. include the suggestion of a budget? _____yes _____no

16. invite the reader to his/her presentation (including date, time, and location)? _____yes _____no

17. include a list of References prepared according to APA standards with a minimum of eight sources and at least 50% cited from scholarly work? _____yes _____no

18. appear in full block form and include all six elements (return address, date, recipient's address, salutation, body, closing)? _____yes _____no

Is the document . . .

1. signed? _____ yes _____ no

2. free of all grammatical and typographical errors? _____ yes _____ no

3. four to five pages in length, not including the References page(s), in 12-point Times New Roman font with one-inch margins? _____ yes _____ no

1. What parts of the draft are most effective?

2. What parts of the draft need the most improvement?

3. What three suggestions could you provide to strengthen this letter of inquiry?

# Chapter 5 ■ The Letter of Inquiry Peer Review Workshop

Please fill out the following form for your partner. Feel free to write comments on the draft as well.

Does the document . . .

1. directly address the funding source? _____yes _____no
2. catch the attention of the reader? _____yes _____no
3. discuss why the reader is appropriate? _____yes _____no
4. include specific and descriptive headings to help guide the reader? _____yes _____no
5. express a clear command of population and problem? _____yes _____no
6. adequately define and document a problem for a specific location and population? _____yes _____no
7. appropriately quantify the problem? _____yes _____no
8. argue in a way that would appeal to the audience? _____yes _____no
9. refer to specific evidence? _____yes _____no
10. offer examples and/or details from sources? _____yes _____no
11. cite each source in-text according to APA format? _____yes _____no
12. describe a particular paradigm? _____yes _____no
13. offer a researched rationale for the plan? _____yes _____no
14. present a plan which follows logically from the research? _____yes _____no
15. include the suggestion of a budget? _____yes _____no
16. invite the reader to his/her presentation (including date, time, and location)? _____yes _____no
17. include a list of References prepared according to APA standards with a minimum of eight sources and at least 50% cited from scholarly work? _____yes _____no
18. appear in full block form and include all six elements (return address, date, recipient's address, salutation, body, closing)? _____yes _____no

Is the document . . .

    1. signed?                                                       \_\_\_\_\_yes \_\_\_\_\_ no

    2. free of all grammatical and typographical errors?    \_\_\_\_\_yes \_\_\_\_\_ no

    3. four to five pages in length, not including the References page(s), in 12-point Times New Roman font with one-inch margins?    \_\_\_\_\_yes \_\_\_\_\_ no

    1. What parts of the draft are most effective?

    2. What parts of the draft need the most improvement?

    3. What three suggestions could you provide to strengthen this letter of inquiry?

# Chapter 5 ■ The Letter of Inquiry Peer Review Workshop

Please fill out the following form for your partner. Feel free to write comments on the draft as well.

Does the document . . .

1. directly address the funding source? _____yes _____no
2. catch the attention of the reader? _____yes _____no
3. discuss why the reader is appropriate? _____yes _____no
4. include specific and descriptive headings to help guide the reader? _____yes _____no
5. express a clear command of population and problem? _____yes _____no
6. adequately define and document a problem for a specific location and population? _____yes _____no
7. appropriately quantify the problem? _____yes _____no
8. argue in a way that would appeal to the audience? _____yes _____no
9. refer to specific evidence? _____yes _____no
10. offer examples and/or details from sources? _____yes _____no
11. cite each source in-text according to APA format? _____yes _____no
12. describe a particular paradigm? _____yes _____no
13. offer a researched rationale for the plan? _____yes _____no
14. present a plan which follows logically from the research? _____yes _____no
15. include the suggestion of a budget? _____yes _____no
16. invite the reader to his/her presentation (including date, time, and location)? _____yes _____no
17. include a list of References prepared according to APA standards with a minimum of eight sources and at least 50% cited from scholarly work? _____yes _____no
18. appear in full block form and include all six elements (return address, date, recipient's address, salutation, body, closing)? _____yes _____no

Is the document . . .

1. signed? _____yes _____ no

2. free of all grammatical and typographical errors? _____yes _____ no

3. four to five pages in length, not including the References page(s), in 12-point Times New Roman font with one-inch margins? _____yes _____ no

1. What parts of the draft are most effective?

2. What parts of the draft need the most improvement?

3. What three suggestions could you provide to strengthen this letter of inquiry?

# The Oral Presentation

*Chapter*

## The Assignment

The oral presentation is a 10- to 15-minute spoken proposal addressed to your patron (i.e., the person or people who might fund your idea). The 10- to 15-minute parameter does not include time spent setting up and breaking down the necessary materials. This limit also does not include the time required for questions from the audience. This is a formal presentation, and you must use visual aids to help convey information clearly and effectively. The point of the presentation is to make a leadership statement for a specific audience that puts information into action by proposing a research-justified solution to a well-defined problem.

The oral presentation is both a useful step in the process of developing your project and a unique assignment for which you will receive a grade. It therefore serves two, sometimes competing, purposes:

- As an "oral draft" of the proposal project, it's an opportunity to rehearse your audience-awareness, to organize your research, to develop your plan, and to get feedback from the class and the instructor on how to improve your project. A significant amount of your grade will be based on how well you have researched your topic and how well prepared you are to put together the project proposal.

- As an exercise in public speaking, it's a chance to practice the arts of oral persuasion. Your level of success will be partly based on how well you perform as a speaker.

While instructors will generally focus their grades and their remarks on the strength of your content, offering advice on revision, they will also take notice of your form and poise. Usually, those students who have the strongest content do best overall.

The basic parts of the presentation are laid out in the sections that follow. I suggest that you carefully read over the advice offered here, especially if this is the first time you have ever spoken before a group.

# The Basic Parts of the Presentation

Every presentation will have to take its own form, based on the situation and the topic. If you are addressing a potentially resistant audience, for example, you may have to begin by winning them over or addressing possible objections they might have to your idea. Therefore, you should recognize that you cannot always adhere to a single form for the talk, and the outline below may have to be adapted to your particular needs.

As part of the drafting process of your proposal, the oral presentation gives you a chance to firm up your project and work out all of the parts. You should therefore keep in mind the Six P's of the project proposal: patron, population, problem, paradigm, plan, and price. Each of the Six P's should be represented in your presentation. Your talk should suggest the basic form of the project proposal and should do these nine basic things:

1. Announce your topic with a "title slide," which should display your name and the title of your talk. This corresponds to your title page in your proposal.

2. Begin by addressing your specific audience, explaining why they should be interested in your project. This corresponds to the letter of transmittal in the project proposal, where you address the Patron.

3. Give your audience some sense of how you'll proceed, perhaps with an outline, or presentation agenda. This corresponds to the table of contents in the project proposal. This could be presented on a slide, in a handout, or both.

4. Define the problem and try to quantify it in some way. This corresponds to your introduction section of the project proposal, where you will generally lay out the Problem.

5. Present your research, being sure to cite sources in the proper format. This will correspond to the research or literature review section of the project proposal, which is where you develop your Paradigm.

6. Describe your plan of action. This corresponds to your plan or procedures section, where you set forth the Plan.

7. Tell us about your budget and explain the Price.

8. Close with a call to action, which might correspond to your discussion section of the project proposal.

9. Along the way, be sure to use visual graphic aids, just as you will in your project proposal.

The two main differences, then, between the oral presentation and the project proposal is (1) that the oral is spoken and (2) that it is missing a list of references. You must, however, cite any published material used in your presentation.

# How to Prepare

As with all assignments, you will have to prepare in the ways that have worked for you in the past. But here is some advice if you don't know where to start:

- **Research your imagined audience.** Who do you imagine might come to your talk? What is their degree of prestige and power? What level of knowledge or technical sophistication do they possess? What are their names? Many people like to begin their talk by welcoming the people in the imagined audience and thanking some of them by name for coming. This could appear on the title slide, as well. The more specifically you can imagine your audience the better your talk will be.

- **Plan ahead.** You can't wait until the last minute to prepare for a talk, and the sooner you start the better. The most important things to work on ahead of time are your visual aids, especially any visual graphic aids you want to use, such as PowerPoint slides, video, and/or audio. The sooner you begin putting your materials in order, the more secure you will feel about the presentation itself.

- **Focus your talk around key points or examples.** Remember that you can't cover everything in your talk, but you will be able to cover the major points of your argument and the chief examples that support you (which you should be able to discuss in detail). If you can establish these points on paper, you will be able to focus your work.

- **Prepare an outline.** You will definitely want to prepare an outline for yourself, and you likely will want to provide your audience with an outline as well so they can follow you more easily. As you outline, pay attention to the logic and flow of your talk.

- **Develop solid visual graphic aids.** Remember one rule of thumb: if it can be represented visually, then it should be. You should have at least three visual graphic aids (visual representations of numerical information), but if your talk will cover technical information or you will be referencing numerical information you may need to use more than that. These should be effective and useful to your talk.

- **You might prepare notecards for details.** You shouldn't read your talk, but you may need to write some things down for reference. You may want to use notecards to remember numbers, names, and key details you want to cover. Number your notecards so you can keep them in order, and try to key them to your outline for easy use.

- **Know your information and examples so you can talk about them freely.** One of the best ways to prepare for the talk is just to read over your research so that you know your topic well. If you can talk about your key examples off the cuff, then you will do fine. This skill will prove to be vital in the question-and-answer part of the presentation.

- **Rehearse the talk out loud.** The key to preparing any fine performance is a dress rehearsal. Practice in front of the mirror or, better, in front of a friend. Time your talk to make sure it will not run over 15 minutes (you will be surprised how easy that is to do), and so you have a better sense of time management. If you are especially nervous about speaking in a classroom, rehearse your talk in an actual classroom.

- **Get some sleep the night before.** A good night's sleep may be the best preparation for any situation where you will be the center of attention.

- **Double-check everything.** Make a checklist for yourself. Are your slides in order? Do you have your notecards? Make sure you have everything covered. Arrive early to test and set up any equipment you plan to use.

- **Back up all software**. You can't afford delays due to fumbling with technology. Most likely, you won't get an opportunity to reschedule your presentation.

## The Question of Delivery

Delivery is all about ethos. Do we believe you? Do you impress us? Do you know what you are talking about? Like the way you package and present your project proposal, the way you present your information will go a long way toward keeping their interest and attention. Here is some general advice on delivery:

- **Dress the part.** Students always ask, "Do we have to dress up for our presentation?" I usually respond, "It depends on your imagined audience." If you research your patron properly, you will know what they expect. You should definitely wear clothes that are appropriate to the context. If you want to make a good impression, it's generally a good idea to break out some of your better clothes. Sweatpants will not reflect well on you in any situation. For men, a tie is always best, but an outfit you would wear on a casual Friday at an office job might do. For women, any outfit you would wear to an office job should be sufficient. Ask your instructor for specific guidelines.

- **Create the context.** Clothes are only part of setting the stage for your talk. You will also want to indicate your imagined audience and acknowledge their interests whenever possible. Highlight the fact that you know your imagined audience well and make sure that you keep them in mind throughout.

- **Use a tone appropriate to your imagined audience.** One way of keeping the audience in mind is by using the same language and tone that you'd use if they really were in the room.

- **Enunciate and speak clearly.** This doesn't always mean speaking loudly, but you should speak clearly enough so that everyone can hear you.

- **Make eye contact.** Try to make eye contact with everyone in the room at some point during your talk.

- **Don't rely too much on notes.** Organize your presentation around an outline and use notecards, but *do not write out or read the presentation.* In other words: speak it, don't read it. You should know your information well enough at this point to be able to speak with confidence and knowledge using only an outline and visual aids to support and guide you. If you need to write down facts, figures, names, or an outline, use notecards because they are relatively unobtrusive. Try not to put too much between yourself and the audience . . . and NEVER read the slides to your audience.

- **Project energy and "sell" your idea.** If I have one major criticism of student presentations, it's that they rarely give off much energy. Imagine that you are really asking someone for money. You have to sell them on your plan. Turn any nervousness you have about the talk into energy and put a little bit of performance into your presentation. It will count for a lot with your audience and will keep them interested.

- **Ignore distractions and mistakes.** Everyone slips up here and there. Don't draw attention to mistakes, but move on so that both you and your audience can leave them behind.

- **Move for emphasis only—don't pace.** Everyone has tics and idiosyncratic actions that come out when they speak before a group. One person I know always holds a cup of water between himself and the audience as a sort of shield. Odd tics are usually an unconscious way of defending yourself from the people you're addressing. Pacing, for example, presents your viewers with a moving target so they can't hit you if they start to throw vegetables or bricks. Try to recognize these actions ahead of time and work through them. You have nothing to fear from your listeners, so try generally to stand still. Just don't stand in front of the screen too often or you'll be blocking people's view of your visual aids.

- **Be careful with humor.** Many guides to giving oral presentations will tell you to begin with a joke to loosen up your audience. What if you're talking about an especially serious topic? Use humor in moderation and only where appropriate.

## Advice on Using PowerPoint Slides

Since most students rely almost exclusively on PowerPoint, or some other commercially-available presentation software, for their visual aids, here is some advice on preparing and using them:

- **Begin with a title slide**. Be sure to have a title slide that sets the stage for your talk and introduces yourself and your topic. It also helps to make a good first impression—especially if it is well prepared. The title slide, like a title page, should display your title, your name, and your organization. Welcome your patron and make him/her/them comfortable. Use white space, graphics, color, or design elements that are consistent with your other slides to make it attractive.

- **Use a slide for each section of your talk.** Each section of your talk—or even every topic you cover—should have its own slide. This way you can mark the turns in your argument by changing the visual image, and you can help guide your audience through each part.

- **Have one theme per slide.** Remember not to crowd too much information onto each slide. It's best to just try to cover one theme on each one. Be wary of **text-heavy** slides.

- **Give each one a header (and number them if it helps you).** Each of your slides should have its own head line or header, indicating the topic it covers. You might want these headers to correspond to the outline you presented earlier to make your talk easier to follow. Headers should have a consistent style and form and should give a good idea of what you'll cover in that section of your talk.

- **Be sure to cite sources on charts, graphs, paraphrases, or quotes.** Each visual graphic aid that uses information derived from a source should have a "source" reference at the bottom, fully visible to your audience.

- **Use large letters and a clear font.** Remember that your slides have to be seen in the back of the room as well as the front. Make them as clear and as large as possible, yet strive for an attractive appearance.

- **Maintain a consistent font and style.** All of your slides should have the same font and if you use a border it should be the same on each one. Often it is less important to follow any rule than it is to be consistent in the styles you choose. Such consistency helps to project a sense of unity to your presentation.

- **Try a unifying border or logo.** To help further project that image of unity, you can use a logo or border on each slide. This is especially useful when you are representing a company, where you may want to have your company logo or a border with colors or a style consistent with your company image.

- **Jazz it up with color if you can.** There is no question that people are impressed by color, and your presentation will stand out more if you use color in your slides and in your visual aids.

- **Strive for active voice.** Use active voice forms in your slides whenever possible, just as in all professional writing.

- **Put numbers in a visual graphic form.** Remember that if something can be illustrated it probably should be illustrated. A picture is not always worth a thousand words, but it will usually keep you from using a thousand words to say the same thing. If a number or an idea or a definition or a procedure can be illustrated, it probably should be.

- **Let the audience absorb each slide.** Too often students don't leave their slides up long enough, often because they are hurrying through the presentation. Try to manage your time well and use a slide for each section of your talk, leaving each one on the screen until you raise a new topic.

- **Point to your slides for reference.** Draw your audience's attention to key aspects of your slides by interacting with them. You can do this in several ways—on screen, with the mouse, with a shadow, or with a light pen.

# Some PowerPoint Slide "Don'ts"

- **Don't use all caps.** Studies show that people can distinguish words and parts of sentences more easily if you use both lowercase and capital letters. Readers also perceive text written in all capital letters as shouting.

- **Don't put too much information on each slide, or use long sentences, because viewers cannot absorb it all.** Try to put no more than short phrases on each slide, and don't overcrowd them. If you find yourself putting a lot of information on a slide, then likely you need to break that information up to fit on several.

- **Don't use characters smaller than 20-point.** Remember that the people in the back of the room will have trouble with small text.

- **Don't violate the rule of parallel form.** Each slide should have information that fits together in such a way that you can list it using phrases in parallel form. This helps the audience to see connections and to organize information.

- **Don't be inconsistent in capitalizing words.** In fact, don't be inconsistent about anything.

- **Don't forget to proofread for typos.** Typos on a presentation slide are like an unzipped fly: they destroy your ethos and make you look silly.

# Final Words of Advice

### Recognize that it's normal to be nervous.

Most people feel a bit nervous whenever they have to speak before an audience, especially the first few times they have to do so. Remember that this is normal. If fears persist, though, here are a few thoughts that might help you get past your fears:

- Remember that you know more about your topic than anyone in the room. Just try to make yourself clear and you will automatically have something to offer the audience.

- Your listeners take your nervousness for granted. In fact, since most student listeners are not used to giving presentations themselves, they expect everyone to be nervous and will either overlook or identify with your situation.

- This might be the friendliest audience you will ever face. As fellow students, your listeners are on your side and generally want to give you high marks: I often notice that student reviewers generally see the most positive aspects of individual talks and tend to overlook problems (even after I have urged them to offer critical comments).

- Recognize that if this is your first talk it is a necessary rite of passage. The more practice you have giving presentations, the easier they will get and the less nervous you will feel each time.

- Turn fear into motivation. Nervousness can be a spur to greater preparation. Fear is not necessarily a negative thing, but the way you respond to it has to be positive. One common negative response to fear is procrastination, which is merely avoidance behavior (a variation on running away). The best response to fear is work, which can only help you in developing your project and bolstering your confidence in your subject knowledge.

If you still have worries or fears, talk them over with your professor or with friends. The more you face your fears, the better off you'll be in the long run.

### Don't talk down to your audience, but challenge them to follow.

The biggest mistake that students make in presenting a technical subject is trying to get their audiences "up to speed" by giving lots of background information, usually in the form of textbook knowledge, before they begin the presentation itself. Excessive background information should not be presented at the start, for several reasons:

- It destroys the fiction you are trying to create that you are speaking to a knowledgeable audience. Right away, you have confused your listeners as to who your audience really is. Chronologically speaking, your audience has read your letter of inquiry and are there to hear more.

- It sets the wrong tone, making your audience feel like they are being talked down to by a schoolmaster. Treat your audience as equals and they will prick up their ears in order to become equal to your conception of them.

- It underestimates your audience's intelligence. Because you are speaking to a college-educated audience, most of your listeners will already possess much of the basic knowledge needed to follow your talk. There may even be some audience members as expert as yourself in your field of study. Listeners will feel insulted by your explanations of "osmosis," for example, and will tune you out. Challenge them to tune in instead.

- It wastes time that you will need to present your idea. Remember that you only have a maximum of 15 minutes to give your talk. How can you present everything you learned about your topic in such a short time? You can't, so don't try.

- It mistakenly tries to anticipate questions that are best left to the question-and-answer period. Remember, if someone in the audience doesn't understand something they can always ask about it afterward. And what question is easier for you to handle than the most basic questions where you get to show off the breadth of your knowledge?

- It will not make sense in the abstract. Because information is never useful except in context, audiences have a very difficult time understanding definitions, explanations, or lessons offered in report form apart from the flow of argument.

- It is unnecessary. If a presentation is organized logically, your audience will follow your argument even if they do not understand all of the details. If you feel it is necessary to explain certain technical ideas, remember that it is much more useful to offer such explanations briefly in the context of your argument (or in the question period after) than it is to give them ahead of time. Just do your thing with confidence and your audience will be impressed, especially if they don't understand all the details.

**Logic should govern above all.**

This point was brought home to me once while listening to a student presentation on training co-op students to use proper care and technique in recording information in the field so as to comply with government regulations. Basically, these students were making many small mistakes (such as recording temperatures in Fahrenheit instead of Centigrade) that were destroying the integrity of whole projects. What could be more understandable? Yet the speaker began by presenting "background information" about the types of studies the students were doing and the specific data they were collecting. By the time she had finished offering that long explanation, she had to rush through her plan to train these students in better data-collecting techniques. As one reviewer in the audience noted, "I had no idea what she was talking about until she said that these students were using felt-tipped pens on rainy days to write down information." Basically, the audience did not need to know what was being written down with that felt-tip pen to understand that such pens posed a problem in the field.

**State your argument up front; don't keep your audience in the dark.**

You will never have your audience's attention more than you do at the outset of your talk. So tell them as much as you can up-front. Someone once said that the best advice for giving a talk is to do three things: "One: tell your audience what you're going to say; two: say it; and three: tell them what you said." While following that advice literally will lead you to an overly formulaic presentation, it does suggest the importance of leading your audience clearly through your argument with all of the forecasting statements and signposts you can muster. As I suggest above, one of the easiest ways of helping your audience to follow your talk is to provide an outline at the outset and then use slides to signal your transitions (just as you should use strong topic sentences to signal your transitions at the opening of a new paragraph in writing).

**Focus on your evidence.**

The most important aspect of the presentation is that you show that you have the evidence and research to support your assertions. Just as you would do in a written form, be sure to cite your sources. Name the authorities who inform your paradigm. Name the sources for all statistical data you cite. Name the authors of studies or experiments that you reference. Describe examples or models you reference in specific detail. Emphasize that there is a wide array of evidence to support you in your claims.

**Illustrate your budget with a pie chart.**

As part of your plan, you must include a budget, since it is one of your imagined audience's biggest concerns. Since this is one place you will always have numbers to work with, why not use a nice pie chart or other visual aid to sum up your budget? A pie chart is most appropriate because it lets you enumerate both the total and the parts.

**Close with a polished call to action.**

The closing of your presentation should sum up the plan you have in mind and urge your audience to act upon it. Hence the content of your close should focus on what needs to be done, and it should take a form that tries to influence your audience to act. Use whatever rhetorical powers you can muster to get them to listen. Listeners tend to remember best what comes at the beginning and at the end of a presentation more than anything in between. Therefore, in the same way you should strive to make a good first impression, you should close your talk with words that reflect well upon you as a speaker and offer up the "take home" message of your talk in a memorable way. Some speakers actually write out their closing words in order to polish and hone their form and tone. A strong close also signals clearly the end of your talk and lets the audience know it is time to applaud.

# Using Presentation Software to Develop a Presentation

You are required to use visual aids in your presentation, including at least three visual graphic aids (such as graphs or charts). There are a number of computer programs that can help you put together a coherent slide show that combines words and images. One of these programs, PowerPoint, offers both the graph-making abilities of Excel and the text-making abilities of Word while giving you powerful tools for keeping your slides consistent in layout and design.

## *What to Include on Your Slides*

Do not try to put everything you want to say on your slides or you will overwhelm your audience with information. Instead, your slides should emphasize the major points and primary evidence that you want your audience to remember. Focus your presentation slides around key points or examples. Ideally, you should try to limit each slide's content to four to five bulleted points (never more than seven) that are about five words each (the sound bite version of your talk). This way your audience will be able to focus on what you are saying rather than focusing on reading the slides.

Because writing and presenting is an active decision-making process, you want to control the content-making process so that your presentation best suits your audience's needs. A design template may offer you a professional-looking presentation. However, these templates are somewhat generic and are usually recognized by business professionals, so you might consider creating your own template.

## Creating a Title Slide

You should begin your presentation with a title slide that sets the stage for your talk and introduces you and your topic. A good title slide will also help you make a good first impression. The title slide, like a title page, should display your title, your name, and your organization. This is also a good opportunity to welcome your patron. Use white space, graphics, color, or design elements that are consistent with your other slides to make it attractive.

## Organizing the Rest of Your Presentation

Before you select the blank slides for the rest of your presentation, think about the logical progression of your talk. You might find the Six P's a useful basic outlining tool, moving in order through Patron (why did you choose this audience?), Population (who needs help?), Problem (what evidence do you have of a problem?), Paradigm (what research informs your solution?), Plan (how will your course of action be implemented?), and Price (how much will it cost?). Try to chunk major ideas together on each slide, outlining your talk so that the audience can remember its most important points and understand the parts of your argument. For each section, ask yourself what the key ideas are and develop bullet points to represent each one. Spend some time thinking about what visual graphic aids will be the most powerful in persuading your audience. You should especially try to use visual graphic aids to help quantify the problem, since a picture can be a powerful persuader early on in your talk.

## Inserting Tables

Tables are used to show a large amount of numerical data in a small space. They provide more information than a graph with less visual impact. Because of the way they organize information into vertical columns and horizontal rows, tables also permit easy comparison of figures. Be sure to use concise, descriptive table titles and column headings. In addition, arrange the rows of the table in a logical order. When putting dollar amounts into tables, be sure the decimals are aligned for easy addition or subtraction.

## Inserting and Editing Graphs

Before you make a graph, think about the information you want to convey. Draw a picture by hand and think about whether there is room for text on the page as well. You can choose several different graphing options, including bar graphs, pie graphs, line graphs, and even bubble graphs. Select the graph that is best suited to conveying your data. For instance, line charts are generally used to show changes in data over a period of time and to emphasize trends. Bar charts compare the magnitude of items, either at a specific time or over a period of time. Pie charts compare parts that make up the whole. With pie charts, you should start at the 12:00 position with the largest unit and work around in descending order. Whatever chart you choose, be sure to keep it simple. Your goal is to focus the reader's attention on the data in the chart rather than on the chart itself. In addition, you will want to label all charts as figures and assign them consecutive numbers that are separate from table numbers. This way if your audience has a question about a specific image later, they can refer to it by name and number.

## Using Photos and Graphics

The "power" of programs such as PowerPoint comes from the way it allows you to seamlessly integrate text and images. Images can be a powerful support for your message, though they can also distract from what you want to say if they are not well chosen. Ideally, you will want to develop your own original images to use in your presentation. Sometimes, however, sourced graphics and images can be useful.

## *Making a Master Slide*

You can also make any graphic or photo into a background for all of your slides. Sometimes it is hard to see text against an image background. However, if the image is well chosen or especially appropriate to your topic it can help you to create an original background that breaks from the familiar generic backgrounds that most presenters use. Also, there are ways to make a background image fade into the background so that your text and support graphics can take center stage.

## *Adding Text*

Once you have the basic visual layout of your talk, you can add your text. Remember to keep your slides consistent and uncluttered. Keep in mind that you, and not your slides, are delivering your presentation. Develop slides that will help you achieve your independent goals, in support of your proposal.

# The Graphic Aids Assignment

Visual aids are an important part of both your oral presentation and your project proposal. They can provoke an immediate response in your audience in a way that a paragraph of statistics may not. In preparation for your oral presentation, bring in at least three visual aids with written commentary.

For the purposes of this assignment, these three visual graphic aids should be taken from popular sources, such as newspapers or magazines, or printed out from online sources (e.g., *Google* images). They could be ones that you are considering using for your oral presentation and project proposal, but they could also just be interesting examples of graphics. Please do not bring in pictures or photographs for this particular assignment: I would much rather have you find images which are visual representations of statistical information, as in charts, tables, graphs, and so on. You may find certain graphics that you find misleading, or would like to show the class possible "sneaky" tactics used by the presenters. To help you develop strong, informative, attractive visual aids, we will look at your examples and some others in a peer review/class presentation session.

# Sample Oral Presentation Slide Show

You are being provided with an actual student sample of this assignment. To help see the continuity among assignments, this presentation matches the letter of inquiry from the previous chapter. This is a representative sample that is typically seen at this point in the proposal-writing process and has both strong and weak points. Again, annotations based upon the requirements of the assignment are provided. Consult your instructor for number and types of sources required and appropriate citation.

**Slide 1**

> ## Proposal
> ## for First-Generation
> ## College Preparedness in
> ## Lakewood, New Jersey
>
> **By: Luke Dragon**
>
> **Welcome Ms. Rebecca Villarreal, Director of Education
> Grantmaking at Ascendium Philanthropy Group**
>
> 1

Title slide

**Slide 2**

> ## Introduction
>
> **Welcome Ascendium Education!**
> - **Rebecca Villareal**
>   - **Director of Education Grantmaking**
>
> **"We believe in the power of postsecondary
> education and workforce training to create
> opportunity. Through our continued funding of
> evidence-based practices, we look to remove
> barriers to completion of education and career
> goals that matter most."**
>
> 2

Welcome slide, reinforcing choice of patron

**Slide 3**

> ## Presentation Overview
>
> - **National First-Generation Student Issues**
> - **Lakewood Township Socioeconomic Context**
> - **Lakewood High School Survey Results**
> - **Ineffective Models**
> - **Models of Success**
> - **Plan of Action**
> - **Implementation for First-Gen Students**
> - **Budget**
> - **Why We Should Care**
>
> 3

Agenda

**Slide 4**

> ## National First-Generation Student Issues
>
> - **"Students that are pursuing a postsecondary education
>   and their parent(s)/guardian(s) do not have a bachelor's
>   degree."[11]**
> - **Growing emphasis since Federal Higher Education Act.[2]**
> - **Disadvantage with jargon, culture, and application
>   process.[3]**
> - **Lower college GPA[7] and degree completion rate.[5]**
> - **Confusing nature of financial aid applications.[6,12]**
>
> [2] Bowden, A. B., & Belfield, C. (2015)
> [3] Byrd, K., & Macdonald, G. (2005)
> [5] First-Generation Students in Higher Education(2018)
> [6] Gallup-Purdue. (2015)
> [7] Holmes, L., & Slate, D. (2017)
> [11] RTI International. (2019)
> [12] Taylor, Z., Bicak, I., Egetenmeyer, R., & Osborne, M. (2019)
>
> 4

Discussion and analysis of the remaining Five P's, in order, throughout the presentation

**Slide 5**

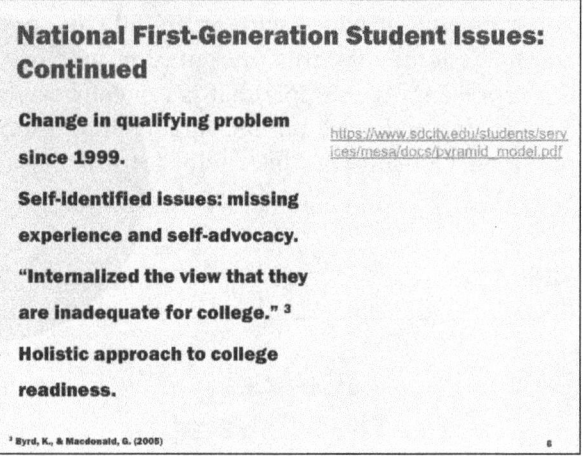

National First-Generation Student Issues

Percent of Students Using Financial Aid Services[5]

Demographic Distribution of College Students[5]

https://firstgen.naspa.org/files/dmfile/NASPA_FactSheet-03_FIN.pdf

https://firstgen.naspa.org/files/dmfile/FactSheet-01.pdf

[5] First-Generation Students in Higher Education(2018)

5

**Slide 6**

National First-Generation Student Issues: Continued

- Change in qualifying problem since 1999.

- Self-identified issues: missing experience and self-advocacy.

- "Internalized the view that they are inadequate for college." [3]

- Holistic approach to college readiness.

https://www.sdcity.edu/students/services/mesa/docs/pyramid_model.pdf

[3] Byrd, K., & Macdonald, G. (2005)

6

**Slide 7**

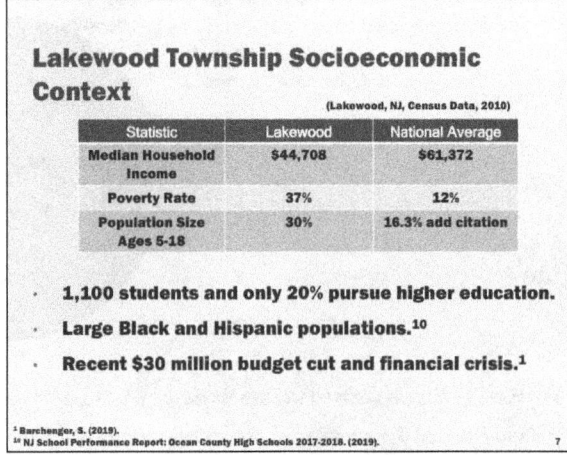

Lakewood Township Socioeconomic Context

(Lakewood, NJ, Census Data, 2010)

| Statistic | Lakewood | National Average |
|---|---|---|
| Median Household Income | $44,708 | $61,372 |
| Poverty Rate | 37% | 12% |
| Population Size Ages 5-18 | 30% | 16.3% add citation |

- 1,100 students and only 20% pursue higher education.
- Large Black and Hispanic populations.[10]
- Recent $30 million budget cut and financial crisis.[1]

[1] Barchenger, S. (2019).
[10] NJ School Performance Report: Ocean County High Schools 2017-2018. (2019).

7

**Slide 8**

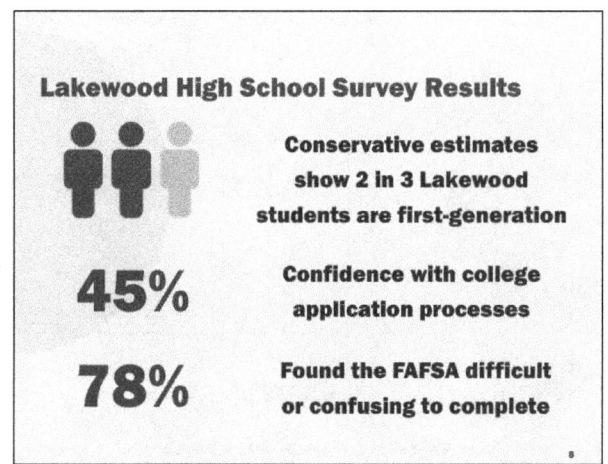

Lakewood High School Survey Results

Conservative estimates show 2 in 3 Lakewood students are first-generation

45% — Confidence with college application processes

78% — Found the FAFSA difficult or confusing to complete

8

**Slide 9**

## 95.8%

Supported a dedicated college readiness program for disadvantaged students

9

**Slide 10**

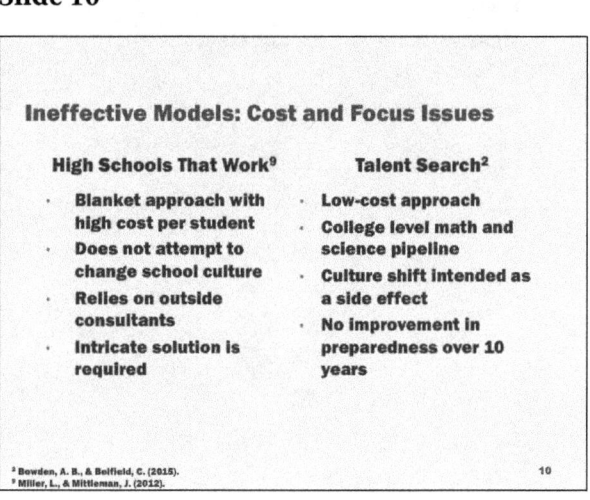

Ineffective Models: Cost and Focus Issues

High Schools That Work[9]

- Blanket approach with high cost per student
- Does not attempt to change school culture
- Relies on outside consultants
- Intricate solution is required

Talent Search[2]

- Low-cost approach
- College level math and science pipeline
- Culture shift intended as a side effect
- No improvement in preparedness over 10 years

[2] Bowden, A. B., & Belfield, C. (2015).
[9] Miller, L., & Mittleman, J. (2012).

10

**Slide 11**

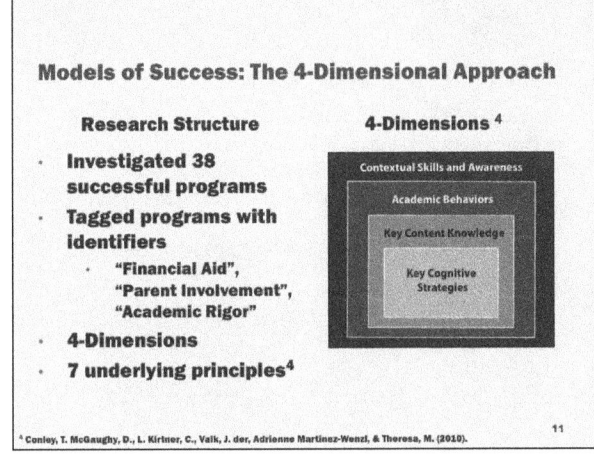

Models of Success: The 4-Dimensional Approach

**Research Structure**    **4-Dimensions** [4]

- **Investigated 38 successful programs**
- **Tagged programs with identifiers**
  - "Financial Aid", "Parent Involvement", "Academic Rigor"
- **4-Dimensions**
- **7 underlying principles**[4]

[4] Conley, T. McGaughy, D., L. Kirtner, C., Valk, J. der, Adrienne Martinez-Wenzl, & Theresa, M. (2010).    11

**Slide 12**

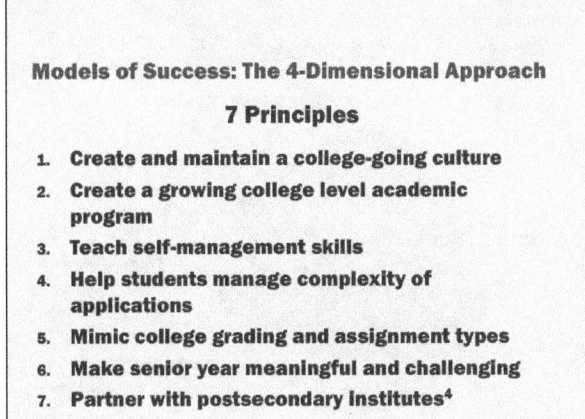

Models of Success: The 4-Dimensional Approach

**7 Principles**

1. **Create and maintain a college-going culture**
2. **Create a growing college level academic program**
3. **Teach self-management skills**
4. **Help students manage complexity of applications**
5. **Mimic college grading and assignment types**
6. **Make senior year meaningful and challenging**
7. **Partner with postsecondary institutes**[4]

[4] Conley, T. McGaughy, D., L. Kirtner, C., Valk, J. der, Adrienne Martinez-Wenzl, & Theresa, M. (2010).    12

**Slide 13**

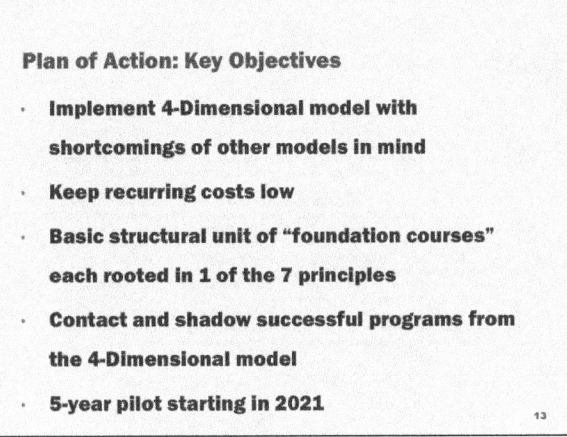

Plan of Action: Key Objectives

- **Implement 4-Dimensional model with shortcomings of other models in mind**
- **Keep recurring costs low**
- **Basic structural unit of "foundation courses" each rooted in 1 of the 7 principles**
- **Contact and shadow successful programs from the 4-Dimensional model**
- **5-year pilot starting in 2021**

13

**Slide 14**

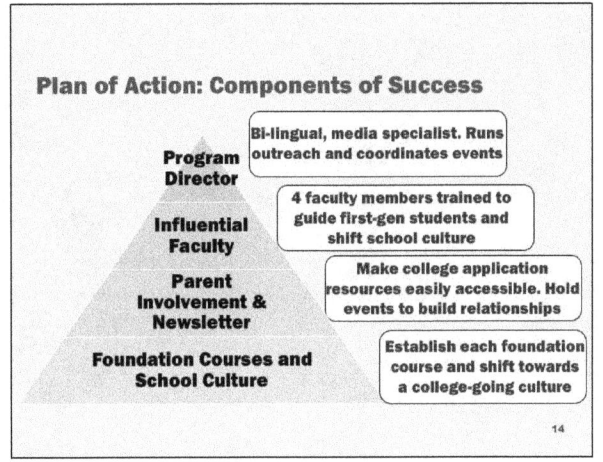

Plan of Action: Components of Success

**Program Director** — Bi-lingual, media specialist. Runs outreach and coordinates events

**Influential Faculty** — 4 faculty members trained to guide first-gen students and shift school culture

**Parent Involvement & Newsletter** — Make college application resources easily accessible. Hold events to build relationships

**Foundation Courses and School Culture** — Establish each foundation course and shift towards a college-going culture

14

**Slide 15**

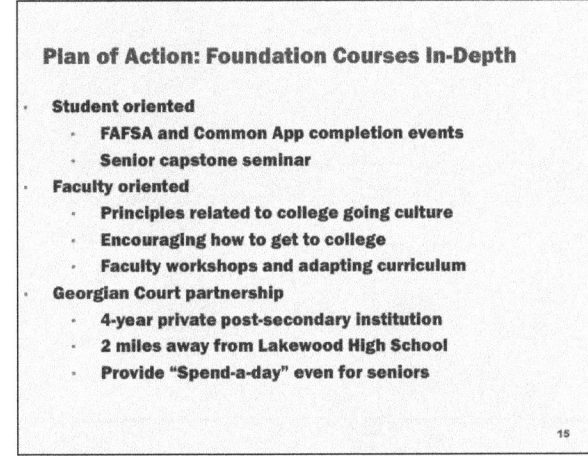

Plan of Action: Foundation Courses In-Depth

- **Student oriented**
  - **FAFSA and Common App completion events**
  - **Senior capstone seminar**
- **Faculty oriented**
  - **Principles related to college going culture**
  - **Encouraging how to get to college**
  - **Faculty workshops and adapting curriculum**
- **Georgian Court partnership**
  - **4-year private post-secondary institution**
  - **2 miles away from Lakewood High School**
  - **Provide "Spend-a-day" even for seniors**

15

**Slide 16**

**Budget**

- **Significantly cheaper than the average federally funded project**
- **In the same range as many similar Ascendium grants**

| Item | Cost Per Year | Years | Total Cost Per Item |
|---|---|---|---|
| Faculty Training | $1,200 | 1,3 | $2,400 |
| Director Stipend | $6,000 | 1-5 | $30,000 |
| "Foundation Course" Materials and Licensing | $1,000 | 1-5 | $5,000 |
| Event Budget | $300 | 1-5 | $1,500 |
| Transportation | $400 | 1-5 | $2,000 |
| Total Cost | | | $40,900 |

16

**Slide 17**

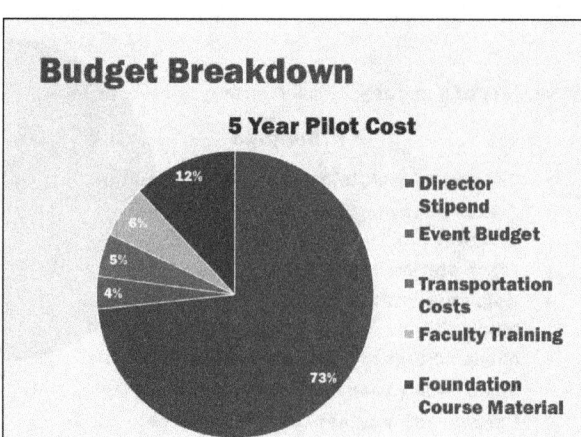

**Slide 18**

Why We Should Care

- Lakewood Township is in dire need of economic support
- Massive budget cuts in recent years
- Large youth population requires immediate action
- First-generation is the best identifier for disadvantaged students
- Social and economic equity through financial mobility

**Slide 19**

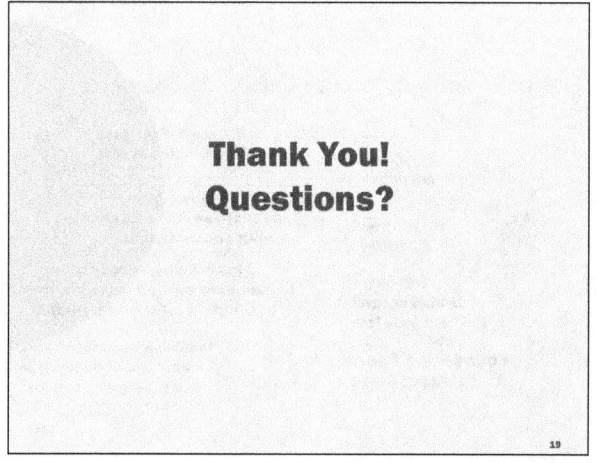

Q&A slide

**Slide 20**

References

[1] Barchenger, S. (2019). Lakewood schools' $30M promised by Murphy cut from new Sweeney budget. Retrieved March 5, 2020, from https://www.app.com/story/news/education/2019/06/19/lakewood-nj-schools-lose-30-million-funding-lawmakers-budget/1483070001/
[2] Bowden, A. B., & Belfield, C. (2015). Evaluating the talent search TRIO program: A benefit-cost analysis and cost-effectiveness analysis. *Journal of Benefit-Cost Analysis, 6*(3), 572-602.
[3] Byrd, K., & Macdonald, G. (2005). Defining college readiness from the inside out: First-generation college student perspectives. *Community College Review, 33*(1), 22–37.
[4] Conley, T. McGaughy, D., L. Kirtner, C., Valk, J. der, Adrienne Martinez-Wenzl, & Theresa, M. (2010). College readiness practices at 38 high schools and the development of the CollegeCareerReady school diagnostic tool. Retrieved March 2, 2020, from https://eric.ed.gov/?id=ED509644
[5] First-Generation Students in Higher Education. (2018). Retrieved March 2, 2020, from https://pnpi.org/first-generation-students/
[6] Gallup-Purdue. (2015). Student loan debt incurred as undergraduates among alumni who graduated between 2006 and 2015. Retrieved February 16, 2020, from https://www.gallup.com/services/185924/gallup-purdue-index-2015-report.aspx

APA-style reference slide(s), listing each source cited, either on the respective slides and/or orally, in the presentation

**Slide 21**

References Continued

[7] Holmes, L., & Slate, D. (2017). Differences in GPA by gender and ethnicity/race as a function of first-generation status for community college students. *Global Journal of Human Social Science Research, 17*(3), 1–5.
[8] Lakewood, NJ Census Data. (2010). Retrieved March 2, 2020, from https://datausa.io/profile/geo/lakewood-nj/
[9] Miller, L., & Mittleman, J. (2012). High schools that work and college preparedness: Measuring the model's impact on mathematics and science pipeline progression. *Economics of Education Review, 31*(6), 1116–1135.
[10] NJ School Performance Report: Ocean County High Schools 2017–2018. (2019). Retrieved February 17, 2020, from https://rc.doe.state.nj.us/report.aspx?type=school&lang=english&county=29&district=2520&school=050&SY=1718&schoolyear=2017-2018
[11] RTI International. (2019). First-generation college students: Demographic characteristics and postsecondary enrollment. NASPA. Retrieved February 16, 2020, from https://firstgen.naspa.org/files/dmfile/FactSheet-01.pdf
[12] Taylor, Z., Bicak, I., Egetenmeyer, R., & Osborne, M. (2019). What is the FAFSA? An adult learner knowledge survey of student financial aid jargon. *Journal of Adult and Continuing Education, 25*(1), 94–112.

# Chapter 6 ■ The Oral Presentation Peer Review Workshop

Please fill out the following form for your partner. Feel free to write comments on the draft as well.

Are the Oral Presentation slides . . .

1. visually appealing? _____yes _____no
2. easy to read? _____yes _____no
3. cited properly in APA format (including text features)? _____yes _____no

Do the Oral Presentation slides . . .

1. have a title slide including the title of the proposal, the presenter's name, the name of the course, the date, and an image related to the topic? _____yes _____no
2. have a slide to welcome the patron? _____yes _____no
3. include the main contents of the presentation clearly outlined on an introductory slide? _____yes _____no
4. have photos/text features, which are easy to see and understand? _____yes _____no
5. have a consistent font style throughout the presentation? _____yes _____no
6. have a cohesive visual theme? _____yes _____no
7. present information in a logical order? _____yes _____no
8. follow the progression of the Six P's? _____yes _____no

1. Does the amount and style of text on each slide inform the audience without distracting them?

2. Is there any additional information that needs to be included in the presentation?

3. Does the author appeal to ethos, pathos, and logos in presentation?

4. Is it clear why the presenter has chosen this particular patron? Explain why or why not.

5. Is it clear that the presenter has adequately researched the population affected by the problem? Explain why or why not.

6. Is the price justified and clearly broken down to explain allocation?

7. What three suggestions could you provide to strengthen this presentation?

# Chapter 6 ◼ The Oral Presentation Peer Review Workshop

Please fill out the following form for your partner. Feel free to write comments on the draft as well.

Are the Oral Presentation slides . . .

| | | |
|---|---|---|
| 1. | visually appealing? | _____yes _____no |
| 2. | easy to read? | _____yes _____no |
| 3. | cited properly in APA format (including text features)? | _____yes _____no |

Do the Oral Presentation slides . . .

1. have a title slide including the title of the proposal, the presenter's name, the name of the course, the date, and an image related to the topic?                                                                          _____yes _____no
2. have a slide to welcome the patron?                     _____yes _____no
3. include the main contents of the presentation clearly outlined on an introductory slide?                              _____yes _____no
4. have photos/text features, which are easy to see and understand?   _____yes _____no
5. have a consistent font style throughout the presentation?   _____yes _____no
6. have a cohesive visual theme?                         _____yes _____no
7. present information in a logical order?               _____yes _____no
8. follow the progression of the Six P's?               _____yes _____no

1. Does the amount and style of text on each slide inform the audience without distracting them?

2. Is there any additional information that needs to be included in the presentation?

3. Does the author appeal to ethos, pathos, and logos in presentation?

4. Is it clear why the presenter has chosen this particular patron? Explain why or why not.

5. Is it clear that the presenter has adequately researched the population affected by the problem? Explain why or why not.

6. Is the price justified and clearly broken down to explain allocation?

7. What three suggestions could you provide to strengthen this presentation?

Reader: _____ Author: _____

# Chapter 6 ■ The Oral Presentation Peer Review Workshop

Please fill out the following form for your partner. Feel free to write comments on the draft as well.

Are the Oral Presentation slides . . .

1. visually appealing? _____yes _____no
2. easy to read? _____yes _____no
3. cited properly in APA format (including text features)? _____yes _____no

Do the Oral Presentation slides . . .

1. have a title slide including the title of the proposal, the presenter's name, the name of the course, the date, and an image related to the topic? _____yes _____no
2. have a slide to welcome the patron? _____yes _____no
3. include the main contents of the presentation clearly outlined on an introductory slide? _____yes _____no
4. have photos/text features, which are easy to see and understand? _____yes _____no
5. have a consistent font style throughout the presentation? _____yes _____no
6. have a cohesive visual theme? _____yes _____no
7. present information in a logical order? _____yes _____no
8. follow the progression of the Six P's? _____yes _____no

1. Does the amount and style of text on each slide inform the audience without distracting them?

2. Is there any additional information that needs to be included in the presentation?

3. Does the author appeal to ethos, pathos, and logos in presentation?

4. Is it clear why the presenter has chosen this particular patron? Explain why or why not.

5. Is it clear that the presenter has adequately researched the population affected by the problem? Explain why or why not.

6. Is the price justified and clearly broken down to explain allocation?

7. What three suggestions could you provide to strengthen this presentation?

# Chapter 6 ■ The Oral Presentation Evaluation

1. **Audience**: How well did the speaker address the funding source?

   1     2     3     4     5     6     7     8     9     10

2. **Eye Contact**: How well did the speaker acknowledge and address those actually present?

   1     2     3     4     5     6     7     8     9     10

3. **Delivery**: How were the speaker's volume, enunciation, posture, appearance, and body language?

   1     2     3     4     5     6     7     8     9     10

4. **Evidence**: Did the speaker support claims, give examples, reference facts, and cite sources?

   1     2     3     4     5     6     7     8     9     10

5. **Organization**: Was the presentation easy to follow? Were all Six P's represented, in the correct order?

   1     2     3     4     5     6     7     8     9     10

6. **Visual Aids**: Were there sufficient, attractive, and useful visual graphic aids?

   1     2     3     4     5     6     7     8     9     10

7. **Preparation**: Did the presentation show careful planning, good time management, and smooth transitions?

   1     2     3     4     5     6     7     8     9     10

8. **Questions**: Did the speaker demonstrate knowledge, confidence, courtesy, and interest?

   1     2     3     4     5     6     7     8     9     10

Additional Comments/Suggestions:

# The Project Proposal

*Chapter* 7

## The Assignment

The project proposal is the final draft of the project you have worked on all term. Like the oral presentation, it should be a leadership statement that puts information into action by proposing a research-justified solution to a well-defined problem. Unlike the presentation, though, it must adhere to a specific format, which is presented below and illustrated in the sample paper that follows. The guidelines for preparing this document may not conform to those of your workplace or those requested for specific grant applications you might be considering. These guidelines, though, should be readily adaptable to any real-world submission. We encourage you to revise your final project for submission in your workplace or in your future graduate work, but for the time being focus on fulfilling the requirements in this chapter. Please consult with your instructor if there are any discrepancies between the parameters presented here and the instructions included in a published Request for Proposals (RFP).

Remember that the heart of the proposal is a problem, paradigm, and plan that work together to create a unified concept. The paradigm should grow organically out of the way you define the problem, and the plan you present should be clearly rationalized by the paradigm. If you unify and focus your argument, you will be able to present a well-organized and logical paper.

The final draft of the project proposal must be from 15–20 pages inclusive, single-spaced (though your References should be double-spaced in keeping with APA guidelines). You should also be sure to do the following:

- Strive for a consistent professional tone throughout.
- Number your pages clearly.
- Provide coherence to your paper using rhetorical, design, and signposting strategies.
- Use clearly distinguished headings and subheads to help guide your reader through the parts of each section.
- When appropriate, use bullets or numbers to list items for easy comprehension.
- Label and number all graphs and figures for easy reference.
- Unify your paper with a consistent typography and style.

- Polish your writing for style and emphasis.
- Proofread for errors in spelling, grammar, and syntax.

# The Parts of the Proposal

The formal aspects of the project proposal help you to present your overall argument in a way that is useful for your reader. There are 13 parts of the project proposal, most of which should be labeled and presented in order (with the exception of visual graphic aids, which should ideally be incorporated into the body of the paper with individual titles):

1. Cover Letter—generally one full page (not numbered or titled)
2. Title Page—one page (not numbered)
3. Abstract—one page (Roman numeral i)
4. Table of Contents—one page (Roman numeral ii)
5. Table of Figures—one page (Roman numeral iii)
6. Introduction—generally two or more pages (Arabic numeral 1·)
7. Literature Review (or Research)—generally two or more pages
8. Plan (or Procedures)—generally one to two more pages
9. Budget
10. Discussion (perhaps including an Evaluation Plan)
11. References
12. Visual Aids (or Figures)—incorporated into the text when possible
13. Appendix (if necessary)

## 1. Cover Letter

Like the cover letter that accompanied your résumé, this letter of transmittal is intended to explain and interpret the attached document. It should explain why the reader has received your proposal, and it should try to persuade the reader to examine it closely, offering details about the content intended to interest or intrigue him or her. This letter of transmittal should respond to the situation of reading and answer the reader's likely questions: "Why is this on my desk?" and "Why should I read this when I have a dozen other things to do?"

The transmittal letter can take the form of a letter (for a reader outside of your organization) or memo (for a reader within your organization). While an increasing number of transmittals are written in e-mail form, where the proposal is usually an attached file, we ask that you adhere to the traditional paper forms for the purposes of this course.

If it is a letter, it should follow the full block style, in which all of the elements are flush with the left margin in this order:

1. Return address (your name and address)
2. Date (for the purposes of the class, use the due date of the project proposal)
3. Recipient's address (including name, title, organization, and business address)
4. Salutation ("Dear" plus formal address and name)

5. Body (see discussion below)

6. Closing ("Sincerely") and signature

If you are using the letterhead of a specific organization, you will not need to include your address. If the cover letter is prepared as a memo, then it should be written on company stationery (or facsimile) and prepared in memo form:

- To: (addressee's full name)

- From: (your full name and handwritten initials)

- Date: (today's date)

- Subject: (a line indicating your proposal topic)

- Body (see discussion below)

Many of the rules for writing the cover letter to accompany your résumé apply here. Since your imagined reader probably attended your presentation (or at least you created a context where he or she was imagined in the room), you may want to begin by reminding the reader of that event, explaining that this is the full version of that proposal. Whether or not you have met your reader before, begin by explaining why you sent him or her your proposal and why it should be of interest. Emphasize what you know about the reader's interests, and highlight the principal ways in which this proposal matches those interests.

The central paragraph (or central two paragraphs) should offer an overview of the project, highlighting salient details about the problem, paradigm, and plan. Again, point to those aspects of your project most likely to interest your reader.

The final paragraph should invite further contact, offering the most convenient way for the reader to get in touch with you (perhaps by phone or email).

## 2. Title Page

The page should include the following information:

- Project title

- Submitted by: Your full name and title (or position)

- Submitted to: Your addressee's full name, title, and business address

- Date

You should also indicate somewhere near the bottom of the page the course for which this paper was prepared, your instructor's name, and any class information requested by your instructor. (This way if your paper gets lost it won't end up on the desk of the imagined audience but will have a chance of being returned.)

The title of your project should be carefully chosen and crafted for maximum communication in the shortest space. It is one of the first things the reader sees of your proposal, and it will become the means of referencing it to others. The more communicative power it has, the more effective it will be. Strive to be both clear and memorable. Remember that you can use a two-part title, especially if you want to give your project a catchy title followed by a more technically specific one.

There are many ways to design the title page, and you should do what looks and works best for your specific project. Use white space, color, and other page elements to design an attractive image that is consistent with the document design as a whole. You might want to use graphics or pictorial lettering to highlight your topic.

## 3. Abstract

The abstract should be clearly labeled as an "abstract" at the top of the page and should be no more than one or two paragraphs in length. The purpose of the abstract is to tell busy people (or their secretaries) how to file your report. It should be written from a disinterested perspective, providing a balanced view of the project idea as though written by an outside party. Usually it is written in the third person or uses passive voice to avoid naming the agent. For the purposes of this class, you should write a relatively long, informative abstract that includes details about your overall argument and covers elements of the problem, paradigm, and plan (in that order). Be sure to indicate your rationale and what specific action you want to take. Aim to be maximally communicative within minimal space—generally between 150 and 300 words.

## 4. Table of Contents

Clearly label and design your table of contents for easy use. Recognize that the table of contents has two main uses: it helps readers locate the information that interests them most (this is especially true of longer proposals) and it gives your reader an overview of the project and its parts. You should list all parts of the project listed above (excluding the cover letter, title page, and visual aids), along with any important subheads. Number the front matter (abstract, table of contents, and table of figures) with small Roman numerals (i, ii, iii) and then use Arabic numbers (1, 2, 3) beginning with the introduction section. Use whatever design elements you can to help make the information clear and usable—indenting subheads, using ellipses to link section names and page numbers, and aligning all related parts. You may want to use dot leaders to align the elements of your table. The style and font should be consistent with the design throughout your document.

You can work up a table by carefully laying out the items in it, but many word processing programs, such as Microsoft Word, will generate a table for you.

## 5. Table of Figures

If your table of contents is short, you might include your table of figures (clearly labeled) on the same page. Otherwise, it should occupy its own page. Ideally, each figure and illustration you use should have a number for easy reference. List the number and title of each figure along with the page on which it appears. Again, dot leaders may be helpful for proper alignment.

## 6. Introduction

There are two purposes for the introduction: to present information about the problem you will address and to forecast your overall argument. Here is where you will want to offer all the information you have on the problem you seek to address. You should try to quantify or define and quantify the problem, as well as offer images that help clarify and emphasize the key aspects of it. Focus on those aspects of the problem that will most interest your reader, and suggest by the way you examine or define the problem a direction for approaching it. Close the introduction with a forecasting statement giving your reader a sense of your argument to follow and providing a transition to the next part.

## 7. Literature Review (or Research)

This is the section in which you present, analyze, and integrate your paradigm research into your proposal. The literature review section should open with some reference to the problem (especially by way of transition from the introduction), but it should focus mostly on the justification for your project. The research you present should explain why you will approach the problem in a particular way; it should also provide a unified rationale for the specific plan of action you describe in your plan.

Thus the paradigm is essential for unifying your paper because it shows how the plan of action you will propose is a logical approach to the problem you have defined. Remember, there are two sides to paradigms—they are represented by a **theoretical framework** and by **multiple models of success**. These elements work together to provide justification for your specific course of action.

While each of you will have to explore research in a way unique to your topic, all of you should strive to show that you are not merely asserting your approach to the problem based on opinion, politics, or personal view, but that there is a consensus of opinion or a well-documented trend or development that supports your idea. You will want to discuss theories that form the basis for your assertion that the plan you have in mind will be effective—offering evidence and authority to show that your plan is responding to a body of knowledge in a particular field. If you are planning experimental work that grows out of a well-established scientific paradigm, you should review the tradition of work in the field that you are building on in your research. You will also discuss examples of similar or related projects you are using as models, focusing on the procedures and plans that worked in those instances and emphasizing the positive results achieved. Remember that the main purpose of the research is to justify your plan of action. Thus, if you plan to educate people about a specific environmental issue, you will likely want to focus more on an effective way (or paradigm) of educating people than you will on that environmental issue (though you will need research on that as well).

One of the purposes of the literature review is to establish your authority, which will stand or fall based on the quality of the research you cite. By demonstrating your command over recognized or paradigmatic research, you show that you have the knowledge and expertise to make valid recommendations. You should strive to find the most useful and authoritative research whenever possible, and you should discuss published research (ideally, research that has been subjected to peer review). Many projects will, however, call for a wide range of research sources, including articles, books, internet sources, published government statistics, interviews, surveys, field studies, calculations, and experimental results. You should do your best to evaluate sources and use only the most solid in building your literature review. To use low-quality materials in constructing your paper is equivalent to using low-quality materials in building a house, and your product will be evaluated and graded accordingly.

## 8. Plan (or Procedures)

The plan should be as specific as possible and should follow logically from your research. How it is presented will depend upon the specific project you have in mind. If you are proposing a workplace project, you might focus on how your idea will be implemented (perhaps providing a flowchart or time line). If you are proposing to do an experiment, you should lay out the specific procedures you will use. If you are building something, you will want to describe how it will be built and provide diagrams. You might wish to reference research to support the specific choices you are making, though the literature review section should provide the bulk of your rationale.

## 9. Budget

The budget should list everything you will need for your project, from salaries to supplies. Some items may require explanation, which you should provide here as well. You should arrange the cost of your budget items in aligned accountant's columns to make your addition clear.

## 10. Discussion (with Evaluation Plan)

Generally your paper should conclude by summing up your project and making a final pitch for its value. If you are proposing a project whose results can be tested in some way, then you should also offer an evaluation plan.

## 11. References

This section should list all sources of information cited in your paper in alphabetical order. The list of references should be prepared according to APA Style, covered in the discussion about the APA Style guide in Chapter 4. For those who want extra guidance, you might consult *The APA Handbook*, which is available in the reference section of any campus library.

## 12. Visual Aids (or Figures)

You should have at least three graphic aids that are visual representations of numerical information. These might include graphs, tables, charts, or maps. In addition to these three, you may include drawings, photographs, flowcharts, maps, organization charts, Gantt charts, timelines, diagrams, or floor plans. Each visual graphic aid should be numbered (e.g., Figure 1, Figure 2, etc.) and should have a title. If the graphic is based on information from a source, then you should have a citation line at the bottom (i.e., Source: Alvarez, 2015, p. 26). If you can incorporate your graphics into the body of the paper, do so. If you cannot incorporate your graphics, then include them at the end in an appendix or inter-paginate them directly following the first reference to them.

## 13. Appendix (optional)

If you have other information that doesn't exactly fit into your text, you could include it as an appendix (which is literally appended to the end of your document). For example, if you cite a map or chart which is too big to be incorporated into the body of your text, you could label it as Appendix A. Be sure to list it under Appendix or Appendices in your table of contents, and refer to it in the text (i.e., See Appendix A, p. 20).

# Sample Project Proposal

What follows is a representative sample of student work, as with the previous assignments, presented for purposes of class discussion. This section is included to generate debate, provide the opportunity for objective critique, and facilitate practicing of peer review. Once again, this assignment is annotated in light of the guidelines of the assignment. This paper has a variety of strong and weak moments. Hopefully, as you prepare to revise your work, this experience will help you to identify the usual moments of achievement, as well as areas that would benefit from improvement.

For the purposes of appropriate formatting for this text, some editorial modifications were made to this student's work. As mentioned earlier, each major section should begin on a new page. Consult your instructor for specific formatting guidelines.

123 Elm Street
New Brunswick, New Jersey 08901

December 1, 2022

Rebecca Villarreal
Director of Education Grantmaking
Education Philanthropy Division of Ascendium Education Group
2501 International Lane
Madison, Wisconsin 53704

**Re: Improving College Preparedness for First-Generation Students at Lakewood High School**

Dear Ms. Villarreal,

Ascendium Education Group is a leader on the front of removing systemic barriers to postsecondary educational success of disadvantaged groups. Your organization has granted millions of dollars for projects dedicated to serving underrepresented demographics which have achieved progress around the country. One of the key populations Ascendium seeks to aid is first-generation high school students and their access to resources necessary for their success. Through my research, I have identified a large population of first-generation students at Lakewood High School that are in dire need of external preparedness intervention that only an organization such as Ascendium can provide. Their overwhelmingly minority and low-income student population consistently struggles to meet state and national college preparedness standards which perpetuates economic hardship. Despite Lakewood's historical issue with college readiness, this school is at its highest potential for long-lasting improvement than it has been in decades and the time to break this cycle of inequality is now.

Building upon the research I presented to you on March 11, 2020, there is substantial evidence to support an overhaul of the current system in place for Lakewood's college preparedness. This involves directly targeting first-generation students who are the best group for creating widespread and lasting improvement given Lakewood's demographics. This project's goal is to implement the 4-Dimensional College and Career Readiness Program which is a synthesis of the most effective aspects of college preparedness programs from 38 high schools around the country. Pairing this with an overall shift in the culture of the school based on the Ramp-Up to Readiness model, Lakewood High School and its surrounding township will see lasting benefits that will improve the opportunity, financial mobility, and education quality of subsequent generations.

This proposal and Ascendium share the same goal of improving social and economic equity through the promotion of postsecondary education. A successful project that transforms Lakewood from an impoverished district to a champion of higher education would not only suit Ascendium's specific resources, but also continue to bolster your international reputation as the top education philanthropy group. Together we can bring these foundational ideas to fruition and give newfound hope to the upcoming generations of Lakewood, New Jersey. If you have any questions, please feel free to reach out to me at dragon@rutgers.edu or call me at (732) 555-1234. Thank you for your time and I look forward to discussing this with you in the future.

Sincerely,

*Luke Dragon*

Luke Dragon

# Improving College Preparedness
# for First-Generation Students
# at Lakewood High School

© fizkes/Shutterstock.com

**Submitted by:**
Luke Dragon
9273 BPO Way
Piscataway, NJ 08855

**Submitted to:**
Rebecca Villarreal
Director of Education Grantmaking at Ascendium Philanthropy
2501 International Lane
Madison, Wisconsin 53704

**Submitted on:**
May 4, 2020

**Prepared for:**
Scientific and Technical Writing
01:355:302
Dr. Francesco Pascuzzi

# Abstract

College under-preparedness is an issue that is amplified amongst many disadvantaged populations, including first-generation, low income, and racial minorities. With Lakewood High School being comprised of 95% Black and Hispanic students as well as a median household income that is $16,664 below the national average, the district is in a very precarious position when it comes to students pursuing higher education (Lakewood, NJ Census Data, 2010). Recent budget cuts eliminated many after-school programs, some of which sought to improve readiness indirectly. Estimates show that between 66 to 91% of these students are first-generation, which is significantly higher than 53% on the national level (Margin of Error Calculator, 2020). Without the pre-exposure brought about by being raised with at least one parent who has been through the college system, these students are at a distinct disadvantage when familiarizing themselves with the jargon, culture, and application process of educational institutes (Byrd & Macdonald, 2005). Lakewood's current school culture and method of student guidance is not conducive to encouraging higher education but can be rectified by a shift in consensus on how to improve pre-college knowledge. Recent studies support the importance of a more holistic approach when serving first-generation students that is centered around personal development and supportive college-going culture rather than solely improving standardized test scores.

First-generation students are the most effective group to target for improving college preparedness as they are statistically more prone to dealing with additional disadvantages. Alongside this, the benefit of a bachelor's degree on their family is significantly more impactful. This proposal highlights the 4-Dimensional College and Career Readiness Model which draws on the most effective aspects of 38 preparedness programs around the country and articulates the best ways to support underrepresented students. Combining this with lessons learned from the structure and implementation of the Ramp-Up model, the following plan was developed for the program. A program director and four influential faculty members are dedicated to leading the implementation and organizing the various components through professional development training. The core dimensions of the 4-Dimensional model serve as the basis for the program curriculum and are: creating contextual skills and awareness, building strong academic behaviors, reinforcing key content knowledge, and employing key cognitive strategies. Each of these dimensions are integrated into seven principles and employed in a foundation course style which features mentorship programs, FAFSA completion events, and a school culture overhaul.

Abstract, presented from a third-person, disinterested point of view

# Table of Contents

Visually appealing and easily navigable table of contents

# Table of Figures

Visually appealing and easily navigable table of figures

# Introduction

Discussion of the affected population and problem to be addressed

## *National First-Generation Background and Statistical Trends*

Since the passage of the Federal Higher Education Act in 1965, there has been a deliberate emphasis to support first-generation students and other disadvantaged groups in postsecondary education (Bowden & Belfield,2015). Without the pre-exposure brought about by being raised with at least one parent who has been through the college system, these students are at a distinct disadvantage when familiarizing themselves with the jargon, culture, and application process of educational institutes (Byrd & Macdonald, 2005). According to the Center for First-Generation Student Success, 24% of college applicants nationwide have parents with no postsecondary experience and 56% have parents without a bachelor's degree (RTI International, 2019). These percentages increase when certain racial and ethnic minorities are isolated, which suggests that many first-generation students must also overcome racial inequalities in order to succeed (First-Generation Students in Higher Education, 2018). Alongside this, research shows that first-generation students access academic resources, like tutoring, less frequently which contributes to significantly lower college GPA's (Holmes & Slate, 2017). Other factors that amplify this situation include that first-generation students have a lower average household income which has been shown to contribute to a 44% lower degree completion rate through their first 6 years of postsecondary education (First-Generation Students in Higher Education, 2018). These circumstances prove that first-generation students struggle on a national scale which requires direct intervention in order to accelerate their performance.

### Figure 1: First-Generation Race/Ethnicity Distribution

https://firstgen.naspa.org/files/dmfile/FactSheet-01.pdf

(First-Generation Students in Higher Education, 2018)

### Figure 2: First-Generation Use of Academic Services

https://firstgen.naspa.org/files/dmfile/NASPA_FactSheet-03_FIN.pdf

(First-Generation Students in Higher Education, 2018)

## *Lakewood Demographics*

Lakewood Township is in a very disadvantaged and impoverished situation that does not lend well to the production of college graduates. The town has a median household income of $44,708 and a 37% poverty rate which is significantly worse than the national average of $61,372 and 12%. Pairing this with over 30% of the population being between the age range of 5–17, the township is in a precarious economic situation, but has significant potential with a sizeable upcoming generation (Lakewood, NJ Census Data, 2010). Given the strong correlation between a bachelor's degree and increased lifetime earnings, putting an emphasis on first-generation students is crucial for the financial mobility of disadvantaged populations, like Lakewood (Byrd & Macdonald, 2005). However, according to a 2015 Gallup-Purdue poll, it is evident that first-generation students are 10% more likely to graduate with debt which lessens the positive economic impact brought about by continuing education (Gallup-Purdue, 2015). This is where the essential problem exists, that economically distressed communities remain in the cycle of poverty because the benefits that should come immediately after obtaining a degree wind up being delayed, or "sticky." This higher frequency of loans and "stickiness" is directly related to the confusing and cumbersome nature of financial aid applications, like the Free Application for Student Aid or FAFSA. A 2019 experiment tested the financial literacy of adult aged first-generation students and found that they performed significantly worse and missed more critical information as compared to continuing generation students. The study concluded that "financial wellness and knowledge programming should focus on adults in poverty to bolster their sense of financial wellness and knowledge and assist during the federal student aid application process" (Taylor et al., 2019). This conclusion applies to parents of first-generation high school students as it suggests that they will have equal or less knowledge than the adult aged students surveyed and thus provide less effective advice to their children. A weaker understanding of the financial aid system leads to less aid awarded, greater and more frequent loans, and the perpetuation of income inequality amongst disadvantaged populations.

**Figure 3: First-Generation Use of Financial Aid Services**

https://firstgen.naspa.org/files/dmfile/NASPA_FactSheet-03_FIN.pdf

(First-Generation Students in Higher Education, 2018)

## *Lakewood High School Survey Results*

In order to more accurately understand the statistic's related to Lakewood's first-generation population, a survey was conducted with a few distinct goals: quantify the percentage range of first-generation high school students, assess self-perceived confidence with college academics and application processes, probe support for the creation of a new program, and compare these figures to the national level related to race and ethnicity. With a sample size of n = 24 and a diversity profile reflective of the school, it estimated a first-generation population between 66 to 91% (Margin of Error Calculator, 2020). At the very least, this is 10% more than the national average and with a significantly lower household income, this can only serve to compound such disadvantages. Also surveyed was the self-identified confidence these students had with completing the Common App and the FAFSA. As shown in Figures 4c and 4d, this confidence was on average reported to be below adequate and illuminates the lack of preparation being done to provide students with the information necessary to make an informed decision on attending college. This lack of confidence and preparation is reaffirmed by the overwhelming support of 95.8%, shown in Figure 4e, to implement a college preparedness program at Lakewood High School.

**Figures 4 a,b,c,d,e: Lakewood High School Survey Results**

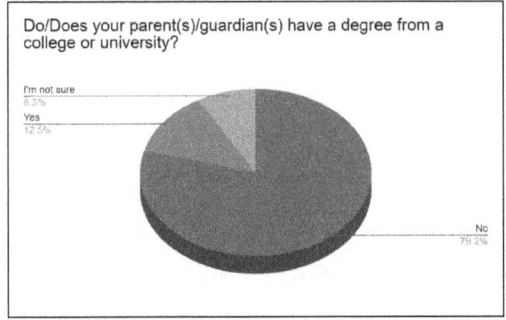

Do/Does your parent(s)/guardian(s) have a degree from a college or university?

I'm not sure 8.3%
Yes 12.5%
No 79.2%

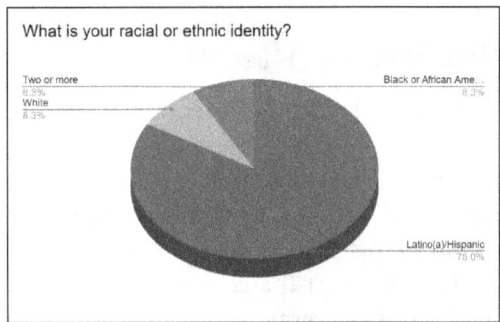

What is your racial or ethnic identity?

Two or more 8.3%
White 8.3%
Black or African Ame... 8.3%
Latino(a)/Hispanic 75.0%

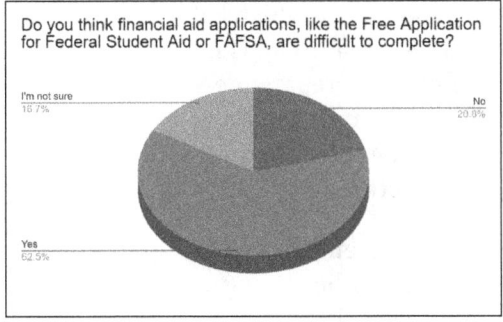

Do you think financial aid applications, like the Free Application for Federal Student Aid or FAFSA, are difficult to complete?

I'm not sure 16.7%
No 20.8%
Yes 62.5%

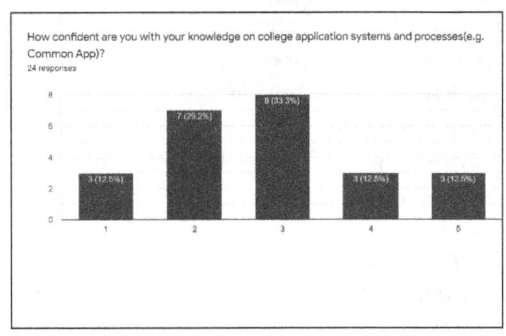

How confident are you with your knowledge on college application systems and processes(e.g. Common App)?
24 responses

1: 3 (12.5%)
2: 7 (29.2%)
3: 8 (33.3%)
4: 3 (12.5%)
5: 3 (12.5%)

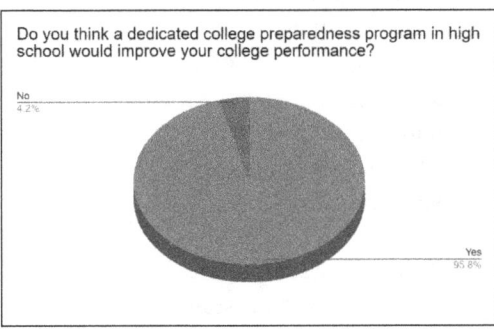

Do you think a dedicated college preparedness program in high school would improve your college performance?

No 4.2%
Yes 95.8%

(Margin of Error Calculator, 2020)

## Shift in Problem Qualification

Within the last two decades, a shift in the perspective of qualifying this problem has occurred. Originally the problem was quantified by a plethora of statistics related to the lower academic performance of first-generation students. Early efforts sought to improve standardized test scores as the most common solution. However, in 1999 there was a shift towards studying the more interpersonal and social aspects of the high school to college transition. A keystone paper by Kathleen Byrd and Ginger Macdonald published in 2005 began to qualify issues outside of academics through interviewing first-generation juniors and seniors in college. They found that the most challenging self-identified learning curve was not a student's scholastic abilities, but rather absent experience with college and inability to self-advocate. Self-advocacy was noted as particularly important given their missing background knowledge of "the college system to understand resources such as advising, financial aid, and student-professor relationships" (Byrd & Macdonald, 2005). This puts many students behind and contributes to a psychological trend that they have "internalized the view that they are inadequate for college" (Byrd & Macdonald, 2005). Since this article's publication, there has been a significant increase in case studies to support a more holistic approach when serving first-generation students. See Figure 5 in Appendix for a visual breakdown of the key components of this consensus shift.

# Literature Review

Section presenting the proposal's paradigm, including at least one guiding theory and a multiple models of success

## *Costly and Ineffective Models*

In terms of pre-existing federal programs that support first-generation students and their access to college, there exists a trend of low or even negative benefit to cost ratio. One specific study on the "Talent Search" model created by the United States Department of Education found that the program offers too much variety. "Talent Search" seeks to provide counseling to high school students only when they need assistance rather than attempting to adapt the community or school culture. This led to implementation sites having either average or inconsistent results due to resources not being properly allocated. The observed cost per student in the program was $3,580 which led to cumulative expenses becoming out of control. Research concluded that there is no discernible evidence to decide whether this "blanket" method of college preparedness is effective (Bowden & Belfield, 015). From this model, it is clear that simply throwing money at this problem does not directly solve anything, but rather an intricate solution tailored to the specific district is needed in order to be cost-effective.

While the aforementioned "Talent Search" model is too broad to be effective, it is also possible for models to treat preparedness as an indirect benefit of other changes. The "High Schools That Work" model represents a low-cost approach that attempts to expose students to a rigorous college-based math and science course progression, known as a pipeline. The goal is that this curriculum will strengthen academic skills through a "student effort-based" method. This method eliminated a progression tracking system in favor of sheer repetition in hopes that students will learn lessons through their own experience. However, a 10-year cycle of the model showed that there was no significant improvement in college readiness or pipeline progression. Reasons for this suggest that the program's reliance on outside consultants thwarted faculty development and thus the intended cultural shift was missed (Miller & Mittleman, 2012). The takeaway from this model is that college preparedness cannot be relied on as a side effect of solely academic improvement. Instead, it requires a much more deliberate combination of targeted areas including adaptation of school culture.

## *4-Dimensional College and Career Readiness Model*

One of the most prevalent studies of the most effective college preparedness programs was a comprehensive research effort that investigated 38 high schools across the nation. Site visits were employed to accurately assess how students responded to and performed in different types of programs in districts that varied in socioeconomic settings. Each program was coded with at least 1 of 50 different identifiers such as "Parent Involvement," "Financial Aid/College Cost," and "Academic Rigor" which assisted in drawing broader conclusions related to categorial success. The study found seven principles that defined every successful preparedness program and broke them down into a 4-dimensional model for high schools to bolster college readiness.

Principles one, two, and five are centered around constant promotion of a "pre-college" culture and a progressive increase in academic rigor that eventually meets college standards. One key takeaway from the initial principles is the need for faculty to discuss how students should prepare for college before recommending whether they should attend or not. Self-management skills are the core of the third principle and findings display that districts that make a deliberate effort to highlight and reward strong organizational skills achieve success. Other notable attributes related to this principle include isolating students on the border of success to take "foundation courses designed to reinforce self-management and self-advocacy skills." This is especially important for underfunded and economically strained districts where a higher portion of students remain in this border state. The fourth principle includes directing students through the college application process by making it a part of their curriculum. Outstanding results were achieved when application tasks like writing one's Common App essay or filling out the FAFSA were made into school assignments. One district in New Mexico published a monthly newsletter named the "Counselor's Corner" which was highly effective at informing parents of important "deadlines, developments, and recommendations regarding college, scholarship, and financial aid applications" (Conley et al., 2010). Principle six is perhaps the most applicable to this specific problem given it is a result significantly amplified amongst first-generation and low-income students. This issue revolves around the tendency of high school seniors to stop challenging themselves. The study found that schools that deliberately engaged seniors with a capstone project and simulated college seminars had better postsecondary performance. The final principle of partnering with a local postsecondary program was highly effective at bridging the gap between academic expectations and enabling students the opportunity to have a fully immersive college experience.

These seven principles and techniques for successful college readiness have contributed to a 4-dimensional model on what high schools without an existing program should focus on in order to improve preparedness. They are academic behaviors, contextual skills and awareness, key content knowledge, and key cognitive strategy. Academic behaviors include training students to overcome obstacles and encourage self-perseverance through adversity. Contextual skills and awareness refer to correcting the gap displayed in students who are "raised outside of the college-bound cultural or social capital network and must rely more heavily on their high schools to provide access to both" (Conley et al., 2010). Essentially the study found that schools that could achieve this had the highest success rates for first-generation students across the board. The latter two dimensions of this model draw on using "human-centered learning" as a means of reinforcing a consistent learning structure through "foundation courses". This implements an interdisciplinary psychological approach to learning theory in which thinking skills and intelligence are considered teachable through a standard structure of processing and retaining information (Conley et al., 2010).

## Long-Term Socioeconomic Analysis and First-Generation Mentorship Model

On the national and state fronts, the direct impact of a bachelor's degree on lifetime earnings is overwhelmingly positive, especially in New Jersey. A 2012 study that broke down yearly earnings of high school and various postsecondary degrees demonstrates New Jersey as the second highest median salary amongst individuals with college degrees. Over the average 40 years of employment, this correlates to a roughly $442,680 lifetime increase for an associate's degree and $837,480 for a bachelor's degree as compared to high school graduates (Zaback et al., 2012). While the long-term benefits may clearly outweigh the average net cost of a 4-year bachelor's degree from public and private institutions, $61,600 and $109,600 respectively, there still exists issues with getting students, especially low income and first-generation, to pursue postsecondary degrees (Trends in College Pricing: College Board, 2019). In order to rectify this, many institutions have begun to implement mentoring programs in order to build a mutual trust between first-generation students who are considering college and those who are currently attending or have attended college (Smith, 2007).

**Figure 5: New Jersey and National Earnings by Degree Type**

**Figure 5a:** See Appendix C here: https://files.eric.ed.gov/fulltext/ED540267.pdf

**Figure 5b:** See Chart 6 here: https://files.eric.ed.gov/fulltext/ED540267.pdf

(Zaback et al., 2012)

The framework for the Smith model lies within the importance of a social capital network, something absent in the experience of first-generation high school students. A common solution to this issue is mentoring programs with the mission of "closing the gap between a student's home culture (i.e., embodied cultural capital) and culture of the school (i.e., institutional cultural capital)" (Smith, 2007). In the mentoring relationship, it is key for both the mentee and the mentor to understand their roles based on the inherent understanding that social capital is not to be thought of as a "single entity," but rather a function of "multiple entities." This includes "that individuals can access one another's human capital (the embodiment of skill sets and knowledge bases) and other valuable resources (e.g., prestige, status, and money)"(Smith, 2007). Through mentoring, these gaps in a first-generation student's network can begin to be filled and their access to opportunities will increase. Once this access is realized, these students are more inclined to perceive increased benefits to the associated risks of attending college, such as cost of attendance and FAFSA knowledge, and thus are more likely to pursue higher education.

This study also establishes a model for effective mentoring relationships and broke them down into four essential functions: establishing norms, sanctions, closure, and information channels. First, this study mainly focuses on first-generation and other disadvantaged student populations, making it especially relevant to the students at Lakewood High School. In these mentoring relationships, it was crucial for both participants to not only share some sort of initial commonality, like hobby or academic interest, but also to have the same commitment expectation and level of trust. Those relationships that could get to the level of sharing personal and powerful stories with each other had the most lasting and beneficial mentorships. The concept of "real" and meaningful exchange of experience and knowledge was the driving factor behind the most successful relationships and directors must be careful not to interfere in these relationships too much (Smith, 2007). This ties into the four essential functions given that they are meant to set a solid foundation for this meaning and importance. Establishing norms that "emphasize the importance of maintaining regular contact with their mentor/mentee and respecting each other's confidentiality" were a requirement of the program (Smith, 2007). These norms were intended to be enforced through sanctions; however, many mentors felt these sanctions should be integrated within mutual trust. Once a relationship created this trust, the sanctions transformed more from the guilt of violating this trust into mentees realizing how valuable and "real" these relationships are. Closure is the essential confidentiality that must exist in order to expand upon the initial foundation and create a lasting bond. Finally, information channels correspond to the belief that mentors truly have the "knowledge, skill sets, and resources" that mentees consider a worthy tradeoff for their time. The larger takeaway from these channels is that the mentor must not only be well connected in multiple areas, but also be very willing and capable of sharing that with their mentee. Overall, this is an effective strategy to not only complete the goal of bolstering college readiness for first-generation students, but also encouraging more of these students to choose higher education over a trade (Smith, 2007).

## *Ramp-Up to Readiness and Insights on Implementation*

Ramp-Up to Readiness is a college preparedness program model developed by researchers at the University of Minnesota that has already been studied for its implementation effectiveness at 52 schools. Although the model is not specific to disadvantaged students, it is based on the same underlying principles as the 4-Dimensional Model and provides valuable evidence for the most effective methods of implementation and program structures. What makes Ramp-Up unique to this project's analysis is its relationship to the previously evaluated "Talent Search" model as it is generally considered to be its more effective alternative given its school-wide approach.

In Figure 6, the Ramp-Up program structure is laid out and demonstrates a very strong consensus with what was presented in the 4-Dimensional Model. This includes the three pillars on the right of the figure related to curriculum content, content delivery, and postsecondary planning tools. The 4-Dimensional Model agreed with all the key areas of academic focus as well as the inclusion of parent contact and early postsecondary planning. This also extends to the methods of delivery which include workshops analogous to foundation courses. The left two pillars serve as a basic structure for how to organize these types of programs and lay an evidence-based foundation as to why it is effective. This structure is mostly reliant on a small group of dedicated staff that direct the program outward to other faculty and downward to students. In order to develop the skills for these staff members, professional development must be required and supplemented if requested by the program leadership team (Lindsay et al., 2016).

### Figure 6: Ramp-Up Program Structure

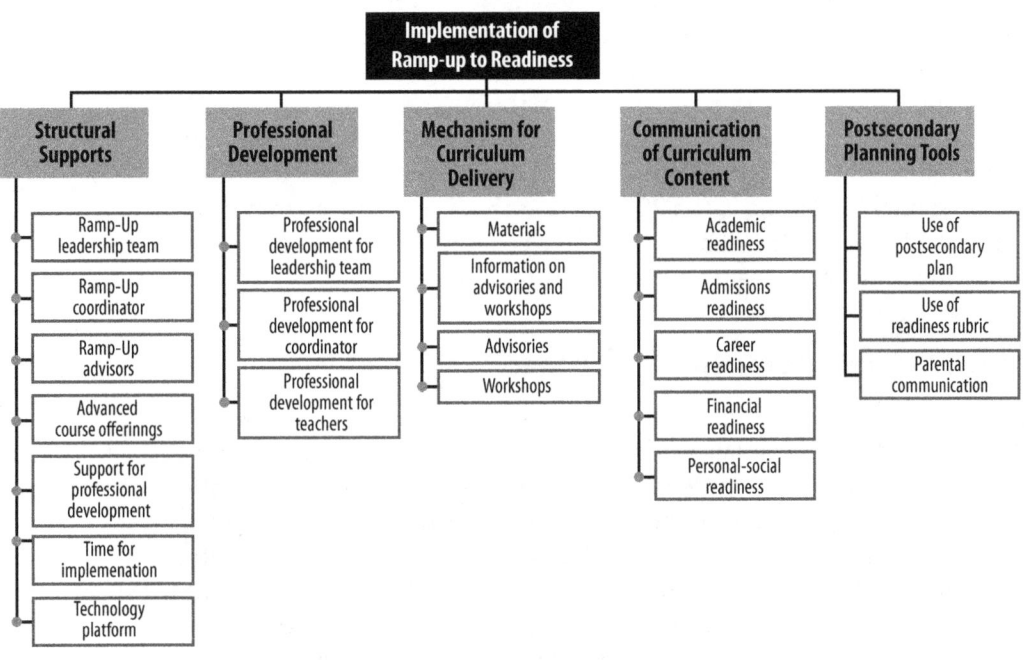

(Lindsay et al., 2016)

In the implementation case studies of the Ramp-Up model, there was support across the board from faculty feedback about the structure of this program. Independent analysis from a separate study on Ramp-Up found "excellent implementation" of structural supports and professional development in a few schools with the average being above adequate (Lindsay et al., 2016). Faculty feedback after the first year remarked that program delivery and method of leadership were especially effective at improving student engagement through primary interaction and discussion. The efficiency of the structure allowed the core leadership and director to focus on the organization of the program while the remaining faculty did the leg work with implementation. Having a few of these implementing faculty take professional development classes was crucial to contributing to a cultural shift and widened the reach of the director. While Ramp-Up has an excitingly positive contribution to this specific project, it also mentions several essential things to keep in mind during implementation. This includes making sure that staff feel within their realm of expertise when teaching this new curriculum as to maintain "buy-in" and not being discouraged by stagnation with initial results. According to testimony of staff not in leadership roles within the program, some teachers were reluctant to adjust their content and style of instruction. A strong program coordinator was essential to handing out responsibilities fairly and knowing the strengths and weaknesses of their other faculty members. In terms of seeing quantitative results for improvement of preparedness, this study makes sure leadership is aware that this will take at least 2 years. All instructors need to be patient and ensure that they are making their best effort to provide these students with skills essential to their future success (Lindsay et al., 2016).

# Plan of Action

Detailed and delineated plan

## Putting the Pieces Together

In order to improve first-generation college preparedness at Lakewood High School, a program that combines the findings of the 4-Dimensional Model with the implementation of Ramp-Up will be put into action with the faults of Talent Search and High Schools That Work models in mind. These four models will work together with the model supporting an included mentorship program with the goal of increasing college enrollment percentages through transfer of primary stories of success. This proposal will be presented for approval to the Lakewood Board of Education immediately after it is funded for a 5-year pilot beginning in the 2023–2024 school year. The culmination of this project will serve Lakewood's community of first-generation students for years to come and have an immeasurable positive impact on hundreds of lives.

## Step 1: Appointing Leadership Positions

Given the structure outlined by the Ramp-Up model, it is clear that picking a program coordinator with the necessary credentials is of the utmost importance. I see the opinion of Ascendium being crucial in this process given your advanced experience with these sorts of projects. This program coordinator must be primarily driven by an inner motivation to help first-generation students and should be able to empathize with their situation. They must also be bilingual in Spanish in order to communicate with non-English speaking parents and technologically savvy in order to leverage online resources. This will come into play with the distribution and delivery aspects of curriculum and preparation material which is essential given Lakewood's low income-high minority socioeconomic context.

In addition to the coordinator, four influential faculty members will serve as part of the leadership committee for the program and spearhead the cultural shift. These individuals will play the role of liaisons between the regular teachers and the program coordinator in order to gauge program progress. All five members of the leadership team will undergo two rounds of training in years one and three of the pilot and will be provided with any supplemental training they request. This committee will meet every other week with formally recorded meeting minutes which are made available to regular instructors upon request.

## Step 2: Integrating the 4-Dimensional Model Into the Curriculum

When considering Lakewood's low-income economic situation, there must be certain adaptations made in order to keep renewing costs low so that the program lasts past its initial funding. To achieve this, each of the seven principles of the 4-Dimensional Model will be rooted in the aforementioned "foundation courses" which will serve as the basic structural unit of the curriculum. Given that the population at hand is statistically predisposed to unpreparedness, "foundation courses" should be applied across the board as basic college knowledge cannot be assumed. Each of the remaining six principles will have their own "foundation courses" with some of them being directly applied to students while others are used as training opportunities for Lakewood faculty. For example, the first principle related to creation of a "college-like" culture would be faculty oriented given that it was used to change school atmosphere and attitude when initiated by guidance counselors (Conley et al., 2010). On the other hand, principle four about bringing the application process to first-generation students would be better served by a "foundation course" in which application completion events are held for students. Principle seven falls slightly outside of these restrictions as it will include partnering with a local 4year postsecondary institution. The majority of the "foundation course" materials already exist and will be directly sourced from Ramp-Up and schools that employed the 4-Dimensional Model. It is the responsibility of the director to delegate who is responsible for which principles and ensure that they are fulfilling their obligations to the program.

## Step 3: Creating a Relationship With Georgian Court University

Georgian Court University is a small private postsecondary institution less than 2 miles from Lakewood High School. Establishing a connection with Georgian Court would not only be important for the execution of principle seven, but also serve as the preferred partner institution for the mentorship program. Although any first-generation individuals who have already completed a college degree may participate as mentors in this program, having that direct link will make it more accessible. Accessibility is an overarching goal of the program and this mentorship program will ensure to achieve that goal through equitable opportunity, experience, and guidance. This bridge between Georgian Court and Lakewood High School would prove invaluable in bolstering primary experience with first-generation students as its "foundation course" would be straight from a 4-year university. This could include "spend a day" events where interested high school students would be able to shadow a Georgian Court student and be exposed to their daily schedule. Other contributions from Georgian Court will come in the form of Dual-Enrollment programs for students to obtain college credit before graduating.

# Budget

Fully detailed and supported final budget for project

The costs associated with this program include supplemental funding necessary to run a 5-year pilot of this preparedness model at Lakewood High School. To obtain the most accurate estimates for this budget, a public high school accountant with more than 20 years of experience was consulted as well as the 2018–2019 budget for Lakewood High School (Personal Communication, April 2020, Maureen Martin, Avon Board of Education). Estimations for professional development were sourced from Ramp-Up. Cumulative cost for 5 years is $40,900 which is significantly less than average for similar federally funded projects. This is important given the district wide $30 million budget cut mentioned in the introduction.

### Figure 7a, b: Budget Breakdown

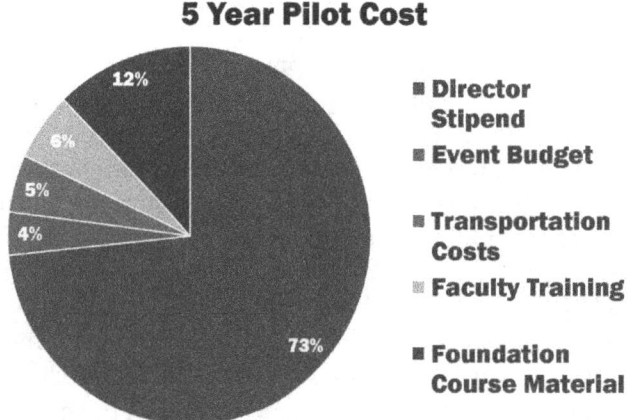

**5 Year Pilot Cost**

- Director Stipend
- Event Budget
- Transportation Costs
- Faculty Training
- Foundation Course Material

| Item | Cost Per Year | Years | Total Cost Per Item |
|---|---|---|---|
| Faculty Training | $1,200 | 1–3 | $2,400 |
| Director Stipend | $6,000 | 1–5 | $30,000 |
| "Foundation Course" Materials and Licensing | $1,000 | 1–5 | $5,000 |
| Event Budget | $300 | 1–5 | $1,500 |
| Transportation | $400 | 1–5 | $2,000 |
| Total Cost | | | $40,900 |

(NJ School Performance Report: Ocean County High Schools 2017–2018, 2019)
(Lindsay et al., 2016)

The director stipend is based on standard pay for two seasons of an extracurricular, sport, or club leadership role such as a coach. While the rest of the leadership group does not receive a stipend, their other duties, such as hall monitoring or covering as a substitute, will be reduced as compensation. The event budget is intended as petty cash for the program director to use for bonding events in order to build better relationships with parents. Transportation is the bussing budget for up to 52 students four times a year to go to Georgian Court as part of the mentorship program.

# Discussion

Evaluation of plan

This well-established plan of action and budget will serve as the face of the proposal when it is presented to the Lakewood Board of Education. Putting certain measures in place to ensure that this proposal is properly implemented to its fullest potential is essential to protecting the program and bolstering its image. At every 6-month increment along the program's timeline, it will be reevaluated in terms of its successes and failures. Amongst hundreds of statistics to be collected a few key ones are feedback from student focus groups and faculty, duration of individual component implementation, and cost per student. The principle of the high school, board of education, superintendent, and full leadership committee must be in attendance for these meetings. This will serve as a checks and balances system to ensure the funding Ascendium works incredibly hard to provide is being used for its intended purpose of helping first-generation students who need it.

College preparedness of first-generation students is a solvable problem that plagues many underrepresented districts around the country. Lakewood is in dire need of economic support, especially with recent budget cuts. It is our responsibility to do what is right for the young people who struggle accessing the opportunities they deserve. Any contribution, specifically in the form of social capital, will go a long way to improving the financial mobility of subsequent generations. Selecting first-generation students as the target population provides the most widespread support of disadvantaged students and will continue to last for generations to come. With a large youth population, Lakewood is at its highest point of potential to make lasting change and the time to act is now. Implementation of the 4-Dimensional Model combined with Ramp-Up's structure and a dedicated program director will put these students in a position to succeed. Together we can promote social and economic equity in Lakewood by investing in a population which has been left out of society's push towards economic success.

# Appendix

**Benefit to Cost Ratio:** summarizes the overall relationship between relative costs and benefits of a proposed project. Can be expressed in monetary or qualitative terms. If the ratio is greater than 1.0, the project is expected to deliver a positive net present value to a firm and its investors. Required for a project to receive federal funding (Taylor et al., 2019).

**First-Generation:** students that are pursuing a postsecondary education and their parent(s)/ guardian(s) do not have a bachelor's degree (RTI International, 2019).

**Foundation course:** a college or university level course that introduces students to a subject and prepares them for studying it at a higher level (Foundation Course, n.d.).

**Title I:** a federally funded supplemental program to assist school districts with the highest concentrations of student poverty to meet educational goals (Title I School, n.d.).

**Sticky:** a general economic theory that can apply to any financial variable that is resistant to change (Taylor et al, 2019).

### Figure 8: Consensus Shift Visual Breakdown

https://www.sdcity.edu/students/services/mesa/docs/pyramid_model.pdf

(Byrd & Macdonald, 2005)

## References

APA-style reference page, listing each source cited in-text

Bowden, A. B., & Belfield, C. (2015). Evaluating the talent search TRIO program: A benefit-cost analysis and cost-effectiveness analysis. *Journal of Benefit-Cost Analysis, 6*(3), 572–602.

Byrd, K., & Macdonald, G. (2005). Defining college readiness from the inside out: First-generation college student perspectives. *Community College Review, 33*(1), 22–37.

Conley, T., McGaughy, D. L. Kirtner, C., Valk, J. der, Adrienne Martinez-Wenzl, & Theresa, M. (2010). College readiness practices at 38 high schools and the development of the CollegeCareerReady school diagnostic tool. Retrieved March 2, 2020, from https://eric.ed.gov/?id=ED509644

First-Generation Students in Higher Education. (2018). Retrieved March 2, 2020, from https://pnpi.org/first-generation-students/

Foundation Course. (n.d.). In Cambridge Dictionary Online. Retrieved March 2, 2020, from https://academicanswers.waldenu.edu/faq/73139

Gallup-Purdue. (2015). Student loan debt incurred as undergraduates among alumni who graduated between 2006 and 2015. Retrieved February 16, 2020, from https://www.gallup.com/services/185924/gallup-purdue-index-2015-report.aspx

Holmes, L., & Slate, D. (2017). Differences in GPA by gender and ethnicity/race as

    a function of first-generation status for community college students. *Global*

    *Journal of Human Social Science Research, 17*(3), 1–5.

Lakewood, NJ Census Data. (2010). Retrieved March 2, 2020, from https://datausa.io/

    profile/geo/lakewood-nj/

Lindsay, J., Davis, E., Stephan, J., & Bowdon, J. (2016). Stated briefly: Ramping up to

    college readiness in Minnesota high schools: Implementation of a schoolwide

    program (REL 2016–184). Washington, DC: U.S. Department of Education,

    Institute of Education Sciences, National Center for Education Evaluation and

    Regional Assistance, Regional Educational Laboratory Midwest. http://ies.

    ed.gov/ncee/edlabs.

Margin of Error Calculator. (2020). Retrieved May 2, 2020, from https://www.survey-

    monkey.com/mp/margin-of-error-calculator/

Miller, L., & Mittleman, J. (2012). High schools that work and college preparedness:

    Measuring the model's impact on mathematics and science pipeline progres-

    sion. *Economics of Education Review, 31*(6), 1116–1135.

NJ School Performance Report: Ocean County High Schools 2017–2018. (2019).

    Retrieved February 17, 2020, from https://rc.doe.state.nj.us/report.aspx?type=-

    school&lang=english&county=29&dis trict=2520&school=050&SY=1718&-

    schoolyear=2017-2018

RTI International. (2019). First-generation college students: Demographic character-

    istics and postsecondary enrollment. NASPA. Retrieved February 16, 2020,

    from https://firstgen.naspa.org/files/dmfil e/FactSheet-01.pdf

Smith, B. (2007). Accessing social capital through the academic mentoring process,

    *Equity & Excellence in Education, 40*(1), 36–46.

Taylor, Z., Bicak, I., Egetenmeyer, R., & Osborne, M. (2019). What is the FAFSA? An

    adult learner knowledge survey of student financial aid jargon. *Journal of Adult*

    *and Continuing Education, 25*(1), 94–112.

Title I School. (n.d.). In US Legal Definitions Online Dictionary. Retrieved March 2, 2020, from https://definitions.uslegal.com/t/title-1-school/

Trends in College Pricing, College Board. (2019). Retrieved May 2, 2020, from https://research.collegeboard.org/pdf/trends-college-pricing-2019-full-report.pdf

Zaback, K., Carlson, A., & Crellin, M. (2012). The economic benefit of postsecondary degrees: A state and national level analysis. Retrieved May 2, 2020, from https://eric.ed.gov/?id =ED540267

# Chapter 7 ▪ The Project Proposal Peer Review Workshop I

Please fill out the following form for your partner. Feel free to write comments on the draft as well.

## Cover Letter and Title Page

Does the cover letter . . .

1. directly address the funding source? _____yes _____no

2. explain why the reader has received this proposal? _____yes _____no

3. persuade the reader to examine this plan closely? _____yes _____no

4. offer details about the content of the plan? _____yes _____no

5. appear in full block form and include all six elements

   (return address, date, recipient's address, salutation, body, closing)? _____yes _____no

Is the cover letter . . .

1. signed? _____yes _____no

2. free of all grammatical and typographical errors? _____yes _____no

Does the title page . . .

1. include all five elements (project title, name of sender, name of
   recipient, date, return information)? _____yes _____no

2. catch the attention of the reader? _____yes _____no

3. have a title appropriate to the plan? _____yes _____no

Is the title page . . .

1. visually appealing? _____yes _____no

2. free of all grammatical and typographical errors? _____yes _____no

1. What parts of the draft are most effective?


2. What parts of the draft need the most improvement?

# Abstract

1. Is the document clearly labeled as an "Abstract" at the top of the page? _____ yes _____ no
2. Is the document written from a third-person perspective? _____ yes _____ no
3. Does the document provide a balanced view of the project idea? _____ yes _____ no
4. Does the document cover elements of the problem, paradigm,

   and plan (in that order)? _____ yes _____ no
5. Does the document indicate a specific course of action? _____ yes _____ no
6. Is the document between 150 and 300 words and no longer

   than two paragraphs in length? _____ yes _____ no
7. Is the document single-spaced, in 12-point Times New Roman type? _____ yes _____ no
8. Is the document free of errors in grammar, usage, and/or

   sentence structure? _____ yes _____ no
9. Is the document presented in a clear, readable form? _____ yes _____ no
10. Would this document encourage me to read this plan? _____ yes _____ no

1. What parts of the draft are most effective?

2. What parts of the draft need the most improvement?

# Table of Contents and Table of Figures

1. Are these documents clearly labeled and presented in a logical
   and readable form? _____ yes _____ no
2. Are these documents free of errors in grammar, spacing,
   and punctuation? _____ yes _____ no

Additional Comments/Suggestions:

# Chapter 7 ■ The Project Proposal Peer Review Workshop I

Please fill out the following form for your partner. Feel free to write comments on the draft as well.

## Cover Letter and Title Page

Does the cover letter . . .

1. directly address the funding source? _____yes _____no

2. explain why the reader has received this proposal? _____yes _____no

3. persuade the reader to examine this plan closely? _____yes _____no

4. offer details about the content of the plan? _____yes _____no

5. appear in full block form and include all six elements

   (return address, date, recipient's address, salutation, body, closing)? _____yes _____no

Is the cover letter . . .

1. signed? _____yes _____no

2. free of all grammatical and typographical errors? _____yes _____no

Does the title page . . .

1. include all five elements (project title, name of sender, name of recipient, date, return information)? _____yes _____no

2. catch the attention of the reader? _____yes _____no

3. have a title appropriate to the plan? _____yes _____no

Is the title page . . .

1. visually appealing? _____yes _____no

2. free of all grammatical and typographical errors? _____yes _____no

1.  What parts of the draft are most effective?



2.  What parts of the draft need the most improvement?

# Abstract

1. Is the document clearly labeled as an "Abstract" at the top of the page? _____ yes _____ no
2. Is the document written from a third-person perspective? _____ yes _____ no
3. Does the document provide a balanced view of the project idea? _____ yes _____ no
4. Does the document cover elements of the problem, paradigm, and plan (in that order)? _____ yes _____ no
5. Does the document indicate a specific course of action? _____ yes _____ no
6. Is the document between 150 and 300 words and no longer than two paragraphs in length? _____ yes _____ no
7. Is the document single-spaced, in 12-point Times New Roman type? _____ yes _____ no
8. Is the document free of errors in grammar, usage, and/or sentence structure? _____ yes _____ no
9. Is the document presented in a clear, readable form? _____ yes _____ no
10. Would this document encourage me to read this plan? _____ yes _____ no

1. What parts of the draft are most effective?

2. What parts of the draft need the most improvement?

# Table of Contents and Table of Figures

1. Are these documents clearly labeled and presented in a logical and readable form? _____ yes _____ no
2. Are these documents free of errors in grammar, spacing, and punctuation? _____ yes _____ no

Additional Comments/Suggestions:

# Chapter 7 ■ The Project Proposal Peer Review Workshop I

Please fill out the following form for your partner. Feel free to write comments on the draft as well.

## Cover Letter and Title Page

Does the cover letter . . .

1. directly address the funding source? _____yes _____no

2. explain why the reader has received this proposal? _____yes _____no

3. persuade the reader to examine this plan closely? _____yes _____no

4. offer details about the content of the plan? _____yes _____no

5. appear in full block form and include all six elements

   (return address, date, recipient's address, salutation, body, closing)? _____yes _____no

Is the cover letter . . .

1. signed? _____yes _____no

2. free of all grammatical and typographical errors? _____yes _____no

Does the title page . . .

1. include all five elements (project title, name of sender, name of recipient, date, return information)? _____yes _____no

2. catch the attention of the reader? _____yes _____no

3. have a title appropriate to the plan? _____yes _____no

Is the title page . . .

1. visually appealing? _____yes _____no

2. free of all grammatical and typographical errors? _____yes _____no

1. What parts of the draft are most effective?

2. What parts of the draft need the most improvement?

# Abstract

1. Is the document clearly labeled as an "Abstract" at the top of the page? _____ yes _____ no
2. Is the document written from a third-person perspective? _____ yes _____ no
3. Does the document provide a balanced view of the project idea? _____ yes _____ no
4. Does the document cover elements of the problem, paradigm, and plan (in that order)? _____ yes _____ no
5. Does the document indicate a specific course of action? _____ yes _____ no
6. Is the document between 150 and 300 words and no longer than two paragraphs in length? _____ yes _____ no
7. Is the document single-spaced, in 12-point Times New Roman type? _____ yes _____ no
8. Is the document free of errors in grammar, usage, and/or sentence structure? _____ yes _____ no
9. Is the document presented in a clear, readable form? _____ yes _____ no
10. Would this document encourage me to read this plan? _____ yes _____ no

1. What parts of the draft are most effective?

2. What parts of the draft need the most improvement?

# Table of Contents and Table of Figures

1. Are these documents clearly labeled and presented in a logical and readable form? _____ yes _____ no
2. Are these documents free of errors in grammar, spacing, and punctuation? _____ yes _____ no

Additional Comments/Suggestions:

# Chapter 7 ■ The Project Proposal Peer Review Workshop II

Please fill out the following form for your partner. Feel free to write comments on the draft as well.

## Introduction and Literature Review

Does the introduction . . .

1. attempt to define and quantify the problem?  _____yes _____no

2. include visuals that help clarify and emphasize the key aspects of the problem?  _____yes _____no

3. focus on the aspects of the problem that would most interest the reader?  _____yes _____no

4. suggest a direction for approaching the problem?  _____yes _____no

5. close with a forecasting statement giving the reader a sense of the argument to follow and providing a transition to the next section?  _____yes _____no

Is the introduction . . .

1. single-spaced, in 12-point Times New Roman font?  _____yes _____no

2. free of all grammatical and typographical errors?  _____yes _____no

Does the literature review . . .

1. open with a reference to the problem?  _____yes _____no

2. focus on the paradigm of the project?  _____yes _____no

3. explain why the problem will be approached in a particular way?  _____yes _____no

4. provide a unified rationale for the specific plan of action?  _____yes _____no

5. show how the plan of action proposed is a logical approach to the problem defined?  _____yes _____no

6. include the most useful and authoritative sources (especially those subject to peer review)?  _____yes _____no

Is the literature review . . .

1. single-spaced, in 12-point Times New Roman font?  _____yes _____no

2. free of all grammatical and typographical errors?  _____yes _____no

1.   What parts of the draft are most effective?

2.   What parts of the draft need the most improvement?

Additional Comments/Suggestions:

# Chapter 7  ■  The Project Proposal Peer Review Workshop II

Please fill out the following form for your partner. Feel free to write comments on the draft as well.

## Introduction and Literature Review

Does the introduction . . .

1. attempt to define and quantify the problem?                                              _____yes _____no

2. include visuals that help clarify and emphasize the key aspects
   of the problem?                                                                          _____yes _____no

3. focus on the aspects of the problem that would most interest
   the reader?                                                                              _____yes _____no

4. suggest a direction for approaching the problem?                                         _____yes _____no

5. close with a forecasting statement giving the reader a sense of the
   argument to follow and providing a transition to the next section?                       _____yes _____no

Is the introduction . . .

1. single-spaced, in 12-point Times New Roman font?                                         _____yes _____no

2. free of all grammatical and typographical errors?                                        _____yes _____no

Does the literature review . . .

1. open with a reference to the problem?                                                    _____yes _____no

2. focus on the paradigm of the project?                                                    _____yes _____no

3. explain why the problem will be approached in a particular way?                          _____yes _____no

4. provide a unified rationale for the specific plan of action?                             _____yes _____no

5. show how the plan of action proposed is a logical approach
   to the problem defined?                                                                  _____yes _____no

6. include the most useful and authoritative sources (especially those
   subject to peer review)?                                                                 _____yes _____no

Is the literature review . . .

1. single-spaced, in 12-point Times New Roman font?                                         _____yes _____no

2. free of all grammatical and typographical errors?                                        _____yes _____no

1. What parts of the draft are most effective?

2. What parts of the draft need the most improvement?

Additional Comments/Suggestions:

# Chapter 7 ■ The Project Proposal Peer Review Workshop II

Please fill out the following form for your partner. Feel free to write comments on the draft as well.

## Introduction and Literature Review

Does the introduction . . .

1. attempt to define and quantify the problem?                                          _____yes _____no

2. include visuals that help clarify and emphasize the key aspects
   of the problem?                                                                       _____yes _____no

3. focus on the aspects of the problem that would most interest
   the reader?                                                                           _____yes _____no

4. suggest a direction for approaching the problem?                                      _____yes _____no

5. close with a forecasting statement giving the reader a sense of the
   argument to follow and providing a transition to the next section?                    _____yes _____no

Is the introduction . . .

1. single-spaced, in 12-point Times New Roman font?                                      _____yes _____no

2. free of all grammatical and typographical errors?                                     _____yes _____no

Does the literature review . . .

1. open with a reference to the problem?                                                 _____yes _____no

2. focus on the paradigm of the project?                                                 _____yes _____no

3. explain why the problem will be approached in a particular way?                       _____yes _____no

4. provide a unified rationale for the specific plan of action?                          _____yes _____no

5. show how the plan of action proposed is a logical approach
   to the problem defined?                                                               _____yes _____no

6. include the most useful and authoritative sources (especially those
   subject to peer review)?                                                              _____yes _____no

Is the literature review . . .

1. single-spaced, in 12-point Times New Roman font?                                      _____yes _____no

2. free of all grammatical and typographical errors?                                     _____yes _____no

1.   What parts of the draft are most effective?

2.   What parts of the draft need the most improvement?

Additional Comments/Suggestions:

# Chapter 7 ■ The Project Proposal Peer Review Workshop III

Please fill out the following form for your partner. Feel free to write comments on the draft as well.

## Plan, Budget, and Discussion

Does the plan . . .

1. transition logically from the research?                              _____yes _____no
2. focus on how the idea will be implemented?                      _____yes _____no
3. reference research to support the writer's choices?           _____yes _____no
4. present information clearly?                                            _____yes _____no
5. consider all possibilities in justifying its recommendations?   _____yes _____no

Is the plan . . .

1. organized logically?                                                      _____yes _____no
2. free of unanswered questions or areas of confusion?         _____yes _____no
3. single-spaced, in 12-point Times New Roman font?           _____yes _____no
4. free of all grammatical and typographical errors?            _____yes _____no

Does the budget . . .

1. list everything needed for the project?                           _____yes _____no
2. explain items that may be unfamiliar to the reader?          _____yes _____no

Is the budget . . .

1. arranged in aligned accountant's columns?                       _____yes _____no
2. single-spaced, in 12-point Times New Roman font?           _____yes _____no
3. free of all mathematical, grammatical, and typographical errors?   _____yes _____no

Does the discussion . . .

1. conclude by summing up the project?                             _____yes _____no
2. make a final pitch for the value of the project?               _____yes _____no
3. offer an evaluation plan for testing the results?             _____yes _____no

Is the discussion . . .

1. single-spaced, in 12-point Times New Roman font?           _____yes _____no
2. free of all grammatical and typographical errors?            _____yes _____no

1. Which parts of the draft are most effective?

2. Which parts of the draft need the most improvement?

# References

1. Is the document clearly labeled as a list of References at the top of the page? _____ yes _____ no

2. Does the document contain a minimum of 10 sources? _____ yes _____ no

3. Are there various types of sources represented (books to develop a theoretical framework, scholarly journals for detailed models, etc.)? _____ yes _____ no

4. Are at least 50% of the references cited from scholarly sources? _____ yes _____ no

5. Is the document formatted in proper APA citation style (alphabetized, indented after first line, publication elements ordered correctly, etc.)? _____ yes _____ no

6. Is the document correctly spaced, in 12-point Times New Roman type, with one-inch margins? _____ yes _____ no

7. Is the document free of errors in grammar, punctuation, and capitalization? _____ yes _____ no

Additional Comments/Suggestions:

# Chapter 7 ■ The Project Proposal Peer Review Workshop III

Please fill out the following form for your partner. Feel free to write comments on the draft as well.

## Plan, Budget, and Discussion

Does the plan . . .

    1. transition logically from the research?            _____yes _____no

    2. focus on how the idea will be implemented?     _____yes _____no

    3. reference research to support the writer's choices?   _____yes _____no

    4. present information clearly?     _____yes _____no

    5. consider all possibilities in justifying its recommendations?   _____yes _____no

Is the plan . . .

    1. organized logically?     _____yes _____no

    2. free of unanswered questions or areas of confusion?   _____yes _____no

    3. single-spaced, in 12-point Times New Roman font?   _____yes _____no

    4. free of all grammatical and typographical errors?   _____yes _____no

Does the budget . . .

    1. list everything needed for the project?   _____yes _____no

    2. explain items that may be unfamiliar to the reader?   _____yes _____no

Is the budget . . .

    1. arranged in aligned accountant's columns?   _____yes _____no

    2. single-spaced, in 12-point Times New Roman font?   _____yes _____no

    3. free of all mathematical, grammatical, and typographical errors?   _____yes _____no

Does the discussion . . .

    1. conclude by summing up the project?   _____yes _____no

    2. make a final pitch for the value of the project?   _____yes _____no

    3. offer an evaluation plan for testing the results?   _____yes _____no

Is the discussion . . .

    1. single-spaced, in 12-point Times New Roman font?   _____yes _____no

    2. free of all grammatical and typographical errors?   _____yes _____no

1. Which parts of the draft are most effective?

2. Which parts of the draft need the most improvement?

# References

1. Is the document clearly labeled as a list of References at the top of the page? _____ yes _____ no

2. Does the document contain a minimum of 10 sources? _____ yes _____ no

3. Are there various types of sources represented (books to develop a theoretical framework, scholarly journals for detailed models, etc.)? _____ yes _____ no

4. Are at least 50% of the references cited from scholarly sources? _____ yes _____ no

5. Is the document formatted in proper APA citation style (alphabetized, indented after first line, publication elements ordered correctly, etc.)? _____ yes _____ no

6. Is the document correctly spaced, in 12-point Times New Roman type, with one-inch margins? _____ yes _____ no

7. Is the document free of errors in grammar, punctuation, and capitalization? _____ yes _____ no

Additional Comments/Suggestions:

# Chapter 7 ■ The Project Proposal Peer Review Workshop III

Please fill out the following form for your partner. Feel free to write comments on the draft as well.

## Plan, Budget, and Discussion

Does the plan . . .

1. transition logically from the research? _____yes _____no
2. focus on how the idea will be implemented? _____yes _____no
3. reference research to support the writer's choices? _____yes _____no
4. present information clearly? _____yes _____no
5. consider all possibilities in justifying its recommendations? _____yes _____no

Is the plan . . .

1. organized logically? _____yes _____no
2. free of unanswered questions or areas of confusion? _____yes _____no
3. single-spaced, in 12-point Times New Roman font? _____yes _____no
4. free of all grammatical and typographical errors? _____yes _____no

Does the budget . . .

1. list everything needed for the project? _____yes _____no
2. explain items that may be unfamiliar to the reader? _____yes _____no

Is the budget . . .

1. arranged in aligned accountant's columns? _____yes _____no
2. single-spaced, in 12-point Times New Roman font? _____yes _____no
3. free of all mathematical, grammatical, and typographical errors? _____yes _____no

Does the discussion . . .

1. conclude by summing up the project? _____yes _____no
2. make a final pitch for the value of the project? _____yes _____no
3. offer an evaluation plan for testing the results? _____yes _____no

Is the discussion . . .

1. single-spaced, in 12-point Times New Roman font? _____yes _____no
2. free of all grammatical and typographical errors? _____yes _____no

1.  Which parts of the draft are most effective?




2.  Which parts of the draft need the most improvement?




# References

1.  Is the document clearly labeled as a list of References at the top of the page? _____ yes _____ no

2.  Does the document contain a minimum of 10 sources? _____ yes _____ no

3.  Are there various types of sources represented (books to develop a theoretical framework, scholarly journals for detailed models, etc.)? _____ yes _____ no

4.  Are at least 50% of the references cited from scholarly sources? _____ yes _____ no

5.  Is the document formatted in proper APA citation style (alphabetized, indented after first line, publication elements ordered correctly, etc.)? _____ yes _____ no

6.  Is the document correctly spaced, in 12-point Times New Roman type, with one-inch margins? _____ yes _____ no

7.  Is the document free of errors in grammar, punctuation, and capitalization? _____ yes _____ no

Additional Comments/Suggestions:

**Reader:** _____     **Author:** _____

# Chapter 7 ■ The Project Proposal Evaluation

1. The proposal includes all necessary sections and is within the page-length requirement.

   1   2   3   4   5   6   7   8   9   10

2. The proposal strives to persuade (and address the needs of) its audience.

   1   2   3   4   5   6   7   8   9   10

3. The proposal clearly defines and quantifies a viable problem, using published research and fieldwork.

   1   2   3   4   5   6   7   8   9   10

4. The proposal attempts a challenging and/or original task.

   1   2   3   4   5   6   7   8   9   10

5. The proposal is based upon relevant and/or innovative scholarly research.

   1   2   3   4   5   6   7   8   9   10

6. The references page includes the required number of sources and is presented in APA format.

   1   2   3   4   5   6   7   8   9   10

7. The research is organized into a clearly and carefully delineated paradigm.

   1   2   3   4   5   6   7   8   9   10

8. The plan of action follows logically from the research and is specifically described to the audience.

   1   2   3   4   5   6   7   8   9   10

9. The proposal places sources in logical relation to each other and to the project as a whole.

   1   2   3   4   5   6   7   8   9   10

10. The proposal is fully justified by the published research.

    1   2   3   4   5   6   7   8   9   10

11. The proposal engages possible complications suggested by the research or the plan.

    1   2   3   4   5   6   7   8   9   10

12. The transitions and headings help guide the reader through the project.

    1     2     3     4     5     6     7     8     9    10

13. The visuals are appropriate and effective at conveying information to the reader.

    1     2     3     4     5     6     7     8     9    10

14. The writing is fluent and virtually error-free.

    1     2     3     4     5     6     7     8     9    10

15. The proposal exhibits an overall attractive appearance and visually appealing design.

    1     2     3     4     5     6     7     8     9    10

# Index

CPSIA information can be obtained
at www.ICGtesting.com
Printed in the USA
LVHW062350070822
725061LV00005B/5